Blueprint Reading for Construction

Blueprint Reading for Construction

James A. S. Fatzinger, CPE, ME
American Society of Professional Estimators

Prentice Hall

Upper Saddle River, New Jersey   Columbus, Ohio

Library of Congress Cataloging-in-Publication Data

Fatzinger, James A. S.
Blueprint reading for construction / James A.S. Fatzinger.
    p. cm.
Includes index.
ISBN 0-13-531542-5
1. Building—Details—Drawings. 2. Bluepirints.   I. Title.
    TH431.F38   1998
    692'.1—dc21

97-24598
CIP

Cover photo: Art Tilley/FPG
Editor: Ed Francis
Production Editor: Stephen C. Robb
Design Coordinator: Julia Zonneveld Van Hook
Cover Designer: Brian Deep
Production Manager: Laura Messerly
Marketing Manager: Danny Hoyt
Production Supervisor: Custom Editorial Productions, Inc.

This book was set in Schneidler, Humanist 777, and Courier by Custom Editorial Productions, Inc., and was printed and bound by Courier/Kendallville Company. The cover was printed by Phoenix Color Corp.

© 1998 by Prentice-Hall, Inc.
A Pearson Education Company
Upper Saddle River, New Jersey 07458

Printed in the United States of America

10 9 8 7 6 5 4 3 2

ISBN: 0-13-531542-5

Printed with corrections, June 1999

Prentice-Hall International (UK) Limited, *London*
Prentice-Hall of Australia Pty. Limited, *Sydney*
Prentice-Hall Canada, Inc., *Toronto*
Prentice-Hall Hispanoamericana, S. A., *Mexico*
Prentice-Hall of India Private Limited, *New Delhi*
Prentice-Hall of Japan, Inc., *Tokyo*
Pearson Education, Asia Pte. Ltd., *Singapore*
Editora Prentice-Hall do Brasil, Ltda., *Rio de Janeiro*

PREFACE

To an inexperienced person, a *blueprint* is nothing more than lines, numbers, letters, arrows, short statements, abbreviations, and pictures on large sheets of blue or white paper. This text is written to explain the information on these sheets of paper so that one can begin to visualize and understand the meanings. These are the two purposes of *blueprint reading* —to establish a picture of the structure in one's mind so that the construction team can make the picture a reality and to show the necessity for coordination between trades so that the structure can be finished with the fewest problems and the most cooperation.

FEATURES OF THE BOOK

Part I, "Introduction to Blueprint Reading," focuses on the basics. Chapter 1, "Blueprint Reading Fundamentals," explains the physical appearance of blueprints, their components, and their meanings.

Part II, "Residential Blueprint Reading," transports the reader from the drawing table to the job site. There the reader can relate the plan to the process and thence to the product. All phases of construction of a home—from before the first spadeful of earth to the last nail in the last roof shingle and afterward—are examined, and their origins are traced from the blueprint. Chapter topics include surveying, site improvement, below-grade construction, above-grade construction, and plumbing, mechanical, and electrical systems. Chapter 8, "The Lee Residence and Specifications," is especially helpful to readers because it relates all systems and construction phases to the blueprints and plans for one particular home.

Readers can gain insight into the complex legal issues and multiparty interrelationships of nonresidential construction in Part III, "Commercial Blueprint Reading." The lead-off chapters examine the legal documents and contracts, the project manual, and site improvement. Two ensuing chapters review the similarities and differences in planning and constructing two major families of commercial projects: office complexes and manufacturing/warehouse facilities.

Four appendixes conclude this thorough book. The first is an optional review chapter, "Fundamental Everyday Mathematics." The other useful appendixes include construction abbreviations, reference tables, and bid documents. Finally, the glossary defines common terms used in architecture and the construction trades.

A picture is indeed worth a thousand words, especially in the construction industry when one is endeavoring to communicate an idea, show it to other participants with varying skills and individual areas of expertise, and enable them to transform that idea into a physical reality. Therefore, *Blueprint Reading for Construction* relies heavily on schematics in general and blueprints in particular. Foremost is the set of large-scale illustrations reproduced from architectural drawings for the Lee Residence (note the tie-in with Chapter 8) that is shrink-wrapped with this book. As a further aid to the reader, each chapter concludes with exercises that promote better understanding of the material covered.

The author has practical experience in construction as a crew member in the field as well as a contractor and professional estimator. This text is written based on the knowledge gained from these experiences and professional guidance from friends in the industry.

ACKNOWLEDGMENTS

The author sincerely thanks the following reviewers for their insightful critiques and helpful suggestions: Marcal E. Sammut; H. Thomas Gillespie, Portland Community College; Marvin Maziarz, Niagara Community College; George B. Schramm.

James A. S. Fatzinger

CONTENTS

P A R T I

Introduction to Blueprint Reading

CHAPTER 1
Blueprint Reading Fundamentals

1

Blueprint Reading Fundamentals

The urge to produce a design drawing (plan) for a construction project is as old as time. The ancient structures of the Middle East, such as the pyramids, Nebuchadnezzar's palace, and many other magnificent structures, indicate that a great deal of planning went into logical layout and construction of temples, palaces, and whole communities. The same is true of structures built by the Polynesians, Incas, Mayans, and Aztecs: the Incan temples and communities in the Andes Mountains of Peru, the Taj-Mahal of India, and the temples of Indonesia. Some plans were engraved in stone and others were painted on walls, examples of which still exist today.

As humankind continued to dream of larger structures, details were written (specifications) describing exactly how the structure was to be built. One of the best examples of such instructions is found in the Bible for Solomon's temple. The necessity to actually design a structure became stronger as people discovered better writing utensils and materials (ink, graphite, and papyrus) which were used to better describe their thoughts. Projects of today, too, are designed on paper and built to the specifications and drawings of the architect and engineer. The development and improvement in paper quality (vellum, mylar, and the like) and the variety of available blueprinting processes have increased the ability to make plans for all types of structures. These plans are called **blueprints.**

THE BLUEPRINT

The term *blueprint* has two definitions. The first refers to the initial *blueprint sheet*, a drawing developed from a blueprint process. The individual blueprint sheet, best described as a *plan* or *drawing*, is but one part of the whole design.

One drawing, such as a floor plan, expresses only one view of a project.

The second meaning of the term *blueprint* infers a *composite* of several plans (such as the foundation, elevations, and so on) which must be assembled into a *set of drawings* to show as much about a project as can be placed on paper in one- or two-dimensional views. It is a complete pictorial description of a construction project prepared by a construction designer, an architect, or an engineer, and is designed for use by the owner, contractor, subcontractor, estimator, and the manufacturers and suppliers of materials, as well as all construction field personnel.

COMPUTER-AIDED DRAFTING (CAD) AND DESIGN DRAFTING (CADD)

See figure 1–1. The growth of the personal computer industry has resulted in the development of a **computer-aided drafting (CAD)** program, used for standard two-dimensional drawings, and a **computer-aided design drafting (CADD)** program, used for both two-dimensional and three-dimensional design development. Today most drawings in use in construction are produced from these programs. A draftsperson with computer experience can produce a drawing or set of drawings in a much shorter time than it takes to produce the drawing(s) manually. A completed drawing can be revised simply by making a computer command change. Plans can be changed or components relocated in a fraction of a second. The completed plans can be saved within the computer itself or by placing the information on a *disc* instead of a vellum or mylar that requires filing the sheets in large storage cabinets.

See figure 1–2. The computerized drawings can also be drawn on paper in black and white or in color, as desired, by use of a *plotter*, a machine designed for the purpose of producing the finished computer drawing on paper. The plotter is connected to the computer; by the push of a button or a command signal, the plotter draws the plans as directed by the computer. The drawings

FIGURE 1–2
Inkjet technology is used in the HP DeskJet 600 plotter, a high-resolution monochrome inkjet plotter with fast output. It uses commonly available media and offers better print quality than its predecessor.

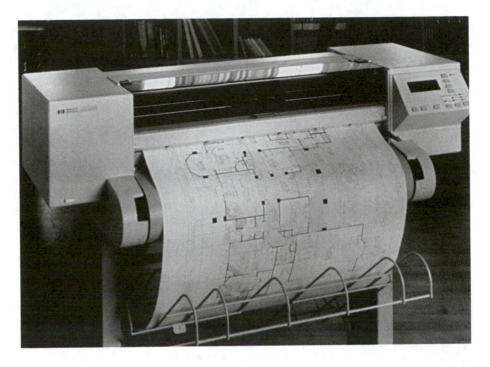

can then be reproduced by standard copy methods rather than through the use of blueprint machines.

THE PLAN GROUPS

There are six major plan groups in a complete set of plans. The groups include Civil, Architectural, Structural, Mechanical, Plumbing, and Electrical. A breakdown of the groups is as follows:

1. Civil Plans (work that has to do with construction in or on the earth)
   a. Site or Survey Plans (natural contours, property dimensions, azimuths, and possible legal description)
   b. Plot Plan (finish grades, structure location, landscaping layout)
   c. Utilities layout
   d. Paving
   e. Street improvements[1]
   f. Sections and details for each plan as required
   g. Landscape[1] (hardscape[1] and softscape[1])
2. Architectural (the plans that comprise the project design)
   a. Floor plan (bird's-eye view—horizontal room layout)
   b. Exterior elevations (pictorial views of size of structure and finishes)
   c. Interior elevations (details of individual room finishes and designs)
   d. Roof plan (indicating shape and finish materials necessary)
   e. Reflected ceiling plan

---

1. Each of the plans indicated may also be an independent set of plans designed by others.

      f. Door, window, hardware and room finish schedules[2]

      g. Sections (how the structure is to be built)

         (1) Longitudinal: parallel to ridge of a gable structure or the longest cutting plane

         (2) Transverse: perpendicular to the longitudinal section

         (3) Partial wall: a section of any portion of any wall of a structure

3. Structural (the engineered plans to match the architectural design)

    a. Structural general notes[3]

    b. Foundation plan (concrete footings, slabs, foundation walls; steel girders, columns or beams; reinforcement)

    c. Structural floor plan (wood or metal joist framing and underlayment)

    d. Walls (concrete, masonry, wood or steel framing, and accessories)

    e. Roof framing (sloped, flat; ceiling joists and roof rafters; trusses)

    f. Structural sections (same as architectural sections showing only the structural requirements)

    g. Structural schedules (reinforcement, footings, beams, piers, columns, lintels, joists, and so on)[3]

    h. Miscellaneous structural details (for better understanding of connections, accessory attachments, and so on)

4. Mechanical (engineered plans for heating, ventilation, and air-conditioning [HVAC])

    a. Layout (floor, reflected ceiling, roof, as required)

    b. Equipment schedules (HVAC, air-handling units)

    c. Control schematics (mechanical and electrical connections)

    d. Mechanical details (safing insulation, equipment mounts, and so on)

5. Plumbing (engineered plans for water supply and waste disposal)

    a. Isometric potable water plan (identifying supply connections and sizes)

    b. Isometric waste disposal plan (identifying all connections and sizes)

    c. Fixture and equipment schedules

6. Electrical (engineered plans for all electrical power and supply)

    a. Exterior lighting layout (if necessary)

    b. Power and lighting layout (lights, receptacles, and so on)

    c. Equipment schedules (service entrance panel, and so on)

    d. Details and schematics (electrical diagrams)

    Each project is individual in design and criteria, therefore, each may use all, or part, of the above listings for the set of plans. Large *commercial* and *industrial* construction projects are likely to incorporate all of the above plans in a project. There is also a difference between the plans used for residential as compared to those listed above.

Commercial Plans

Commercial plans may include *any structure of four stories or more developed for living purposes* such as multi-story apartments, condominiums, or hotels. Both commercial and industrial plans may include any *nonhabitable* structure one

---

2. The schedules may be noted separately in the plans, may be found in the specifications in a project manual, or both.

3. The schedules may be located in the General Notes sheet(s) or may be noted on individual plan sheets.

or more stories high, such as offices, warehouses, manufacturing plants, and so on. In addition, a separate book of information, called the *project manual*, is included with most commercial and industrial construction plans. The project manual states all of the legal requirements, conditions of the contract, a list of the organizations whose instructions are to be followed throughout all of the construction, and a format of specifications supplying material, labor, and equipment requirements necessary for the project.

Residential Plans

Residential plans are smaller in size since only portions of the plan groups are utilized. A plot plan, floor plan, roof plan, elevations, and one or two sections are normally all of the architectural plans drawn. Minimal structural, mechanical, plumbing, and electrical plans are utilized. Much of the work is accomplished through the workmanship clauses in construction associations and according to local codes and ordinances.

THE TITLE BLOCK

See all Plans and figure 1–3. General information regarding the project is found in the title block of each drawing. The block may be located along the bottom or the right side of the sheet. Included in the title block should be the following information:

1. Name of project.
    a. Owner's name and project address is also included.
2. Name of architect and/or engineer, address and telephone number.
    a. A certification or confirmation such as a state seal indicating the architect's or engineer's registration.
3. Project (drawing) number of architect and/or engineer.
4. Date plans are completed.
5. Initials of draftsperson and date.
6. Initials of plan checker and date.
7. Revision(s) and revision date(s) noted, if any.
8. Scale of plan.
    a. If more than one scale is used on the plan (such as found on detail sheets) the space for indication of scale should read "as shown" or "as noted."

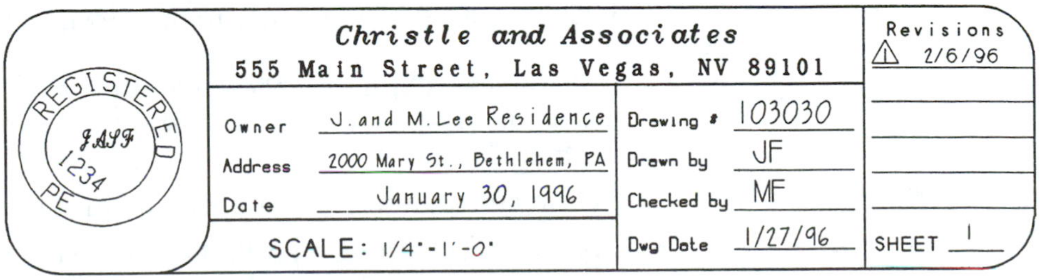

FIGURE 1–3
Typical Title Block.

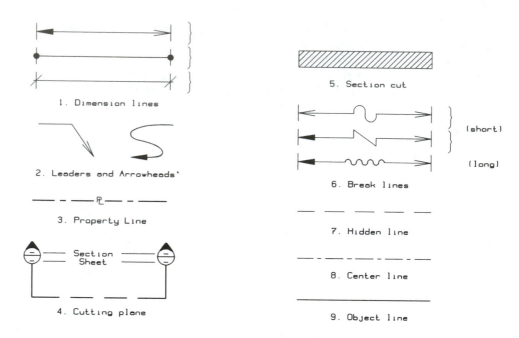

FIGURE 1–4
Lines of Construction

LINES OF CONSTRUCTION

See figure 1–4. It is necessary for the draftsperson and the blueprint reader to understand how lines play a very important part in defining meanings on a drawing. Identification of some of the more common types are as follows:

1. Dimension lines. Used to establish the dimensions of a portion of a structure and terminated with arrows (open or closed), dots, or slashes at a termination line drawn perpendicular to the dimension line and concluding at a desired point.

2. Leaders and arrowheads. Indicate the location of a specific part of the drawing for identification purposes. Used with words, abbreviations, symbols, or keynotes (see the following sections).

3. Property lines. Define the perimeter and the perimeter direction.

4. Cutting planes. Lines drawn to aid in the location and identification of an area of a drawing that is to be shown in a separate *plan* or *section* view.
   a. Plan view. A bird's-eye view identified from an elevation view.
   b. Section view. An elevation view showing interior construction criteria.

5. Section cut. Shows areas not included in the cutting plane view.

6. Broken line. Identifies a portion of a drawing that is not included.

7. Hidden line. Identifies a portion of a structure that is not visible.

8. Center line. Identifies symmetry about an object, such as the center line of a wall.
9. Object line. Identifies the object of primary interest or closeness.

Note that each line has a specific design and thickness that identifies it from other lines. Some of the lines may be used for the identification of off-site utilities. There may be an identification on the cover sheet and/or on the civil plans where they are used. This identification is referred to as the *legend*.

ABBREVIATIONS, SYMBOLS, AND KEYNOTES

Architects and engineers have devised systems of abbreviations, symbols, and keynotes to remove the clutter of wordy descriptions, making plans easier to read and understand.

Abbreviations

See appendix II. Abbreviations used in blueprint reading are a shortening of common construction terms. For example, the term *flush on* (or *face of*) *slab* is abbreviated as *F.O.S.* Abbreviations should always be written in upper-case (capital) letters. Abbreviations for a specific project should be noted on the title sheet or other introductory drawing. There are books available offering construction abbreviations and their definitions. It is not recommended that these abbreviations be memorized; usage will make them easier to remember.

Symbols

Symbols are used as part of the drawings to designate a particular material required for that portion of the project. A combination of these symbols, expanded and drawn to a specific size to match other material sizes on a drawing, make up the pictorial view of the plan. Symbols have been established for the architectural *(figure 1–5)*, civil and structural *(figure 1–6)*, mechanical *(figure 1–7)*, plumbing *(figure 1–8)*, and electrical *(figure 1–9)* plan groups. Some symbols may vary slightly in meaning from one geographic locale to another. The symbols used for each set of plans should be indicated on the title sheet or other introductory drawing. By so doing, the person reading the set of plans can better identify the object or material indicated. Many code books, manufacturers' brochures, and specifications also include symbols and their meanings.

Keynotes

See figure 1–10. A more recent trend to reduce cluttering a plan is the *keynote*. A number or letter (usually located in a square or circle) with a leader and arrowhead is used to identify a specific object. A portion of the drawing sheet is set aside for the *keynotes* (usually located on the right-hand side of a drawing) with corresponding numbers or letters. These corresponding keynote numbers or letters describe the item identified on the plan. The descriptions will normally include the use of abbreviations.

PLAN VIEWS

General
Brick similar)

Structural
Clay Tile
Masonry

Block-CMU

Batt or Blanket
Insulation

Cement
Plaster

ELEVATION VIEWS

Sheet Metal
Flashing

Masonry

Window

Horizontal Siding
or
Shingle Roofing

Tile
Roofing

SECTION VIEWS

Continuous
Rough Lumber

Blocked

Finish Lumber

Drywall

Plywood

Rigid
Insulation

Steel

Concrete
(w/aggregate)

Block-CMU
Masonry

Earth
(Finish Grade)   (Rough Grade)

FIGURE 1–5
Architectural Symbols

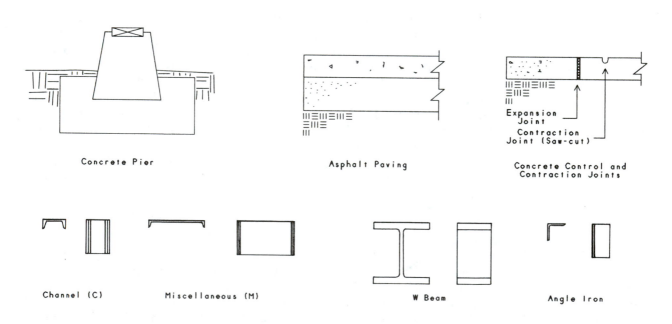

Concrete Pier

Asphalt Paving

Expansion
Joint
Contraction
Joint (Saw-cut)

Concrete Control and
Contraction Joints

Channel (C)

Miscellaneous (M)

W Beam

Angle Iron

Structural Steel

FIGURE 1–6
Civil and Structural Engineering Symbols

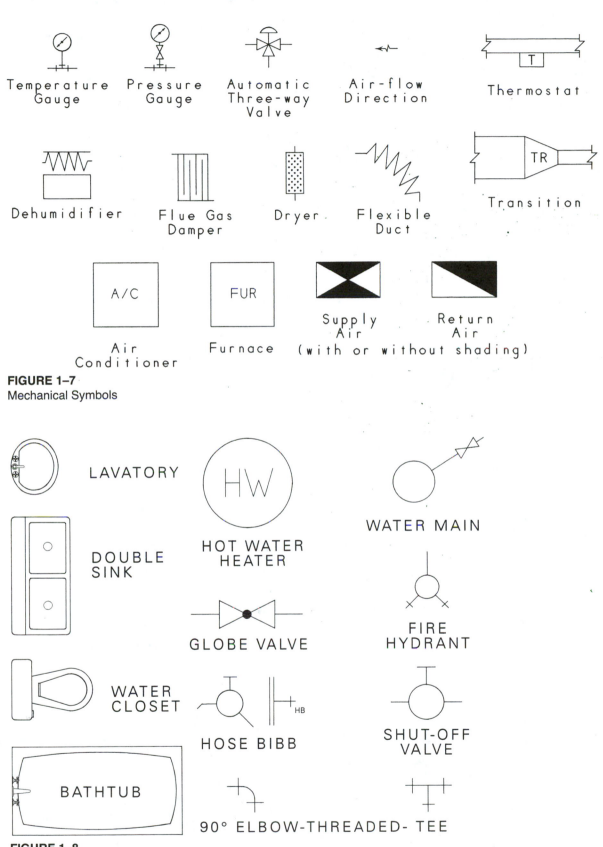

FIGURE 1–7
Mechanical Symbols

FIGURE 1–8
Plumbing Symbols

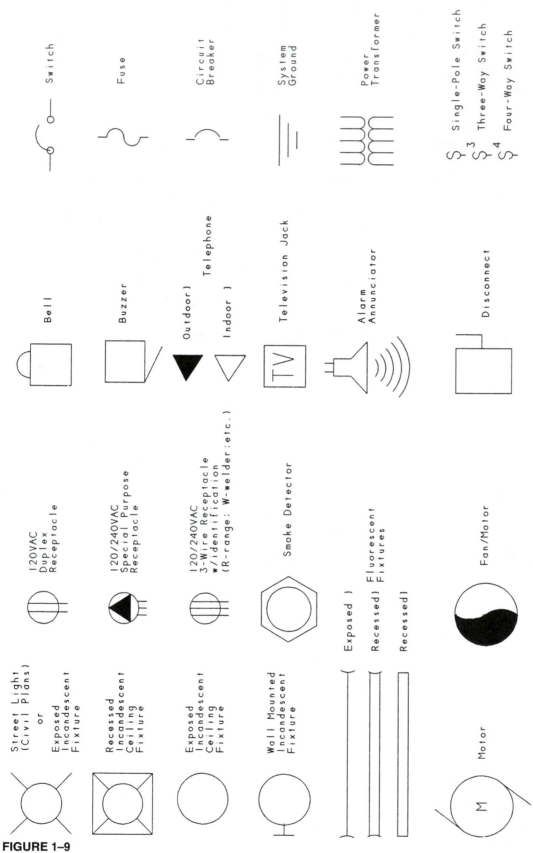

FIGURE 1–9
Electrical Symbols

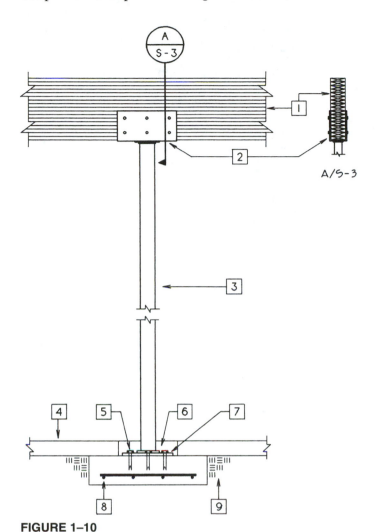

KEYNOTES

1. 6⅛" x 18" glulam beam
2. 6⅛" end cap
3. 6"DIA pipe column
4. 6" concrete slab w/6x6-W2.9 x W2.9 WWF
5. ⅝" DIA expansion bolt (typical of 6)
6. Seismic opening (to be filled with concrete)
7. ½" steel plate column base
8. 1'-0" x 4'-0" concrete footing w/4-#5 rebar each way
9. Natural or compacted grade

FIGURE 1–10
Keynotes

THE CSI FORMAT

See figure 1–11. Much of the above plan grouping has been produced through the efforts of architects and engineers resulting in a format to aid contractors and estimators regarding the requirements for each trade included in the project. An organization known as the Construction Specifications Institute is an outgrowth of these efforts. This organization is made up of architects, engineers, contractors, estimators, manufacturers, suppliers, and others interested in the development of a universal systematic construction and estimating procedure. This format is followed informally in residential construction but is strictly adhered to in commercial and industrial construction. The format includes sixteen divisions. The specifications in this text are examples of these formats using the *broadscope*, the *mediumscope,* and the *narrowscope* specifications. Figure 1–11 shows the divisions as they are listed in the broadscope specification. The mediumscope breaks the sections down into major subsections with numbers and titles. The narrowscope breaks the work down into paragraphs under the subsections. For example:

Division 1 - General Requirements

01010 Summary of Work
01020 Allowances
01025 Measurement & Payments
01030 Alternates/Alternatives
01040 Coonlimttlon
01060 Workmen's Comp. & Ins.
01200 Project Meetings
01300 Submittals/Substitutions
01400 Quality Costrol
01500 Construction Facilities
01600 Materials & Equipment
01700 Contract Close-out

Division 2 - Sitework

02000 Scope of Work
02010 Subsurface Investigation
02100 Site Preparation
02200 Earthwork
02500 Paving & Surfacing
02900 Landscaping

Division 3 - Concrete

03000 Scope of Work
03100 Concrete Formwork
03200 Reinforcement
03300 Cast-In-Place Concrete
03400 Precast Concrete

Division 4 - Masonry

04000 Scope of Work
04100 Mortar and Grout
04200 Brick
04300 Concrete Masonry Units

Division 5 - Metals

05000 Scope of Work
05100 Structural Metal Framing
05200 Structural Light Gauge Metal Framing

Division 6 - Wood and Plastics

06000 Scope of Work
06100 Rough Carpentry
06200 Finish Carpentry

Division 7 - Thermal and Moisture Protection

07000 Scope of Work
07100 Waterproofing
07200 Insulation
07300 Roofing Tile
07600 Sheet Metal
07900 Sealants & Caulking

Division 8 - Doors and Windows

08000 Scope of Work
08100 Metal Doors & Frames
08200 Wood & Plastic Doors
08250 Door Opening Assemblies
08500 Metal Windows

Division 9 - Finishes

09000 Scope of Work
09200 Lath & Plaster
09250 Gypsum Board (OWB)
09300 Tile
09500 Acoustical Treatment
09650 Resilient Flooring
09680 Carpet
09900 Painting
09950 Wallcovering

Division 10 - Specialties

10000 Scope of Work
10500 Lockers
10800 Toilet & Bath Accessories

Division 11 - Equipment

11000 Scope of Work
11700 Medical Equipment

Division 12 - Furnishings

12000 Scope of Work
12100 Office Furniture
12200 Draperies
12300 Rugs
12400 Art Work

Division 13 - Special Construction

13000 Scope of Work
13100 Boiler
13200 Incinerator

Division 14 - Conveying Systems

14000 Scope of Work
14100 Elevators
14200 Hoisting Equipment
14300 Conveyors

Division 15 - Mechanical

15000 Scope of Work
15050 Basic Mechanical Materials & Methods
15100 Heating, Ventilation & Air Conditioning
15400 Basic Plumbing Materials & Methods
15450 Plumbing

Division 16 - Electrical

16000 Scope ofWork
16050 Basic Electrical Materials & Methods
16400 Service & Distribution
16500 Lighting
16600 Special Systems
16700 Communications

FIGURE 1–11
CSI Master Format

Division:	DIVISION 4 - Masonry	}		}	}
		}Broadscope	}		}
Section:	04000 Scope of Work	}		}Mediumscope	}
			}		}Narrowscope
Subsection:	04010 General Requirements		}		}
					}
Paragraph:	1.1 Division 1 shall be considered a part of this Division.			}	

Division 1 in the CSI format contains information about the responsibilities and limitations of the owner, contractor, subcontractor, and specific details for submitting product information sheets, alternate and alternative proposals, allowances for special equipment, materials, change orders and work authorizations, specific insurance requirements, payment procedures, quality control, and temporary facilities.

Divisions 2 through 16 specify the materials and equipment required, installation procedures, code requirements, and standards of good construction practice. Instructions for a trade or combination of trades are included in each division. Each contractor or subcontractor bids the work according to the division and/or section of a division pertaining to the trade or trades in which the company is involved. For example, Division 7, Thermal and Moisture Protection, includes work pertaining to thermal insulation, underground moisture protection, roofing, sheet metal flashings, roof accessories, and caulking and sealants. Specialty contractors (subcontractors) working in insulation will bid those portions of the division pertaining to the insulation materials and working requirements. Manufacturers or suppliers specializing in roof accessories, such as prefabricated roof hatches or skylights, may also bid their own products directly to the contractor.

The CSI is constantly working to simplify the format and place new products into the proper categories. The format may have some minor changes in the latest update of the CSI, but the broadscope format shown is much the same as the new format.

DRAWING SCALES

The three drawing scales commonly in use for the development of plans are the architectural, civil engineering, and metric scales. The scales may be designed in triangular (open-divided) or flat shapes. Each type includes varying measurements indicated on each face of the scale. The open-divided triangular scales are 12″ in length, whereas, the flat or bevel scales may be 4″ to 18″ in length. Some scales are made into tape measures and others are included in wheels. These other scales do not include all of the scales identified in the open-divided scale as listed in the following paragraphs.

Many architects also include a statement warning everyone working with the drawings that *"dimensions shown on the plans take precedence over scaling."* The term *scaling* means to measure with some form of scale (architectural, engineering, metric, measuring wheel, or tape measure) rather than reading the dimensions.

Architectural Scale

See figure 1–12. Most plans are designed by the architect. A set of scales used to aid in producing drawings has been developed by the architects referred to as

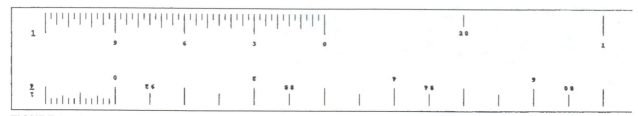

FIGURE 1–12
Typical Architectural Scale

the *architectural scales,* designed to measure both feet and inches. The scales are designated by a fraction of an inch equal to one foot, for example, ¼″ = 1′-0″, which is actually ¹⁄₄₈ of one foot (4 [¼″ per inch] x 12″ = 48, therefore ¹⁄₄₈, or 1:48 scale). The open-divided architectural scale includes four[4] measurements on each face, for a total of twelve scales. They are as follows:

Face 1:

Full Scale = 12″
¹⁄₁₆″ = 1′-0″ (the "16" marked on the Full Scale)[4]
³⁄₃₂″ = 1′-0″
³⁄₁₆″ = 1′-0″

Face 2:

⅛″ = 1′-0″
¼″ = 1′-0″
½″ = 1′-0″
1″ = 1′-0″

Face 3:

⅜″ = 1′-0″
¾″ = 1′-0″
1½″ = 1′-0″
3″ = 1′-0″

Because the architectural scales are challenging to read, an explanation of the meaning of the scales and the lines follows. On an open-divided scale, each line of scales on every face except the full scale (12″ ruler) contains the same information. The left and right ends show a small ruler broken down into either inches or inches-and-fractions-of-an-inch. The size of the scale is also designated on each end. The larger the scale, the larger the spacing, and the more fractions of an inch can be measured. The smaller scale on each level of each face is always half the size of the larger scale; that is, ³⁄₃₂″ and ³⁄₁₆″ are on one level; ⅛″ and ¼″ on another; ⅜″ and ¾″ on a third; and ½″ and 1″ on a fourth; and, finally, 1½″ and 3″ on the fifth. The remaining two scale are the "full scale" (12″ ruler) broken down into ¹⁄₁₆″ increments.

4. This scale is not recognized by most architects as a scale on this face, but many plans have been drawn to this ¹⁄₁₆″ = 1′-0″ scale and is, therefore, to be considered.

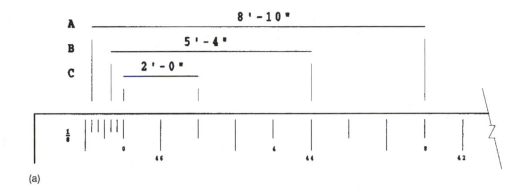

(a)

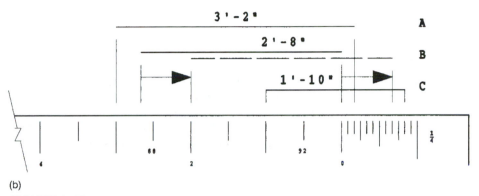

(b)

FIGURE 1–13
Reading Architectural Open-Divided Scale

The sizes indicated on the two drawings are for the ⅛″ = 1′-0″ and ¼″ = 1′-0″ scales. Both scales are on the same face and on the same level of the face.

See figure 1–13a. This drawing shows a portion of the ⅛″ scale. The very small lines left of the zero represent increments of 2″, adding up to 1′-0″. Reading from the zero on the left toward the right, there are two different size lines and two groups of numbers with differing values. The space between *all* of the lines (shortest and longest) is the ⅛″ = 1′-0″ scale. Starting at the zero and reading from left to right, each fourth line is numbered starting with 4 (lineal feet) and ending with 92 (lineal feet).

See figure 1–13b. The drawing shows a portion of the ¼″ scale. The breakdown for the very small lines from the zero to the right shows 1″ increments, totaling 1′-0″. Starting at the zero and reading from right to left, the numbers start with 2 and end with 46. Only the larger lines on the scale represent the ¼″ scale.

To read a measurement with the scales, use the following procedure:

1. Place the zero (0) on the end of the line to be measured or drawn.

2. If the line ends on one of the vertical scale lines, read the length.

3. Where the line extends beyond one of the scale indicators but does not extend to the next longer measurement, use the following procedure:
   a. Move the scale so that the end of the line is located at the nearest lower measurement. This moves the end of the line at the zero into the inch increments.
   b. Read the number of inches and/or fractions of an inch and add them to the foot measurement to which the scale is moved.

For example, the length of line "C" in figure 1–13a (the ⅛" scale) is exactly 2 lineal feet (lf). All other lines are longer and include both feet and inches, that is, line "A" is 8'-10" long and line "B" is 5'-4". Figure 1–13b (the ¼" scale) shows how these measurements are obtained. Line "B" on the right extends beyond the *nearest lower whole foot*. In this case the nearest lower whole foot is 2 lf. The scale is moved (see arrows) so that the left end of the line aligns with the 2 lf mark. The reader then looks to the right of zero to see how many inches, or fractions of an inch, the line extends into the ruler on the right. In this case it extends 8". The line, therefore, is 2'-8". It is in this same manner that all lines are measured. No matter which scale is used, align the *nearest lower whole foot* to the left or right (depending upon the scale) with the end of the line being measured and read the inches to the left or right of the zero.

Civil Engineering Scale

See figure 1–14. Site plans and city engineering developments such as street improvements and utility installations are frequently much too large for the architectural scales. Therefore, engineers have developed their own scales designed to measure feet per inch only (for example, 1" = 10 lf). The engineering scale, similar to the triangular-shaped architectural scale, has six scales on the three faces. They are as follows:

Face 1:

1" = 10'-0"

1" = 50'-0"

Face 2:

1" = 20'-0"

1" = 40'-0"

Face 3:

1" = 30'-0"

1" = 60'-0"

Each line on any scale is equal to 1 lineal foot. The lines that are numbered must have the zero (0) added. Thus, number 1 = 10 lf, 2 = 20 lf, and so on, no matter which scale is read.

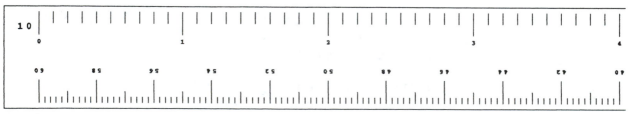

FIGURE 1–14
Typical Engineering Scale

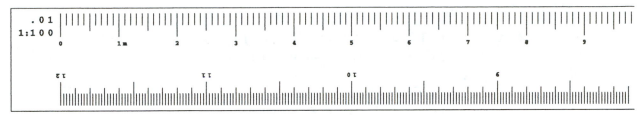

FIGURE 1–15
Typical Metric Scale

Metric Scale

See figure 1–15 and appendix III. Many countries have been using the Systeme International (SI) metric system. Appendix III identifies some metric measurements and their English equivalents. Metric scales are now required in the United States for all federal government plans for the purpose of establishing metrics as a standard for *all* plans. Some architects and engineers are also using metrics on nongovernmental projects, although in many cases the use of metrics is being resisted for private construction projects. As with the architectural and civil engineering scales, there are variations in the shapes of the metric scales, but the scale used for explanation is the triangular open-divided scale. The metric scale has a total of six measurements on three faces.

The metric drawing scale uses the millimeter as the base linear measurement. Metric measurements are in multiples of 10. Numbers are expressed in whole and decimal parts of whole numbers. For example:

1 millimeter (mm) = $\frac{1}{10}$ centimeter (cm) = $\frac{1}{100}$ decimeter (dm) = $\frac{1}{1000}$ meter (m)

1 centimeter (cm) = $\frac{1}{10}$ of a decimeter (dm) = $\frac{1}{100}$ of a meter (m)

1 decimeter (dm) = $\frac{1}{10}$ of a meter (m)

10 meters (m) = 1 decameter (dcm)

100 meters (m) = 10 decameters (dcm) = 1 hectometer (hm)

1000 meters (m) = 100 decameters (dcm) = 10 hectometers (hm) = 1 kilometer (km)

Square and cubic measures are calculated in the same manner as the English measure. The same measurements indicated above for linear measure also hold true for liquid measure (volume), except that the term *liter* is used in lieu of *meter*.

Fractions are described as decimals in the following manner:

500 millimeters
{ 0.5 meter
{ 5.0 decimeters
{ 50.0 centimeters

The decimals located on the faces of the scales—.01, .0125, .02, .025, and .05—indicate the decimal length of a meter on the scale. The ratios indicate the ratio of the scales to a meter; that is, on the scale with a ratio of 1:100, 100 mm = 1 m. The faces of a metric scale are as follows:

Face 1:

.01 - 1:100　　(where 100 mm = 1 m)
.025 - 1:40　　(where 40 mm = 1 m)

Face 2:

.0125 - 1:80　　(where 80 mm = 1 m)
.02 - 1:50　　(where 50 mm = 1 m)

Face 3:

.05 - 1:20　　(where 20 mm = 1 m)
1:331/3　　(where 30 mm = 1 m)

CHAPTER EXERCISES

1. What do the following abbreviations mean?

a. CJ	e. HDW	i. L	m. DIA
b. FTG	f. TOP	j. MO	n. DO
c. GI	g. BM	k. CC	o. ENCL
d. d	h. REINF	l. A.F.F.	p. SHTHG

SCALES

The student should already have the three scales, or the instructor may supply scales for the following examples.

Architectural Scale

1. Draw a line that is 6³⁄₁₆″ long. Using an open-divided architectural scale, determine the length of the line for each scale below in inches, feet, or feet and inches.

a. ⅛″ = 1'-0″ scale _____	g. ⅜″ = 1'-0″ scale _____
b. ³⁄₃₂″ = 1'-0″ scale _____	h. 1″ = 1'-0″ scale _____
c. 1½″ = 1'-0″ scale _____	i. ½″ = 1'-0″ scale _____
d. ³⁄₁₆″ = 1'-0″ scale _____	j. ¹⁄₁₆″ = 1'-0″ scale _____
e. ¼″ = 1'-0″ scale _____	k. ¾″ = 1'-0″ scale _____
f. Full scale _____	l. 3″ = 1'-0″ scale _____

Engineering Scale

1. Draw a line that is 5⅞″ long. Using an open-divided civil engineering scale, determine the length of the line for each of the following scales in feet only.

a. 1″ = 10' _____	d. 1″ = 50' _____
b. 1″ = 60' _____	e. 1″ = 20' _____
c. 1″ = 30' _____	f. 1″ = 40' _____

Metric Scale

1. Draw a line that is 7″ long. On the metric scale, this line measures:

a. .025 (1:40) scale = _____ m	d. .02 (1:50) scale = _____ m
b. 0.30 (1:33 ⅓) scale = _____ m	e. .0125 (1:80) scale = _____ m
c. 0.05 (1:20) scale = _____ m	f. .01 (1:100) scale = _____ m

General Exercises

1. Figure 1–16 is a *footprint* of a structure with various measurements indicated by letters only. Using the following architectural scales give the length of the line corresponding with the letter next to the scale:

   a. ⅛″ =1′-0″ _____   i. ³⁄₃₂″ =1′-0″ _____
   b. 1″ =1′-0″ _____   j. 3″ =1′-0″ _____
   c. 1½″ =1′-0″ _____   k. 1″ = 60′ _____
   d. ½″ =1′-0″ _____   l. ³⁄₁₆″ =1′-0″ _____
   e. ¾″ =1′-0″ _____   m. ¹⁄₁₆″ =1′-0″ _____
   f. 1″=10′ _____   n. ⅜″ =1′-0″ _____
   g. ¼″ =1′-0″ _____   o. 1″ = 40′ _____
   h. 1″ = 20′ _____   p. 1″ = 30′ _____

2. Name the six major plan groups and describe the drawings that make up each group of a complete set of plans.

3. Why are both architectural and structural sections drawn in a set of plans?

4. Number and name the divisions per the CSI format. Describe the work included in each division.

5. What is the broadscope version of the format? The mediumscope version? The narrowscope version?

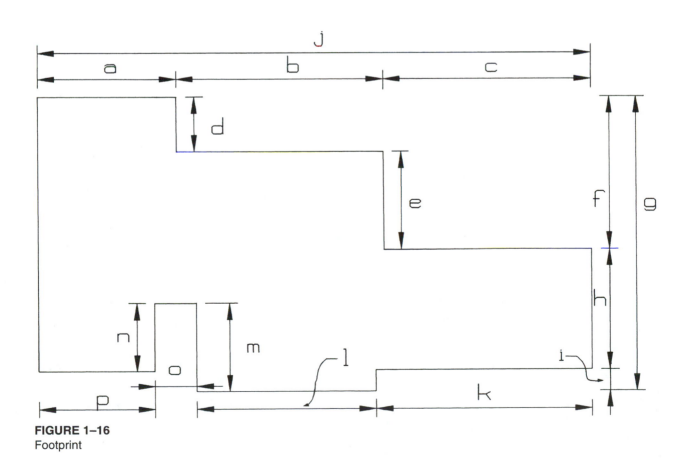

FIGURE 1–16
Footprint

6. Match the components below with the identifying numbers in *figure 1–17*:

a. Concrete wall _____	h. Cased opening _____
b. Combination wall _____	i. Rigid insulation _____
c. Bi-fold door _____	j. Threshold _____
d. FX GL window _____	k. Brick veneer _____
e. Sliding glass door _____	l. Door Opening _____
f. CMU wall _____	m. Exterior plaster _____
g. 2×6 exterior wall _____	n. Drywall (GWB) _____
	o. 2×4 interior wall _____

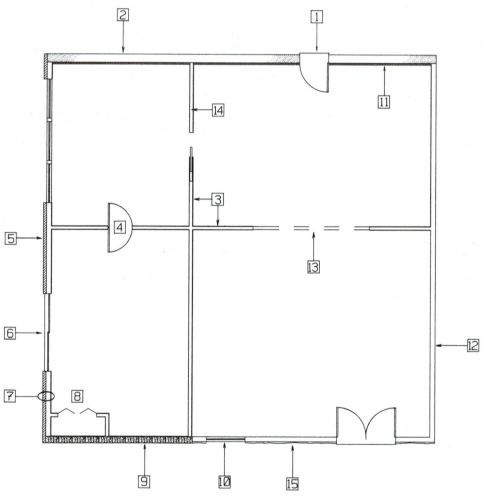

FIGURE 1–17
Wall Components

7. Identify the materials called out below with the wall section in *figure 1–18:*

a. Rafter	_____	n. Foundation wall	_____
b. Stud	_____	o. Sill plate	_____
c. Double top plate	_____	p. Footing	_____
d. Ceiling joist	_____	q. Drywall	_____
e. Sheathing (roof)	_____	r. Subfloor	_____
f. Sole plate	_____	s. Lintel (header)	_____
g. Floor joist	_____	t. Window	_____
h. Beam	_____	u. GI screed	_____
i. Tile roofing	_____	v. R19 insulation	_____
j. Fascia board	_____	w. Rigid insulation	_____
k. Window trim	_____	x. Baseboard	_____
l. R30 insulation	_____	y. Siding	_____
m. Cold key	_____	z. Concrete slab	_____

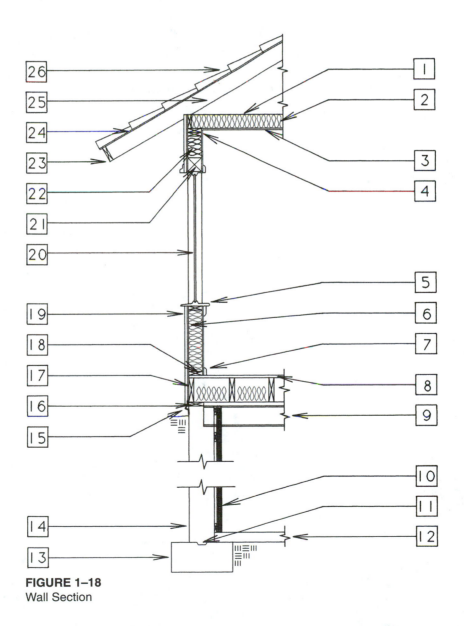

FIGURE 1–18
Wall Section

Refer to figure 1–19 to answer the following questions:

8. The elevation of the finish floor is:
   a. 1101.0'   c. 1133.0'
   b. 1115.0'   d. 1095.0'

9. The lowest point of elevation on the property is located at
   a. Southwest corner   c. Northwest corner
   b. Northeast corner   d. Southeast corner

10. The point of beginning (POB) is located at what point on the property line?
    a. Northwest corner of the footprint
    b. Southwest corner of property
    c. Southeast corner of property
    d. Northeast corner of property

11. The contours are shown in _____ increments.
    a. 0.30 m   c. 4.57 m
    b. 3.05 m   d. 1.49 m

12. The property has:
    a. No right angle corners.   c. Both a and b.
    b. No property line measurements.   d. Neither a nor b.

13. The footprint of the structure:
    a. Follows the shape of the property.
    b. Is at an angle.
    c. Is aligned parallel with the property lines.
    d. None of the above.

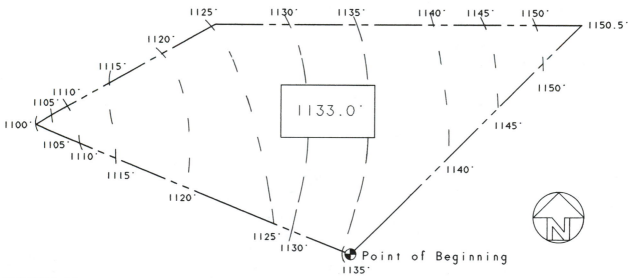

FIGURE 1–19
A Site Plan

P A R T

Residential Blueprint Reading

2

The Survey

Identifying the limits and direction of one's property and property lines has been, and is, important for the owner in many ways. The identification helps prevent encroachment by others onto the property; it aids in the determination of one's wealth; but the *survey,* primarily, secures entitlement to a property. Surveys have been made for these purposes for centuries. A survey accomplishes two purposes: *it is an appraisal of the physical properties of the earth and the determination of dimensions and directions of the perimeter of a specific area.*

One of the earlier types of "survey" was to have someone walk or run as far in one direction in one day (or other specific time sequence) as was humanly possible. This was how the north, south, and west boundaries of at least one of the original states of the United States—Pennsylvania—were identified.

The materials used in earlier times to measure and locate the direction included *rods,* specific lengths of a certain type of *chain* (from which the term *chainman,* for a crew member, developed), and a simple *compass.* The rod, measuring 16'-6", is a part of land measurement still in use today. Another form of the rod is the *Philadelphia rod,* a ruler divided into either ⅛" or ¹⁄₁₀₀" increments and used for determining elevations.

TYPES OF SURVEYS

The Property Survey, Metes and Bounds

See figure 2–1. The *Metes and Bounds* system, in use since colonial times, is commonly used for individual property surveys. Metes and bounds is best described as *the measurement and location of a specific piece of property.* A

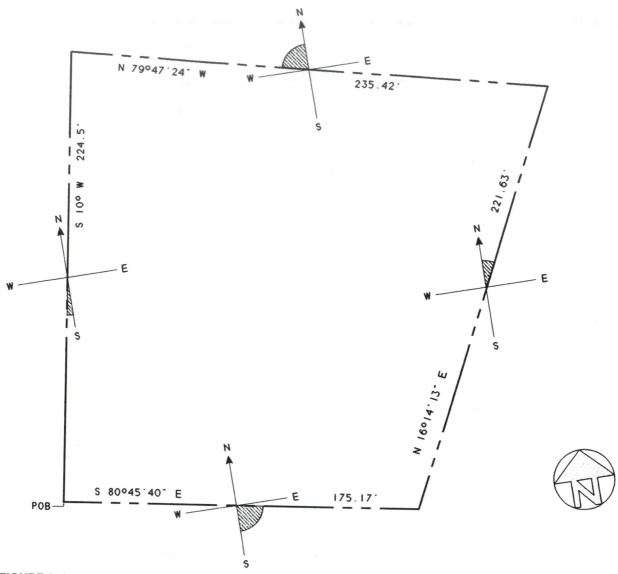

FIGURE 2–1
Metes and Bounds, the "C" Residence

survey team locates, identifies, and uses as a reference point the nearest **datum point** (described in the following sections) to the property. The team then proceeds to locate the distance and direction from that point to the nearest corner of the property, referred to as the **point of beginning** (see later section).

The direction and length of all property lines are determined from this point. The directions are called **azimuths,** and are noted in reference to true North along the property lines. For example, N 25° 33′ 12″ E states the property line is in the direction of: north longitude 25 degrees, 33 minutes ($^{33}/_{60}$ of a degree), 12 seconds ($^{12}/_{60}$ of a minute), in an easterly latitude from the point of reference (point of beginning, or one of the other corners of the property). These references continue until all directions and terminal points are located and plotted. The lengths are determined in feet and decimal fraction of a foot, such as 275.33′.

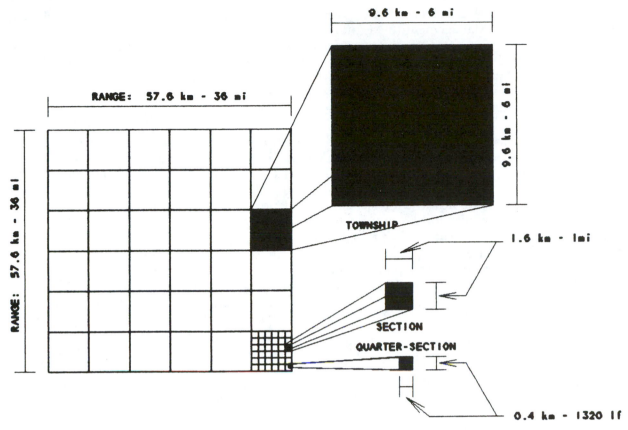

FIGURE 2–2
Range/Township/Section and Quarter-Section

Area Survey, Ranges

See figure 2–2. The second system is the survey used for the location of *ranges*, *townships*, *sections*, *quarter-sections*, and *plats*, for location and identification of areas. The areas are broken down as follows:

1. Ranges, 36 mi by 36 mi, or 1,296 mi² (57.6 km by 57.6 km, or 3,317.8 km²) each

2. Townships, 6 mi by 6 mi, or 36 mi² (9.6 km by 9.6 km, or 92.2 km²) each

3. Sections, 1 mi by 1 mi or 640 acres (1.6 km by 1.6 km, or 3.6 km²) each

4. Quarter-sections, 1,320 lf by 1,320 lf, or 160 acres (0.4 km by 0.4 km, or 0.16 km²) each

5. Plats vary according to the size of the individual property within the quarter-section; that is, a plat may be a single property or may be reduced into a subdivision with many smaller *lots*.

The Benchmark and Datum Point. Each of these areas has a **benchmark** used as the starting point for all surveys within an area. The benchmark usually indicates the lowest elevation above mean sea level for the area. Many of the original benchmarks were established by the United States Army Corps of Engineers. Other government organizations, such as the Bureau of Land Management (BLM), now do their own surveys.

Datum points are also established during the survey. These may be *secondary points* established from a benchmark, or may be a benchmark, indicating the elevation above mean sea level at that point. The additional datum points reduce the distance necessary to locate smaller surveyed areas such as the plats or lots. They are identified on the topographical maps by location and elevation. For example, the location may be indicated by the junction of two rivers or streams or the junction of highway or street intersections. The benchmark may be a marker (such as a steel or wood post) or a concrete or stone monument established for the purpose. The datum points are usually identified by a brass cap located in the center of a street intersection, on a curb near the intersection, or any other location that can be prominently displayed for the surveyors.

The benchmark or datum point nearest a project is usually written on a site or plot plan (see the following sections) indicating its location in relationship to a project. The elevations are noted on the maps as the elevation above mean sea level in feet, and decimal parts of a foot, where necessary, such as elev. 2575.38'. The measurements are identified as the **elevation**, not as the height.

Point of Beginning and Founds. As noted previously, the point of beginning (POB) is usually the corner of a property nearest the datum point where the survey starts. This point should be important to all contractors involved in the project. All site improvements and on-site layouts should be established in reference to this point. Following this procedure ensures fewer errors in layout and work will be more accurate.

The remaining points, at the junction of two property lines, are referred to as **founds**. In the same manner as the benchmark, datum point, or POB, each corner of the property has a found marker and an elevation established for it.

Contours. *See figure 2–3.* The natural **contour lines** are the curved, crooked lines on a topographical map or construction site plan. The contour elevations may be scaled in increments of 1.0', 5.0', 10.0', or larger elevations (for very large topographical maps). The elevation may be noted either above mean sea level or the elevation above the nearest benchmark or datum point.

The example identifies the natural contour elevations in a plan view spaced at 5.0' intervals. A second portion of the drawing shows horizontal lines drawn to the same distance, vertically, as in the plan view. Perpendicular lines are drawn from the ends of the contours on the plan view to intersect with the horizontal lines. When all of the intersections are determined, a line is drawn from intersection to intersection. The line drawn through these intersections produces the profile. This profile is actually an elevation, or a section, of the plan. A second profile, or section, can be done at any angle over the plan in the same manner. The plan view can be dissected even further to get a more accurate picture of the elevations. Reverse the procedure to develop a plan view from an actual elevation.

This is the manner in which civil engineers produce the contours shown on a site plan. The elevations are determined by the readings obtained from the survey. The elevations are plotted and the contour plan produced. All natural contours are normally drawn with dashed lines.

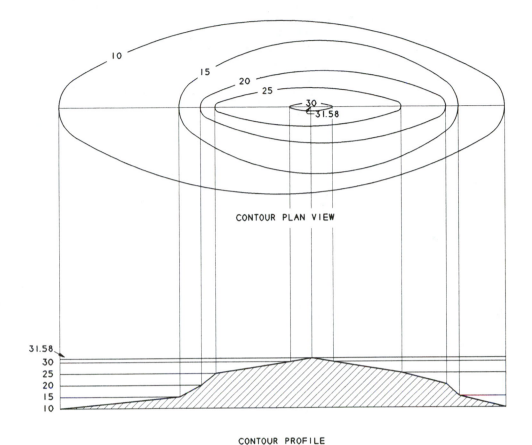

FIGURE 2–3
Development of Contour Profile

THE SITE AND PLOT PLANS

Site Plan

See figure 2–4. The site plan (also referred to as the survey plan) includes the location of the property in regards to the nearest datum point, the perimeter azimuths, the dimensions of the perimeters, and the natural contours developed from a survey. The survey is reproduced into "maps," the civil plans, used for construction.

Plot Plan

See figure 2–5. A plot plan is a layout of a project, including the placement of the residence and/or other structure(s). The finish grade contours indicated are the elevations above mean sea level after excavating and grading work is completed. The finish grades are drawn through the property in the same way as the natural contours, except that solid lines are used. The finish contours are identified in the same manner as the natural contours, that is, as an elevation above mean sea level, or above the nearest datum point, after excavating and grading work is completed.

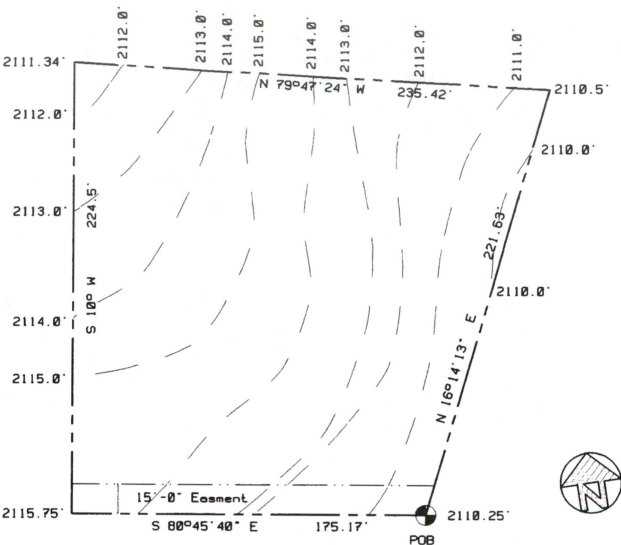

FIGURE 2–4
Site (Survey) Plan, Garland Residence

An alternate to the finish grade contours is the use of grade points. A point, identified thus (+), is drawn with an elevation noted next to it—for example, + 2193.7′ (+ 668.7 m). The points are located at all grade changes for finish surfacing such as asphalt or concrete finish elevations, curbs, and steps. Driveways, sidewalks, landscaping, utility locations, and utility **easements** (see next section) may also be included on the plan.

Easements. An easement is a portion of the property reserved as the *right-of-way* for utilities, whether they are installed above grade, on grade, or below grade. No structures or obstructions may be built by the property owner on the easement, but the area may be landscaped. The exception to the "no structure" regulation may be the installation of property perimeter walls only when permission is granted from the utilities or local authorities.

Set-Backs. A set-back is the distance from the front and from one side of a structure measured from the nearest intersecting property lines. The set-back locations are dependent upon the location and size of the property (tract or

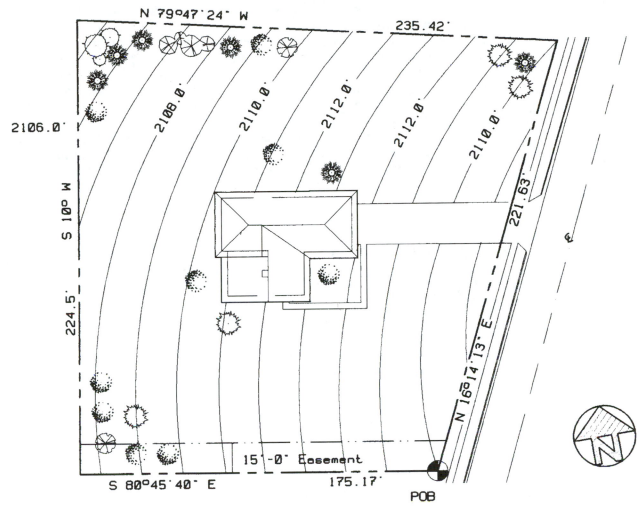

FIGURE 2–5
Plot Plan, Garland Residence

custom construction). If possible, the set-backs should be established from the property lines that intersect at the POB. The set-backs may be noted on the site plan if a structure *footprint* is shown; otherwise they are identified on the plot plan. A footprint is a perimeter outline of the foundation of the structure that may indicate the finish floor elevation—again, above mean sea level, benchmark, or datum point.

Minimum set-backs are established by local codes and ordinances. Where the population is sparse, such as in some suburban areas, the set-back minimums may extend 25'-0" (7.6 m) or more. In locales where high-density construction is allowed, the set-backs may be as little as 2'-0" (0.61 m) or as far as 10'-0" (3.0 m) from the nearest property lines for single-family residences. Density is determined by the number of units per acre allotted by the local authorities.

CONTINUING SURVEYS FOR A PROJECT

Surveying does not stop with the site survey. A survey may be necessary for street improvements, utility installations, and the like. The excavating and grading contractor must continue surveying a project until the earth has been properly graded in accordance with the finish grade elevations. Where a mass excavation (discussed in a later chapter) is required, another survey is necessary for the layout of the area to be excavated. Upon the completion of the excavating and grading, the concrete, plumbing, and electrical contractors must be certain that the trenches are in the proper locations for the structure as well as determining the proper widths and depths for the footings and service installations. And, finally, the proper location of the structure itself requires the services of a survey organization.

The specialty contractors, or subcontractors, use a variety of survey equipment to determine if the floor or ceilings are being installed to the proper levels. The survey equipment varies according to necessity and to how technical the work is, but surveys are necessary from beginning to end of a project.

CHAPTER EXERCISES

Multiple Choice

_____ 1. A property survey is identified as:
   a. A range survey.
   b. A quarter-section survey.
   c. A Metes and Bounds survey.
   d. None of the above.

_____ 2. The base point from which all surveys are made in a specific area is called:
   a. The point of beginning.
   b. The found.
   c. The nearest datum point.
   d. The benchmark.

_____ 3. An area survey includes the following:
   a. Ranges, quarter-sections, and plats only
   b. Townships, sections, and plats only
   c. Ranges and townships only
   d. Ranges, townships, sections, quarter-sections, and plats

_____ 4. The benchmark is also known as one of the following:
   a. A found
   b. A datum point
   c. A secondary elevation point
   d. None of the above.

_____ 5. The property survey includes the following:
   a. The point of beginning
   b. Founds
   c. A datum point
   d. All of the above.

_____ 6. The survey drawing is also referred to as:
   a. The plot plan.
   b. The site plan.
   c. The range layout.
   d. None of the above.

_____ 7. There are two types of contours identified in civil drawings.
They are
a. The natural contours and finish grades.
b. The azimuths.
c. The property perimeter lines.
d. The latitude and longitude lines.

_____ 8. A range map is also referred to as one of the following:
a. A topographical map
b. A plat
c. A subdivision
d. None of the above.

_____ 9. A subdivision is made of individual
a. Townships.
b. Sections.
c. Quarter-sections.
d. Plots.

_____ 10. A site survey is
a. Required on all preliminary property investigations.
b. The determination of the property limits.
c. Both a and b.
d. Neither a nor b.

True or False

T F   1. The natural contours are the finish grades on a plot plan.

T F   2. The utility companies have a "right of way" called the boundary.

T F   3. The individual property survey most commonly uses the system of
Metes and Bounds.

T F   4. The azimuths of a Metes and Bounds survey are the lengths of the
property lines.

T F   5. All latitudes and longitudes are given in reference to true or mag-
netic north.

T F   6. A natural contour is the contour of the land prior to excavating or
grading.

T F   7. A set-back is the distance from the rear and one side of a property.

T F   8. The point of beginning is usually the point nearest the local datum
point.

T F   9. The location of the corners of a property is identified with a found.

T F 10. The number shown at a datum point is identified as the height
above mean sea level.

T F 11. The identification of the direction of a property line is given in
hours, minutes, and seconds.

T F 12. A township is 36 mi by 36 mi square.

T F 13. A plat may be an individual property or subdivided into smaller
plots.

T F 14. An easement is reference to an elevation of a property.

T F 15. The surveyor of a property identifies the angle formed by an azimuth as north-by-east, north-by-west, south-by-east, and south-by-west.

T F 16. Off-site work includes all construction within the project boundaries.

T F 17. The minimum setback for a property in most high-density areas is from 1.5 m to 3.0 m.

T F 18. An easement is a portion of a property used for storage.

T F 19. The point of beginning may be a datum point or a found.

T F 20. A topographical map is the same as a survey map.

Completion

1. The _____ is the area of a property used by the utility companies as a right-of-way.

2. A property line has an azimuth reading, which states that the line is north 35 degrees, 21 minutes, and 30 seconds by west. It is written as _____.

3. The larger survey maps are made up of _____.

4. A quarter-section is _____ in length each way.

5. The original individual property survey, used since colonial times, is called a _____ survey.

6. Surveys were made using chains and _____.

7. The Philadelphia rod is divided into increments of ⅟₁₀₀″ or _____″.

8. The length of a rod in today's survey is _____.

9. A range is _____ mi².

10. A benchmark is normally recorded as the _____ elevation of an area.

3

Off-Sites and Site Improvements

New construction projects require a considerable amount of work on and in the ground before a structure can be built. The work includes both off-site construction and site improvements. Whereas off-sites are not always required, site improvements are. The work may encompass excavating, grading, paving, landscaping, and concrete. Other trades, such as plumbing and electrical, may also be involved. The terms and the work involved are defined and expanded upon in the following sections.

SOILS REPORT

Any contractor involved with work directly on or excavating in the earth must know the soils conditions in which the project is located. This area of instructions must be understood and adhered to prior to any work being started on a construction project. A special report, called the soils report, is included with the legal documents for the project. This report identifies the type, content, and stability of the soil. The types and classifications of soil include:

1. Gravel, a mixture of natural or crushed rock from ¼" (0.64 cm) to 3" (7.62 cm) DIA.
2. Sand, actually, a crushed gravel (rock) that is ⅜" (0.95 cm) DIA maximum, will pass through a no. 4 sieve, but will be retained in a no. 200 sieve.

3. Clay, a compact soil primarily of a silica and alumina mixture. When dry, it is brittle; when wet, very plastic.

4. Loam, a rich, smooth soil consisting of clay, sand, and organic matter.

5. Loam with sand (sandy loam), a mixture of class 2 and class 4.

6. Silt and loam, a very fine sand (passes through a no. 200 sieve) and class 4.

7. Clay and loam, a mixture of class 3 and class 4.

The sieve sizes are designed for soils classifications and range in size from a no. 4 to a no. 200. The sieve is a pie-shaped pan with a wire mesh in the bottom. The sieves are graded as no. 4, no. 8, no. 16, no. 30, no. 50, no. 100, and no. 200 for fine aggregates. There are larger sieves for larger aggregates ranging in size from 6″ (15.24 cm) square to ⅜″ (0.95 cm) square and the no. 4. The smaller sizes are calculated in the number of meshes (openings) in 1 in². The larger sized sieves are square holes of the size indicated.

OFF-SITE CONSTRUCTION

Off-site construction includes all work along the exterior of the perimeter of a property that may be required and any approaches into the property up to the property line. This may include any grading and paving of a public street upon completion of utility work or for street improvement only; curb and gutter installation; driveway entrance aprons; sidewalk improvements and **berms**. Berms are landscaped areas that may be located between the curb and sidewalk or between the sidewalk and the property line. Additional plans may be prepared by the utilities or local authorities to be included with the set of plans, or the requirements may be inferred by local ordinance. Other work and materials that may be included in off-site work are the connections (taps) at the nearest utility location and installation of the utilities from the taps to the structure, including trenching and backfilling.

Street improvements vary with the type of installation. Some tertiary rural roads may only require scarifying of the road surface and installation of gravel for some stability and reduction of dust. Secondary roads, such as asphaltic two-lane rural roads and highways, and local residential streets require the installation of a compacted base material (gravel, Type II soil, and so on), asphaltic surfacing, and sealing. Primary street and highway construction and repairs require much the same materials and installation procedures. The difference is in the type of construction (concrete or cementitious asphalt materials) and the more stringent code requirements.

In urban areas secondary and primary road types frequently require the installation of sidewalks, curbs, and gutters. Landscaping (ground cover, shrubbery, and trees) is also often a major part of such installations. Where utilities have been installed, the work also requires special care, such as inspections to determine the proper installation and protection of the materials and proper compaction to prevent breakdowns from the traffic load on the surface.

SITE IMPROVEMENTS

All construction within the property, including excavating, grading, trenching, landscaping, driveways, sidewalks, and free-standing structures (out-buildings) up to, or a fixed distance from, the main structure(s) are considered *site improvements*. All or part of these items may be identified on the *site plan*, *plot plan*, or both. Where a fixed distance from the main structure(s) is established, it may vary from 4'–0" (1.2 m) to 10'–0" (3.0 m) in all directions from the foundation of the structure(s). The limit may be established by local codes and ordinances, or between the architect/engineer and general contractor prior to construction.

Excavation and Grading

Refer to figures 2–4 and 2–5, Site Plan and Plot Plan, Garland Residence. Any change deliberately created in the earth from the natural grade elevations (site plan) to the finish grade elevations (plot plan) is referred to as *excavating and grading*. An excavating and grading contractor must have a survey (layout) prepared so that the natural contour elevations are removed or relocated to match the specified finish contour elevations on the property.

Earth that is to be excavated or removed from a project is called the *cut*. Earth that is added at any portion of a project is referred to as *fill*. Grading is the leveling and compacting of the fill soils and leveling the excavating to achieve the required finish elevation(s).

See figure 3–1. Any excavation required, such as a subgrade foundation for a subterranean garage or residential basement, is referred to as a *mass excavation*. As previously mentioned, this is one of the areas where the general contractor or excavating contractor must do a special survey to locate the exact

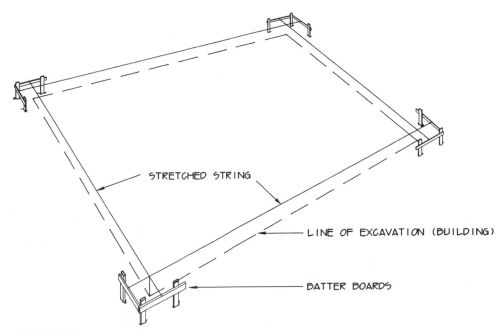

FIGURE 3–1
Mass Excavation Layout

terminal ends of the excavation. The terminal ends are the directions and the distances marked (paint or powder) on the surface of the earth. Stakes, batter boards, and taut strings are placed approximately 2'–0" (0.61 m) from each side of each corner in the manner shown in the drawing. The strings define the outer perimeter of the excavation to identify the layout in the event of weather problems. It is also easier for the equipment operator to see. During the excavation, a checker (one of the crew members) constantly watches and verifies that the work is being done satisfactorily and that the excavation and grading reaches its correct elevation.

Where such work is done, care must be taken to ensure that the earth is sufficiently stable to support itself. Otherwise, forms and shoring may be necessary. Where such materials are necessary, the forms, shoring, or any bracing necessary for concrete or masonry must remain until the concrete footings and concrete or masonry walls are properly cured.

Landscaping

Refer to figure 2–5, Plot Plan, Garland Residence. A plot plan for a single residential project usually shows much of the architect's and/or owner's ideas on at least the tree placement and some shrubbery. Existing trees and/or shrubbery may be required by law to be preserved or may be saved at the request of the owner. The protection for these items must be maintained throughout the whole construction. The protection procedure may be avoidance of the area by all trades involved with earthwork, or by removal, packaging, and saving for later replanting along with any other landscaping proposed and prepared for later installation. Additional landscaping plans may include the specifications for planting soil, ground cover, shrubbery, trees, watering systems (sprinklers), sidewalks, and/or driveways.

OTHER OFF-SITE/SITE IMPROVEMENTS

As mentioned in the introduction to this chapter, there are several other trades involved with the off-sites and site improvements. They include the paving contractor, concrete contractor, plumbing contractor, and electrical contractor.

Paving

See figure 3–2. As previously mentioned, paving includes both asphaltic and/or concrete materials. The normal application for both types of residential paving is indicated in figure 3–2. The applications vary with the expected use. Additional grading and compacting of base materials are required, as noted in the drawing. The quantity of base materials required is dependent upon the use of the paving. For example, asphalt used for vehicular traffic requires a deeper and better compacted base than that used for pedestrian traffic.

Asphalt paving used for vehicular traffic often has cement added, a minimum of one bag (approx. 95 lb [15.6 kg]) per cubic yard of asphalt and aggregate. The aggregate may be crushed rock or slag from ⅜" (0.95 cm) DIA to

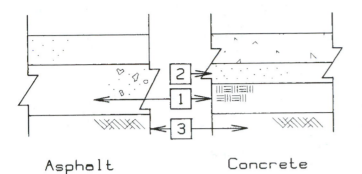

KEYNOTES

1. 6" to 10" compacted base (Type II soil)

2. 4" compacted sand base

3. Natural earth

Asphalt   Concrete

FIGURE 3–2
Paving

¾' (1.91 cm) or larger. This mixture is called a *cementitious asphalt* (*asphalt cement*). The cementitious materials are not necessary but may also be used for walkway installations.

Concrete driveways and sidewalks should have a compressive strength of at least 1800 psi (818.18 kg/6.45 cm²). The lower the compressive strength of the concrete, the less resistance to weight and deterioration it will have. Additional reinforcement, such as welded wire fabric, is used to assist in increasing the resistance to weight. Where deterioration resistance is required or desired, chemical additives are used. The normal application for both types of residential paving is shown in the drawing. The applications vary with the expected use.

Concrete and Masonry

See figure 3–3. The drawing shows an example of a structural concrete retaining wall installation. The procedures for such installations require special inspections for the footing size, wall size, concrete strength, and reinforcement required. They include such items as footings, foundation walls, and/or slabs that are a part of the work on or below grade. Therefore, the concrete contractor must abide with the information in the soils report as well as the specifications. In off-sites and site improvements, these requirements are necessary for free-standing concrete or masonry structural walls, site walls, and retaining walls. The same procedural requirements are necessary for such other items as foundation walls and/or slabs that are a part of the work on or below grade.

See figure 3–4. This drawing indicates a typical masonry retaining wall more than 6'-0" (1.82 m) deep below the highest grade. The procedures for such installations also require inspections for the footing size and placement, the reinforcement required, the sizes of masonry units. In this case 8" × 8" × 16" (20.32 cm × 20.32 cm × 40.64 cm) and 12" × 8" × 16" (30.48 cm × 20.32 cm × 40.64 cm) CMU units are used.

Plumbing

The plumbing trade is divided into two major categories, **plumbing,** including waste disposal, fuel supply (gas and oil pipe, and storage), and water or steam heating; and **piping,** which includes all supply water (potable water). The size of pipe, the type of pipe, plumbing fixtures, accessories, and

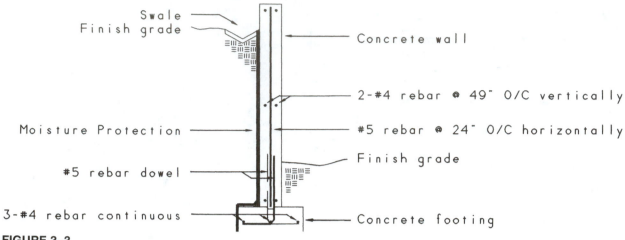

FIGURE 3–3
Concrete Retaining Wall

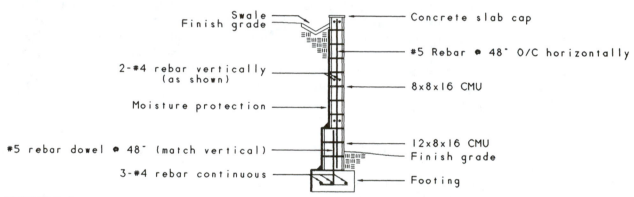

FIGURE 3–4
Masonry Retaining Wall

connections to both water and waste disposal systems are all a part of plumbing. The materials used for plumbing include four basic groups as follows:

1. Cast iron soil pipe and fittings, used solely for waste disposal
2. Galvanized iron (steel) pipe and fittings may be used for waste disposal or for potable water supply
3. Copper tubing (pipe) with solder joint or flare fittings is available in three categories:
   a. Soft copper, bendable by hand
   b. Drawn copper, formed into rigid lengths from 12 lf (4.2 m) to 20 lf (6.1 m)
   c. DWV (drainage, waste, vent), also used for waste disposal and treatment
4. Plastic tubing and piping, which is divided into five categories:
   a. Acrylonitrite-Butabiene-Styrene (ABS) for drainage and waste disposal
   b. Polyvinyl Chloride (PVC) for both cold water supply and drainage or waste disposal
   c. Chlorinated Polyvinyl Chloride (CPVC) used with both cold and hot water supply up to temperatures of 180° F

    d. Polyethylene (PE), for underground water supply (service)
    e. Polybutylene (PB), used for water supply

Supply (Potable) Water

The water supply may be from springs, wells, or piped from water treatment, filtration and purification plants to the consumer. Piped water supply sources are considered utility services owned privately or by local government. Wells and springs large enough to supply a neighborhood or small community may also be owned by private or government utilities. Small springs and wells are normally for use by the property owner only.

Fuel Supply

Both natural gas and liquefied petroleum (LP) gas such as propane and butane and oil supply line installations for residences and light commercial construction, and their storage facilities, are part of plumbing. Liquefied petroleum used by a single owner is supplied from a storage tank set apart from a structure above ground. Oil storage tanks may be installed above ground but are usually installed below ground. Although considered as part of heating, ventilation, and air-conditioning (**HVAC**) installations, the pipe work required for the transmission of liquids for heat-transfer units, air-conditioning, cooling towers, and solar heating panels are specified as a part of plumbing.

Septic Tanks and Leaching Fields (Leach Beds)

See figure 3–5. In rural areas where sewer lines are not available, the homeowner must install a **septic tank** and leaching field in lieu of any sewer connection. Then any part of a septic system, tank and leach field, must be a minimum of 25 lf (7.6 m) from the nearest point of the structure and away from any water supply.

Electrical

See figure 3–6. Electrical blueprints include information for outdoor installations as well as indoor power and lighting. Outdoor installations deal with the site lighting, power and equipment from the utility company power supply (transformer) up to, and including, the service entrance equipment are included as part of the site improvements. The off-site construction (street lighting and power supply installation) are the responsibility of the electric utility or the local authorities. The electrical service entrance equipment (the protection devices for the structure) may be connected from an overhead or a lateral (underground) service.

    Both service installations must meet the standards of the National Electric Code (NEC) and any local codes that may supersede it. The NEC is established by the American Fire Protection Association (AFPA). The code sets the minimum standard procedures and safety regulations for all electrical installations. Any electrical codes written that supersede these standards may not reduce the standards, they may only increase them.

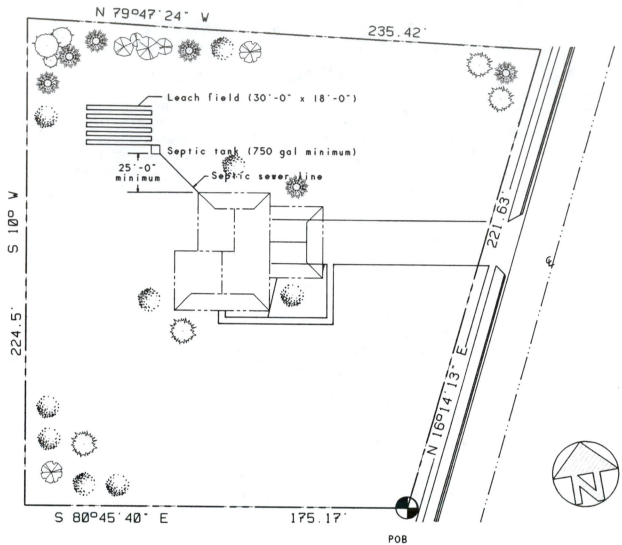

FIGURE 3–5
Leach Field, Garland Residence

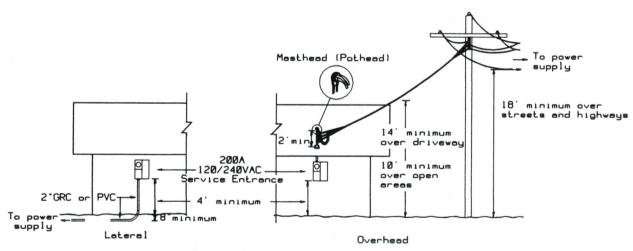

NOTE: Power supply transformers and connections not shown

FIGURE 3–6
Electrical Service Entrance Systems

ALTERNATIVE SOURCES

Fuel-Supplied Generator

If the property is in a rural area where a power supply is not available, an electrical generating system is normally included in the property construction. The most common system is the unit powered by an LP gas or oil-fired engine, both of which are battery started.

Solar Energy

See figure 3–7. Solar energy is a popular source for both heat and power. Solar heating has been in use for centuries. Buildings in ancient times were constructed to retain and absorb as much heat from the sun as possible in the same manner as is used in present-day construction. In addition, solar heating systems use a panel (or panels) to absorb the heat from the sun and convert the water in the panel tubes to a warm water supply. The warm water generated by the sun in these panels is transferred to a pre-heat or storage tank and connected with either a hot water heater (shown) or a heating system to reduce or eliminate the energy required to produce either the hot water or the hot water/steam heating systems from other sources. Such systems have been in use for many years in the southwest regions of the United States.

See figure 3–8. Solar power is common for minimal electrical requirements for residential and some light commercial usage. The disadvantage to such a system is that it will work steadily in regions where it is exposed to the sun for at least some portion of each day for a great part of the year. Solar panels collect the energy (heat) of the sun, which in turn energize the electronic solar cells within the panels, converting the heat energy into electrical energy. The electrical energy, direct current (DC), is transmitted from the panels to storage batteries. Another electronic device, called a *converter*, changes the DC current into alternating current (AC) to be used in the same manner as the power supplied from a standard utility company system.

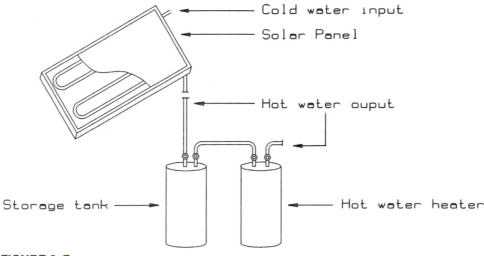

FIGURE 3–7
Solar Heat System

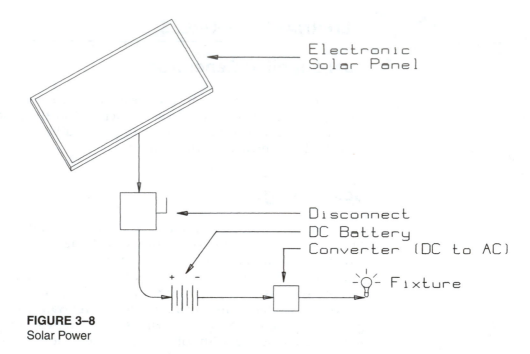

FIGURE 3–8
Solar Power

Utility companies and government agencies are now planning and installing solar collectors in fields of units estimated to be capable of supplying complete power to a city of approximately 100,000 residents. The collectors are connected with one another to transport energy to a transformer to increase the power output that can produce an electrical transmission system. These "fields" are being constructed in the southern California desert and in Nevada at a former nuclear test site.

Wind Generation

Wind generation is also being tested, with fields being constructed of hundreds of wind turbines in areas where the wind is prevalent through most of the year. The fields are constructed of towers and/or poles with airplane-like propellers mounted at the top facing into the prevalent wind direction. The wind turns the propellers which in turn rotate electrical generators mounted at the base of the tower or pole. The combination of multiple generators, like the solar generation system, is also directed into transformers that can increase the power output and produce an electrical transmission system. These fields, too, are located in the desert areas of southern California and Arizona. The prospects of supplying a city of 100,000 residents with full-time generation is also being predicted for the near future.

Other Services

There are at least two other utilities that are or may be involved in site-improvement or off-site work: the telephone cable and the television cable services located along with the other major utilities. These services are frequently excluded from plot plan utilities locations since they are often installed in the same trench or underground areas along with the electrical service in separate conduit or cable and are also installed in accordance with the local utility requirements and ordinances.

In all cases of work being supplied laterally (underground), major caution is needed. Each trade (plumbing and electrical) must know the location of any and all underground conduits, pipes, and so on. prior to any trenching or excavating. A service has been established that supplies information to and from all utilities for protection of the underground services, and the personnel and equipment operating in and around them. No work is to be done until all utilities have been contacted and information returned to a contractor that the work is safe or that someone will be on the project to aid in the location and identification of any utility that may interfere, or be interfered with, during the construction. The telephone number of this service is readily available in every telephone directory and should be known by every contractor. The name given to the service varies from "Call Before You Dig" to "Joint Utility Location Information Exchange (J.U.L.I.E.)".

In the past many underground utilities have been "lost" because of the various developers, building departments, and so on, having misplaced or destroyed records of the installations. It is now necessary by code that a tracer wire (or wires) be placed in all utility trenches for the specific purpose of locating these underground utilities at a future date. This requirement introduces a safety factor never before available. When such future underground work is to be done, using the tracer check with the buried wire and electronic sensing equipment can prevent the destruction of existing equipment and injury, or worse, to those working on the project.

CHAPTER EXERCISES

Completion

1. A _____ is an area located between a sidewalk and curb.

2. The underground electrical service is called a(n) _____.

3. Landscaping includes all trees, shrubs, ground cover, driveways, and _____ where required.

4. A _____ system must be installed where sewer lines are not available to a property.

5. The general contractor is responsible for the installation of all _____ from utilities.

6. Site improvements include any work located _____ the property lines.

7. The point of beginning may be a datum point or a _____ marker.

8. An easement is an area used for the _____ that cut through a property.

9. An identification noted as N 30°22'10" W is called a(n) _____.

10. A _____ is the measurement from a property line to the nearest point on a structure.

11. A footprint indicates the finish floor _____ of a structure on a site plan.

12. The site _____ is done by an engineering company.

13. _____ work includes all construction within the boundaries of the property normally to within 1.5 m of the structure.

14. Landscape plans may include a _____ system for watering the ground cover.

15. A(n) _____ is the direction noted in reference to true north.

16. An _____ excavation requires a special layout.

17. The layout for such an excavation referred to in question 16 is completed using _____ and taut string.

Multiple Choice

_____ 1. The off-site work includes
   a. Street, driveway, and berm improvements.
   b. Work within the property not including the structure.
   c. Work both on and off the property.
   d. Utility construction.

_____ 2. The point of beginning should:
   a. Be a reference for all trades.
   b. Be noted on both the site and plot plans.
   c. Neither a nor b.
   d. Both a and b.

_____ 3. The layout for a mass excavation uses
   a. Taut string and batter boards.
   b. Taut string, batter boards, and stakes.
   c. Wire, batter boards, and stakes.
   d. Wire and batter boards.

_____ 4. Common plumbing pipe used for underground sewer may be
   a. Type K, L, or M copper tubing.
   b. Cast iron, ABS, or DWV pipe.
   c. PVC or CPVC pipe.
   d. All of the above.

_____ 5. There are _____ individual classifications of soil:
   a. No special classifications
   b. Two classifications
   c. Three classifications
   d. None of the above.

_____ 6. A soils engineer is required for:
   a. Identifying soil classifications.
   b. Providing a soils report.
   c. Neither a nor b.
   d. Both a and b.

_____ 7. Modern technologies are now in use, or being tested, to provide electrical power. They include:
   a. Hydroelectric power and nuclear power supply.
   b. Solar and nuclear power supply.
   c. Hydroelectric and wind-driven power supply.
   d. Wind-driven and solar power supply.

_____ 8. Off-sites include
   a. Utilities construction.
   b. Street improvements.
   c. Curb, gutter, and sidewalk improvements.
   d. All of the above.

_____ 9. Site improvements include
   a. The foundation for the structure(s).
   b. The work from the property lines to the structure(s).
   c. Landscaping only.
   d. The utility easement.

4

Foundations and Below-Grade Construction (On-Site)

All work, both architectural and structural, described as the main structure, or within a maximum distance surrounding the structure as prescribed by codes and ordinances, or established by the contractor, are included in on-site construction. All trades from Division 3, Concrete, to Division 16, Electrical, are involved. For example, connections to all the utility services; concrete and/or masonry foundations; below-grade moisture protection; concrete, masonry, or frame walls; the roof structure and roofing; finishes; mechanical; plumbing; electrical; cabinetry; and appliances are all part of the on-site construction work. This chapter includes the study of below-grade installations and the materials necessary for a proper installation.

FOUNDATIONS

See figure 4–1. Weather conditions as well as local codes and ordinances determine the depth of concrete footings. The map shown (or a similar map) is found in many texts, specification pamphlets, and brochures from manufacturers. A study of the map shows that footings in the northern areas of the country must be considerably deeper, 4'-6" (1.37 m) or more, than those located in the southern and southwestern portions that are described as from 1'-0" (0.30 m) to 1'-6" (0.46 m). Exception to the footing depths in the warmer climates are found in the higher altitudes (mountains, and so on) where the weather conditions are similar to those in the northerly areas of the country. The depth of the frost line makes it common practice to build basements in all parts of the northern sections of the country, utilizing these footing depth requirements. In the mountainous areas of the southwestern United States, due to similar frost-line requirements, an owner or builder may

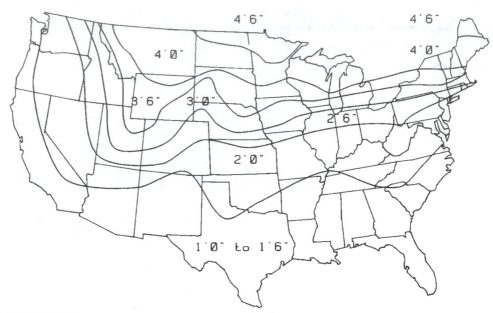

FIGURE 4–1
Average Footing Depths in the United States (Mainland Only)

construct either a full basement or under-floor crawl space to utilize the depth. A crawl space is an open area under the floor up to 3'-0" (0.61 m) deep, usually covering the same surface area as the structure above (to the foundation walls). Under-floor plumbing, piping, electrical, and HVAC installations may be found in these crawl spaces. Thermal protection for these materials is also required in such spaces.

See figure 4–2. The blueprint reader must understand the difference in the terminologies of a footing, a foundation wall, a slab, and a **foundation.** They may be defined as follows:

1. The term *footing* is the foundation support unit that must be sufficiently large and strong enough to support the structure built upon it.

2. The term *foundation wall* is the exterior, below-grade bearing wall placed on a footing. Foundation walls are also referred to as *stem walls.*

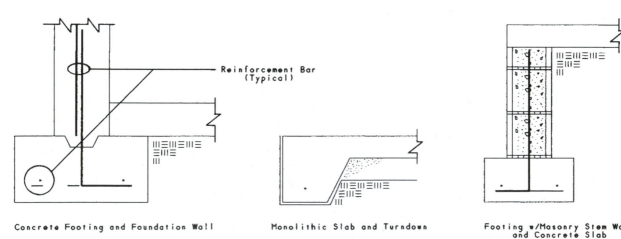

Concrete Footing and Foundation Wall   Monolithic Slab and Turndown   Footing w/Masonry Stem Wall and Concrete Slab

FIGURE 4–2
Foundations

3. The term *slab* is the base horizontal member that may also be the support for interior parts of a structure in conjunction with the footings.

4. The term *foundation* includes *all* of the parts mentioned above.

Items 1 and 3 are constructed of concrete and steel reinforcement. The foundation walls may be constructed using concrete from 6″ (15.24 cm) to 12″ (30.48 cm) thick. These walls are most frequently installed in the colder, more moist climates. Concrete foundation walls are also constructed in other areas of the country, especially for large commercial and industrial applications, as well as some residential construction. Masonry (concrete block— CMU) may also be used in the northern areas of the country, but it is more common to find masonry foundation wall construction in the warmer climates of the southwestern and southeastern United States.

CONCRETE

There are two major classifications given to concrete construction. The first classification is referred to as *structural concrete.* Structural concrete installations for all construction include footings, foundation walls, on-grade slabs, above-grade walls, and above-grade floor or roof slabs. These installations are controlled by rigid codes and regulations governing the mix and compressive strength of the concrete. Compressive strength determines how much weight concrete can withstand before cracking or breaking. The minimum structural compressive strength for residential construction ranges between 2000 psi (909.1 kg/6.45 cm^2) and 2500 psi (1136.36 kg/6.45 cm^2), depending upon local codes and ordinances.

The second classification of concrete is referred to as *nonstructural* concrete. Items used for decorative purposes only and not considered structural support, such as arabesques, exterior window and door trim, balusters, railings, and fireplace trim, do not require the rigid standards of structural concrete. Some of these items may also be included as structural concrete, but most are of the nonstructural classification. The compressive strength of many of these products may be as little as 1000 psi (454.55 kg/6.45 cm^2), or even less, depending upon application.

Steel Reinforcement

See figure 4–3 and appendix III. The most common methods for reinforcing concrete and masonry are the installation of **reinforcement bar (rebar),** both smooth and deformed, and **welded wire fabric** (WWF—mesh). They are also installed for the purpose of controlling the possible spalling and cracking of concrete.

Rebar is manufactured in various sizes and is identified by the diameter of the bar in ⅛″ increments. A #2 rebar (²/₈″ or ¼″ DIA) and #3 rebar (³/₈″ DIA), the smallest sizes, are normally smooth finished and are used to tie the heavier rebar in place until the concrete or masonry grout (a type of concrete) is installed. The #3 rebar may also be available as a deformed bar. All other sizes, #4 rebar (⁴/₈″ or ½″ DIA) and up, are deformed shapes only. The deformed shape is manufactured for the purpose of holding the steel in place in the concrete or grout after curing (setting and hardening of the concrete).

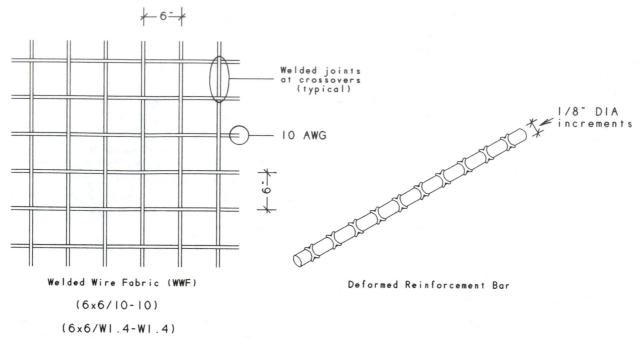

Welded joints
at crossovers
(typical)

10 AWG

1/8" DIA
increments

Welded Wire Fabric (WWF)

(6x6/10-10)

(6x6/W1.4-W1.4)

Deformed Reinforcement Bar

FIGURE 4–3
Steel Reinforcement

Concrete shrinks while curing and can, therefore, release from the rebar. A smooth, straight section of rebar could be removed from the concrete as a result. The deformed rebar has various raised designs built into the bar that will not allow the bar to release upon curing.

Rebar is also identified by its tensile strength, which determines how much stress (stretch) the steel can resist before it breaks. The stress rating is given in kilo-pounds-per-square-inch (kpsi or kps), or classed as the grade of steel. The three most commonly used strengths of rebar installed in residential or commercial construction are 40 kpsi (40 grade), 60 kpsi (60 grade), and 80 kpsi (80 grade).

See figure 4–4. There may be one, two, or more rebar installed horizontally in footings. This depends upon the structural requirements for the building that the footings support. The rebar is laid on chairs (small cementitious blocks to keep the rebar off the ground) before the concrete is placed. Rebar may also be necessary in both horizontal and vertical directions in concrete or masonry walls. Normally, where vertical rebar is installed in a wall, there is also a dowel (see the section on dowels) installed into the footing and tied to the horizontal footing rebar to make a rigid connection between the footing and wall. Where rebar dowels are used, a key is unnecessary (see the section on keyed connections).

Refer to figure 4–3. Installation of welded wire fabric is regularly recommended in commercial construction for concrete slabs wherever there is continuous traffic weighing 3,000 lbs (1363.64 kg) or more, or where heavy machinery (such as presses and stamping machines that can cause considerable vibration) are present.

Like rebar, WWF is also manufactured in various sizes. The wire size and spacing are used to identify WWF. For example, the smallest size WWF is referred to as a 6x6/10-10 or 6x6/W1.4-W1.4. The numbers on the left (6×6) indicate the spacing in perpendicular directions of 6″ (15.24 cm). The numbers

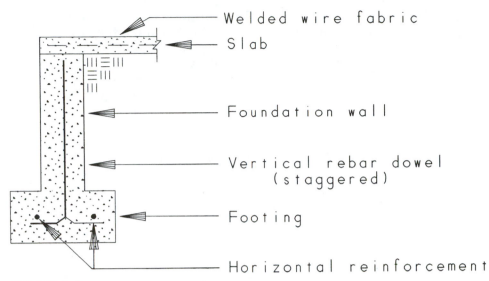

FIGURE 4–4
Footing and Wall Reinforcement

on the right are the wire gauge (10 AWG—American Wire Gauge, or W1.4 mm—metric gauge). Many residential developers and architects also insist upon the use of this size WWF in slab-on-grade construction.

Additives

Chemicals or minerals added to the concrete mixture that are capable of changing texture, curing time, hardness, and so on are called **additives.** One example of an additive is the more recent trend for strengthening concrete that includes a glass or other strong fiber added to the concrete mix, eliminating the necessity for WWF. The mixture is referred to as glass fiber-reinforced concrete (GFRC) or fiber-reinforced concrete (FRC).

The location of the project and the time of year in which the project is under construction determine whether or not an additive is required to achieve the proper compressive strength and finish of concrete. Frost conditions require additives, for example, such as an accelerator like **calcium chloride,** to assist in completing a cure without freezing, whereas desert regions may be more likely to use a retarder, such as **calcium lignosulfonate,** to aid in the curing process during the warmest periods. Care must be taken in the choice and/or quantity of additive so as not to harm the concrete (too quick or too slow a cure time).

Concrete Mixtures

The variation of the mixture of cement, sand, and aggregate (gravel or slag) also helps to determine the compressive strength and curing time of concrete. The normal material mixtures range from a 1:2:4 (one part cement, two parts sand, and four parts aggregate) to a 1:2:6 (one part cement, two parts sand, and six parts aggregate). The quantities determine the fluidity or stiffness of a mix (the common term used by suppliers and contractors).

The water-cement ratio also assists in the determination of the fluidity (how easily the mix will flow and settle), as well as the compressive strength of the mix in terms of the quantity of water (in gallons/liters) per bag of cement. The compressive strength of concrete is inversely proportionate to the water ratio. In other words, the more water used, the lower the compressive strength of the concrete. The average mixture for quality concrete is 18 gallons of water per 10 cubic yards of dry mix.

Keyed Concrete Foundation

See figure 4–5. The concrete contractor is usually responsible for trenching and placement of forms, concrete reinforcement and, where necessary, drainage to protect a basement or other below-grade retaining wall. *Placement* is the preferred term for the installation of the wet concrete.

Footings are placed independent of the foundation walls, that is, installed at separate times. The footings may or may not be keyed to the foundation walls. The key is installed in areas where seismic stability, freezing, or hydrolics (moisture pressure) control are required. Along with a moisture-resistant material (polyethylene or asphalt-impregnated), the key may also be used as a moisture barrier referred to as a *water stop*. The size of footing is determined by the size of the structure to be supported by it.

Monolithic Concrete Placement

See Plan S–1, the Garland Residence. A monolithic placement is one in which a slab and footing are installed simultaneously. The footing and slab edges are formed as a single unit. The footing portion of the monolithic slab is referred to as a turndown. The size of the turndown (width and height) varies with the size of the structure, the materials used for the structural walls, and the stability of the soil surrounding the structure.

Pre- and Post-Tension Reinforcement

Pre-Tensioning. A reinforcing system installed for precast concrete structures used for commercial, industrial, and highway (bridge) construction is called

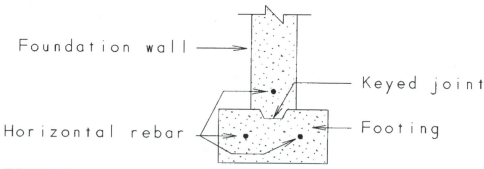

FIGURE 4–5
Dooting and Wall Reinforcement

pre-tensioning. The tensioning is done in the manufacturing plant as the concrete is cured. The reinforcement used is a form of rebar called a *tendon*. When the concrete is completely cured, the tensioning is also completed. The precast product is then placed on site ready for proper connection.

The tendons are placed in much the same manner as horizontal rebar with the exception that they are placed the full length of the slab each way and spaced at various distances from one another. The tendons are woven so that when tension is applied, they stretch against the opposite tendons, giving support to the concrete in the same manner as rebar.

Post-Tensioning. A similar, more recent trend in residential concrete monolithic slab construction is the installation of reinforcement for **post-tensioning.** The reinforcement is placed in the slab similar to the pre-tensioning method. The slab is **tensioned** on-site before the slab is fully cured. This system protects against, or reduces, spalling and cracking of slabs when the structural load is placed upon it.

Dowels

A concrete foundation wall does not require a key in the footing except as mentioned above. Masonry foundation wall construction has no key. The connection between the footings and the foundation walls where no key exists is made with a formed rebar installed in the footing and extending vertically 2'-0" (0.61m) into the wall. The rebar has an angle, referred to as a "hook", from 6" (15.24 cm) to 9" (22.86 cm) long, at right angles to the length of the rebar. The short angle portion of the rebar is tied to the horizontal footing rebar so that the footing and wall are strengthened as a unit. This bent rebar used in this manner is known as a *dowel*. Like the key joint, this system is also used where seismic stability is required.

MASONRY

Brick, concrete masonry units (CMU), and stone are the three basic categories of masonry. The technology of recent years has improved on the old brick as well as having created new brick and concrete masonry units. Both brick and CMU are further categorized as solid-core or hollow-core units. Solid-core units contain 25% or less core (air) space. Hollow-core units contain from 25% to 75% core space. Solid-core units are used for trim or specialty work where reinforcement is unnecessary, such as for decorative finishes like corbels, for filling voids around other structural materials, as well as for veneers and pavers. Hollow-core brick and CMU are used where reinforcement and grout installations are required.

Masonry units are also identified by the **flexural measure (strength)** of the masonry unit. Flexural measure (*f'm*) is a combination of the measure of the compressive strength of a unit and its ability to withstand lateral and vertical stresses without breaking.

Another masonry term, which refers to the thickness of a wall, is the **wythe.** A single wythe wall is one unit thick, a double wythe wall is two units thick, etc. *See figure 4–6.*

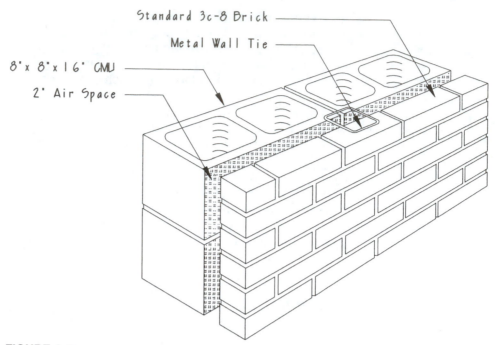

FIGURE 4–6
Double-Wythe Masonry Wall

Concrete Masonry Units

See figure 4–7. CMU is made of concrete mixed with fine aggregates such as crushed rock, cinders, and iron filings or combinations of them, for strength and/or color (natural gray or tinted). They may also be classed as structural or non-structural, depending upon usage. CMU is available in a variety of textures such as smooth-face, split-face, fluted, scored, raked, brushed, or glazed. CMU nominal sizes range from 2" (5.08 cm) high to 12" (30.48 cm) high, from 4" (10.16 cm) wide to 16" (40.64 cm) wide and from 4" (10.16 cm) long to 16" (40.64 cm) long.

CMU is identified in size by width, height, and length (W × H × L). The smaller CMU units (for example, 4" × 2" × 8" [10.16 cm × 5.08 cm × 20.32 cm]) are usually solid-core bricklike concrete units. The larger sizes are usually of the hollow-core variety such as the nominal sized 8" × 8" × 16" (20.32 cm × 20.32 cm × 40.64 cm) block. The actual size of this block is 7⅝" × 7⅝" × 15⅝" (19.37 cm × 19.37 cm × 39.69 cm). The nominal size includes a ⅜" (0.95 cm) thick mortar bed. The mortar is applied to the bottom and one end (head) of a unit to comply with the nominal measurements. (See the sections for mortar and grout use.)

Brick

See figure 4–8. Clay brick, better known as the "red brick," is the oldest and most common masonry unit in existence. Brick may be classed as solid- or hollow-core and is available in nominal sizes ranging from 3¾" (9.53 cm) to 6" (15.24 cm) wide, 2¼" (5.72 cm) to 5¼" (13.34 cm) high and 8" (20.32 cm) to 12" (30.48 cm) long. Brick is also identified in size by width × height × length.

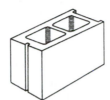
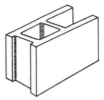
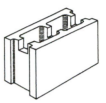

Precision/Smooth Face   Split Face   Fluted

Stretchers

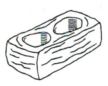

Sash/Jamb   Open End   Bond Beam

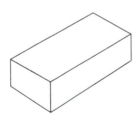
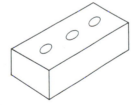

Bullnose   Slumpstone   Lintel

FIGURE 4–7
Typical Concrete Masonry Wall

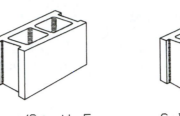
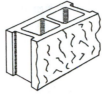
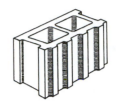

Standard   Modular   Roman

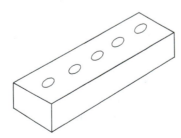
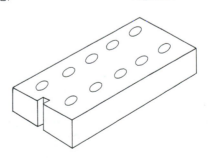

Norman   SCR
(Structural Clay Research)

FIGURE 4–8
Typical Brick Units

The smaller, nominal-size standard brick, 4″ × 2²/₃″ × 8″ [10.16 cm × 6.78 cm × 20.32 cm]), called a *3c-8 brick,* are usually solid-core units used mostly for veneers or pavers. Clay brick is available in many varieties of color from the standard red (terra cotta [clay] color) to variegated tinting and glazing. Brick, too, has a variety of textures such as cut, scored, scratched, broomed, or otherwise roughened surfaces.

See figure 4–9. One of the advantages to brick over CMU is the ability to lay brick in various designs and positions more easily. The three most commonly used positions other than the stretcher course (the standard position of a brick or block) shown in figure 4–9 are the header course, rowlock course, and the soldier course. The header course is most frequently seen as the cap brick on a brick wall, although it is used as a stabilizing unit in double-wythe brick walls as well. The rowlock course is frequently used as the sloped sill water table under exterior windows, or as the edge paver on steps and the like. The soldier course is used for decorative courses throughout a wall, or as the face brick on an arch along with a keystone masonry unit. The other brick positions are also used but are not seen quite as often as those mentioned above.

Structural clay tile brick is classed as a brick although the sizes, shapes, and styles are more in the range of CMU. The difference between normal clay brick and structural clay tile brick is that standard brick is compressed into molds, whereas the tile brick is extruded (forced) under pressure through a machine mold. The extrusion process shapes the tile and compresses the mixture, thereby increasing the structural strength. The remaining manufacturing processes are the same.

Stone

Granite, river rock, marble, slate, strata rock, limestone, and sandstone are all examples of natural stone used in masonry construction. Any of the stone

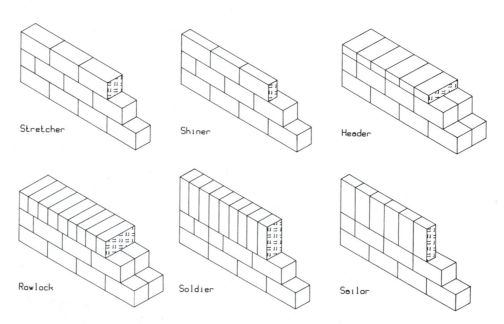

FIGURE 4–9
Brick Positions

types mentioned may be available in any area of the country. Stone may be a structural or nonstructural construction component. Stone may also be cut and set as a veneer over other masonry or frame wall construction.

Marble is primarily used as a facing over other materials, or as a tile, because it can be smoothed and polished into a fine aesthetic appearance. Slate and some strata rock can be obtained in flat sections that may be used for decks, plazas, patios, or entry floors (sometimes referred to as terrazzo decks) because of their structural strength and stability.

Limestone and sandstone are quarried and cut into shapes like brick. The most common treatment of limestone and sandstone is the Ashlar stone finish, which utilizes various pre-cut sizes of stone fitted together in a random design. They may also be sized in Roman and Norman brick sizes for standard bricklike applications. Because of the lack of strength in these materials they are used primarily as a veneer.

Cultured stone is manufactured in panel form using a mix of variegated colored crushed rock and cement compressed and molded to look like natural stone The panels vary in size from $2' \times 2'$ (0.61 m × 0.61 m) to $4' \times 8'$ (1.22 m × 2.44 m) and are approximately 1″ (2.54 cm) thick. The panels may be adhered to the back-up wall material (masonry or frame) by adhesives and/or masonry wall ties.

Masonry Wall Construction

See figure 4–10. Structural masonry walls require a combination of concrete block or brick installed with mortar, grout, and reinforcement. The following sections identify and explain the use of these materials.

Mortar and Grout

A complete masonry installation includes mortar and grout used with the masonry units. Mortar is a concrete mix with a fine aggregate (sand) and may include a *fluidifier* additive to aid in binding the masonry units together. The need for the fluidifier depends upon weather conditions. Just as with concrete, hot, dry areas may require its use while in more moderate and cooler temperatures, it may not be necessary.

Grout is also a concrete mix, similar to regular concrete, with a ³⁄₈″ (0.95 cm) aggregate, with or without a *plasticizer* or other additive. Grout is used to fill the cavities of the hollow-core units containing reinforcement. When used in all wall cavities, grout may increase the strength of the wall. The combination of an $8'' \times 8'' \times 16''$ (20.32 cm × 20.32 cm × 40.64 cm) CMU structural unit (1,535 to 1,565 $f'm$ or better) and grout (2,000 psi [909.1 kg/6.45 cm^2] or greater) can increase wall strength from a nominal 1800 psi (818.18 kg/6.45 cm^2) strength to 3,125 psi (1,420.45 kg/6.45 cm^2) or more. A typical masonry foundation wall is filled solid with grout to strengthen the wall and to aid in moisture resistance.

Reinforcement

The steel reinforcement used in masonry construction includes the rebar previously discussed and horizontal joint reinforcement. Horizontal joint reinforcement is a 9-gauge (AWG) wire system formed in the shape of a ladder or an open-web truss in 10′-0″ (3.05 m) and 20′-0″ (6.1 m) lengths. The width of

KEYNOTES:

1. TILE ROOFING OVER 43# FELT UNDERLAYMENT
    & 1/2" CDX PLYWOOD SHEATHING
2. 2X8 R/S FASCIA BOARD
3. 2-#4 HORIZ. REBAR (CONTINUOUS) - 4 PLACES
4. #5 VERT. REBAR @ 4'-0" O.C. HORIZ.
5. 8X8X16 CMU (SEE SPECS.)
6. 4" HORIZ. REBAR (CONTINUOUS) @ 2'-0" O.C.
    VERTICALLY (SEE NOTE #3)
7. 4" CONC. SLAB W/ 6X6/W1.4XW1.4 WWF
8. #5 REBAR DOWEL ('J' BAR) @ 4'-0" O.C. HORIZ.
    - MATCH VERT. REBAR
9. 2-#4 HORIZ REBAR IN FOOTING (CONTINUOUS)
10. ROOF STRUCTURE - SEE FRAMING PLANS
11. 2X8 TREATED TOP PLATE W/ 1/2"X7" AB @
    4'-0" O.C.
12. DUAL PANE INSULATING GLASS WINDOW
13. 9X4X8 SILL BLOCK
14. 4X4X8 GLASS BLOCK

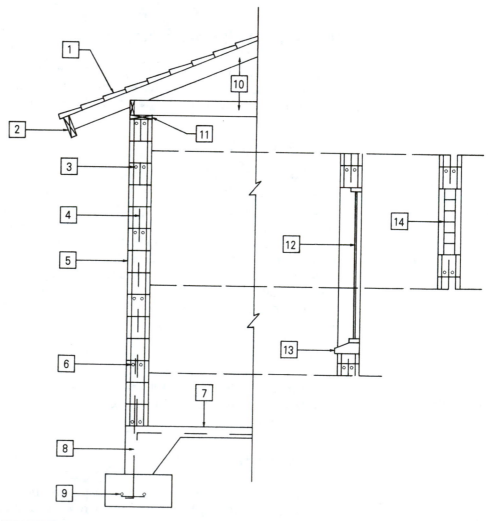

FIGURE 4–10
Masonry Wall Construction

the material varies according to the width of the unit with which it is placed. Horizontal reinforcement is placed in the mortar bed every 16" (40.64 cm) vertically, or between every second course, where an 8" (20.32 cm) high block or brick is installed; it is placed every 12" (30.48 cm) vertically, or between every second course, where a 6" (15.24 cm) high block or brick is installed; and it is placed every 12" (30.48 cm) vertically, or between every third course, where a 4" (10.16 cm) high block or brick is installed. Horizontal reinforcement may reduce, or eliminate, the quantity of rebar required in a masonry wall. The elimination of rebar depends upon the type of structure, its geographic location, and local codes and ordinances.

Accessories

There are two accessory classifications considered in masonry construction, masonry and nonmasonry. Specially formed masonry units such as lintels, sill block, keystones, or other nonstandard block or brick are referred to as masonry accessories. Nonmasonry accessories include all *embeds* such as rebar, horizontal joint reinforcement, wall ties, beam supports, anchor bolts, expansion bolts, and expansion (control) joint inserts. As in concrete installations, many of the embeds are supplied by others to be installed by the brick mason.

MOISTURE PROTECTION

Protection against water (moisture) and weather (moisture and thermal) are included under this heading. The title is correct in that the term *moisture protection* is preferred over the misnomers given to moisture protection, commonly referred to as water*proofing* or damp*proofing,* because there is no product that will completely water*proof* or damp*proof.* Whether the protection is installed below grade or on the roof, the materials used to protect against moisture will only resist or retard penetration for extended periods. The longevity of any protection system depends upon the quality of the materials, proper installation procedures, and continued care and maintenance.

See figure 4–11. Below-grade moisture protection is accomplished through the use of asphalt-based and coal-tar–based materials, concrete additives, cementitious mixtures, and plastics (polyethylene, polyurethane, elastomeric polymers, acrylics, or combinations of them). The products may be manufactured in sheet, roll, rigid board, or in a semi-viscous state for roll-on, brush-on, or spray-on applications.

Asphalt-based and coal-tar–based materials may be hot-mopped or cold-applied with mop or brush and used in combination with asphalt-impregnated felts, fiber mesh, or rubber-based sheets and rolls (neoprene or butylene, for example). Polyethylene is a plastic sheet material (better known as "Visqueen") for use under slabs for added horizontal moisture protection. Polyurethane is most commonly found as foamlike material sprayed on roofs or into wall cavities of exterior walls. Elastomers and acrylics, in liquefied form, are used as spray-on, paintlike materials for weather and moisture protection. Products such as gypsum or regular cement (not concrete), mixed with moisture-retardant additives and allowed to harden like concrete to reduce moisture penetration, are referred to as *cementitious* materials. Such products include both spray-on and hand-applied materials, and cement-impregnated boardlike sheets, called *composite* boards. Several of these products may be available for both moisture and thermal protection.

Hydrostatic Pressure in feet	Materials						Vertical Wall Protection (Layers)
	Cold Applied			Hot Mop			
	Emulsion			Asphalt and Base Sheet			
	Primer	Fabric	Emulsion	Primer	Base Sheet	Asphalt	
1	1	1	2	1	2	3	1
2	1	1	2	1	2	3	1
3	1	1	3	1	2	3	1
4	1	1	3	1	2	3	1
5	1	1	3	1	2	3	1
6	1	1	3	1	3	4	1
7	1	2	4	1	3	4	1
8	1	2	4	1	3	4	1
9	1	2	4	1	4	5	1
10	1	2	4	1	4	5	1
12	1	2	4	1	5	6	1
15	1	3	5	1	5	6	1
20	1	3	5	1	6	7	1
25	1	4	6	1	7	8	1
30	1	4	6	1	9	10	1

FIGURE 4–11
Asphaltic Below-Grade Moisture Protection

CHAPTER EXERCISES

Multiple Choice

_____ 1. On-site construction includes
   a. All work within the boundaries of the property.
   b. All work within a specified distance from a structure.
   c. All work within the structure and for a specified distance in all directions from the structure.
   d. All of the above.

_____ 2. The concrete contractor may be responsible for:
   a. Excavation for all footings.
   b. Supplying all the reinforcement for the concrete footings and stems.
   c. Installing formwork where necessary for both the concrete and masonry work.
   d. All of the above.

_____ 3. All concrete mixes are
   a. 1:2:4 ratio.
   b. 1:2:6 ratio.
   c. Made from a mixture of cement, sand, and aggregate.
   d. 3500 psi (1587.6 kg/6.45 cm²).

_____ 4 Footings may be
   a. Placed where there is less than 95% compaction.
   b. Variable in size dependent upon the soil.
   c. Variable in size dependent upon the soil and the structure above.
   d. All of the above.

_____ 5. The depth of footings:
   a. May be minimum 1'-6" (45.7 cm).
   b. Is determined by the depth of the frost line.
   c. Neither a nor b above.
   d. Both a and b above.

_____ 6. Masonry construction includes
   a. The use of mortar and grout.
   b. CMU or brick.
   c. Stone.
   d. All of the above.

_____ 7. A measure of strength of a masonry unit includes
   a. Its elasticity.
   b. Its flexural strength.
   c. Its impact resistance.
   d. Its expandability.

_____ 8. The purpose of reinforcement is
   a. To make certain that the concrete or masonry properly cures.
   b. To construct a heavier structure.
   c. To add strength to and rigidity to concrete or masonry.
   d. None of the above.

_____ 9. A monolithic placement of concrete
        a. Is a slab and footing placed at the same time as a unit.
        b. Is gigantic.
        c. Requires separate placement of the turndown and the slab.
        d. Requires special concrete mixtures.

_____ 10. The purpose of a key-cold, or keyed, concrete configuration is
        a. The key aids in resistance to seismic pressure.
        b. The key aids in resistance to moisture penetration.
        c. Neither a nor b.
        d. Both a and b.

True or False

T F 1. Divisions 1 through 16 are included in all on-site work.

T F 2. Masonry walls are all single wythe.

T F 3. Stem walls are constructed in concrete only.

T F 4. Concrete slabs are to be a minimum 2000 psi (907.2 kg/6.45 cm²).

T F 5. All masonry walls are solid grouted.

T F 6. The average frost-line footing depth for the state of Maine is 3'-6" (1.07 m).

T F 7. Foundations refer to below-grade walls only.

T F 8. All brick is nonstructural.

T F 9. The basic unit position of brick or block is the stretcher.

T F 10. Reinforcement bar is identified by its grade.

T F 11. The compressive strength of concrete is its ability to resist moisture.

T F 12. Concrete is classified for both structural strength and moisture resistance.

T F 13. Masonry includes brick and CMU only.

T F 14. A 1:2:4 mix in concrete equals 1 part sand to 2 parts aggregate to 4 parts cement.

T F 15. Moisture protection for below-grade installations is necessary for both concrete and masonry walls.

Completion

1. The _____ course is the basic course of masonry installations.

2. The size of an 8" (20.32 cm) concrete masonry stretcher is ___" × ___" × ___".

3. Concrete used for decorative purposes is normally classified as _____.

4. The abbreviation WWF means _____.

5. _____ of concrete can be accomplished by the installation of a special additive such as glass fiber reinforced concrete.

6. Moisture protection for any below-grade wall should have a _____ board.

7. On-site construction includes all work performed within a _____.

8. Most all on-site work includes Division 1 and Division _____ through Division 16.

9. The _____ strength of masonry is its resistance to compressive and lateral stresses.

10. The frost line determines the _____ of a footing.

11. Moisture protection includes all materials required to protect a structure from below-grade _____ and weather.

12. Below-grade protection should include a(n) _____ to prevent damage to the materials.

5

The Structure Above Grade (On Site)

On-site construction further incorporates the building to be installed on the foundation(s) discussed in chapter 4. The construction of all rough carpentry, insulation materials, and light-gauge metal framing are covered in this chapter.

ROUGH CARPENTRY

Rough carpentry includes both wood or **light-gauge metal framing** necessary for the installation of the floor, walls, ceiling, and roof structure. Light-gauge metal framing is referred to later in this chapter. *See Sheet A–1, Floor Plan, Garland Residence,* and *Architectural and Structural Sections figures 5–1 and 5–2.* The basic information in rough carpentry is also the basis for the residential and commercial plans in this text.

See appendix II, Lumber Classifications and Grades. The useful purpose and location of a framing member determines the classification and grade of the lumber. The grade of the lumber is determined by the part of the log from which the member is cut. The closer to the center of the log, the better the material. Thus, the lumber nearest the exterior receives the poorest rating. For example, a **stud** is classified as *stud* or *economy* grade, while joists are classified as *select structural, grades 1, 2, 3,* or *economy.*

The geographic location of the lumber used also determines its *quality classification.* For example, Douglas fir (DF), a west coast and western Canada forest timber, or Pine from the southeast part of the United States (Alabama, Georgia, Tennessee), are both classed as *C or better,* but Pine classifications include a select category that is not extended to Douglas fir. The quality of the lumber is determined by the number of knots in 1'-0" (0.30 m) of board. The fewer the number of knots, the higher the lumber classification.

KEYNOTES:

1. Wood truss w/2x6 top chord and 2x4 bottom chord.

2. 6:12 hip. Wood shake roofing.

3. Vaulted ceiling w/1/2" GWB.

4. 1/2" GWB at all walls (UNO).

5. 6'-0" x 6'-8" cased opening.

6. 4040 FX dual-pane window (typical of 2).

7. 1668 FX dual-pane sidelite (typical of 2).

8. 3068 panel entry door w/entry latch and deadbolt.

9. 4" concrete slab and footing - see plans.

SECTION A-A

FIGURE 5–1
Architectural Section, Garland Residence

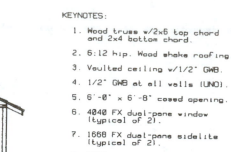

KEYNOTES:

1. 5:12 scissors truss @ 24" o.c. 1/2" CDX plywood sheathing over.

2. 6:12 hip (half) truss @ 24" o.c. 1/2" CDX plywood sheathing over.

3. 2x double top plate

4. 2x6 studs @ 16" o.c. - typical at all exterior walls.

5. 2x4 studs @ 24" o.c. - typical at all partitions UNO.

6. 2x6 mudsill

7. King stud - typical at all openings. Match wall framing.

8. 2x6 DF #2. or better. for all lintels (headers) UNO.

9. 2x8 R/S fascia (typical)

10. 3000 psi concrete foundation slab and footing - monolithic placement.

11. Trimmer stud - typical at all openings. Match wall framing.

SECTION A-A

FIGURE 5–2
Structural Section, Garland Residence

These classifications are governed by the various lumber associations throughout the country.

The wood framing members for all building construction necessary to rough carpentry installations include **sill plates, sole or bottom plates, top plates, floor and ceiling joists, studs, lintels (headers), rafters, subflooring (underlayment),** sheathing (siding and roof), as well as **post and beam** construction. Each of these materials carries one or more of the classifications mentioned in the appendix. Any portion, or all, of the framing members discussed in the following sections may be a part of any one structure.

Plates

Plates are the framing members to which floor, wall, and ceiling framing are attached. They are properly identified by the location and use, such as the sill plate, sole plate, and single or double top plate. Plate stock is usually ordered, shipped, and installed in random lengths (R/L), meaning that the lumber may be in varying lengths ranging from 8 lf (2.44 m) to 24 lf (7.32 m) mixed into a single load. The lumber may be longer, but for normal shipping by truck or rail car, these are the most economical lengths. For smaller work the carpentry contractor may order all plate stock in 16-foot (4.88 m) or 20-foot (6.1 m) lengths.

Sill Plate. *See figure 5–3.* Wherever wood framing meets a concrete or masonry sub-strate, a sill plate is required to protect the framing above from caustic deterioration, where wood comes into contact with the alkaline content of concrete or masonry units. It is also used for protection against termite and rodent infestation. The lumber used may be either redwood or a

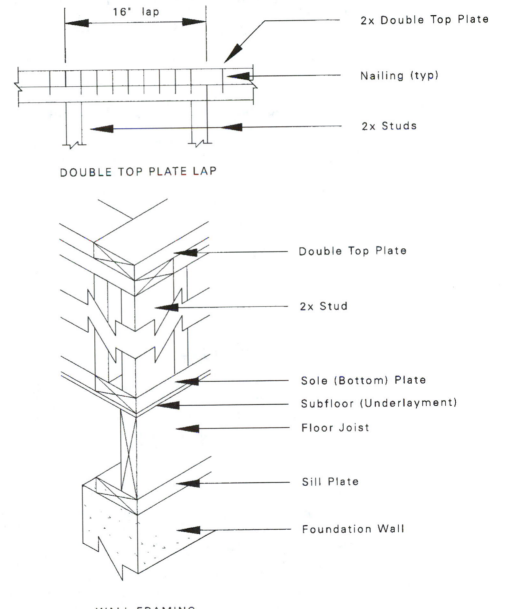

FIGURE 5–3
Basic Framing Components

pressure-treated wood, called a *mudsill*, installed for this protection. The mudsill is produced by a process called Wolmanizing®, in which a salt-based solution is impregnated into units (bundles) of lumber under pressurized heat and moisture inside a tank, then removed from the tank and kiln-dried to remove as much moisture as possible to prevent warping. The treated wood is identified by the letters *PTMS* (*p*ressure *t*reated *m*udsill). Hemlock Fir (HF), utility grade, or Douglas Fir (DF), common, are used for this process. Treated members are required for the exterior bearing walls only. Untreated DF, common, or HF, utility, may be used as the sill plate on slabs for all interior walls.

The size of the standard sill plate may range from a 2×4 (5.08 cm $\times$ 20.32 cm) up to a 2×12 (5.08 cm $\times$ 30.48 cm) to match the surface upon which it is installed, such as a 12″ (30.48 cm) thick concrete foundation wall, or the framing above. The Garland residence requires the 2×6 (5.08 cm $\times$ 15.24 cm) sill plate for all of the exterior bearing walls.

Sole and Top Plate. *Refer to figure 5–3.* Frame walls placed on a wood base (beams, joists, and subflooring) require a sole (bottom) plate. The top of a frame wall also requires a top plate which may be single or double thickness. Exterior wall and interior bearing wall framing require a double top plate. Non-bearing (partition) walls may have a single top plate. The plate materials are normally the same size as the studs, *unless noted otherwise* (U.N.O.). The interior walls of the Garland residence are all on concrete slab. Sill plate is not required for the interior walls. Standard 2×4 (5.08 cm $\times$ 10.16 cm) or 2×6 (5.08 cm $\times$ 15.24 cm) plate stock is used.

All of the walls for the Garland residence are topped with a double top plate. Where the ends of the double top plate members abut one another, the abutting joints must be staggered so there is a minimum of 16″ (40.64 cm) in each direction from the butted joints of the plate stock above or below with a minimum of eight 10d or 16d nails used to secure the plates together. The *d* is the symbol for a *pennyweight*, called a *"penny,"* equal in weight to 2 grams. *See appendix III, Nail Sizes.*

Floor and Ceiling Joists

See figures 5–4 and 5–5. Both floor joists and ceiling joists are the horizontal framing members installed to support some portion of the structure built above. Just as with plate stock, each member should be identified by its use and location on the construction site. For example, floor joists support the floor and all framing above to the top plate, as well as the roof structure. There are no floor joists in the Garland residence since the dwelling is supported by a concrete foundation and slab. Ceiling joists support the floors above in multifloor dwellings, as well as the roof structure. Since the Garland residence is one story, the ceiling joists are the support for the roof structure.

Cut from Western and Canadian forests, joists must meet the minimum standards for Douglas fir construction grade #2, or better, as set by the Western Wood Products Association (WWPA). Both the floor and ceiling joists are classified as a structural grade #2 or better, DF or HF. The term *better* means that a #1 or select grade may be used in lieu of the #2 grade, but no lumber classification lower than a grade #2 may be used. The building codes in each part of the country include charts showing design criteria for framing lumber. Lumber required for joists must meet the minimum qualifications of standards established by the lumber industry and these codes.

1994 DWELLING CONSTRUCTION UNDER THE U.B.C.

TABLE 23-I-V-J-1—FLOOR JOISTS WITH L/360 DEFLECTION LIMITS

The allowable bending stress (Fb) and modulus of elasticity (E) used in this table shall be from Tables 23-I-X-1 and 23-I-X-2 only.

DESIGN CRITERIA:
Deflection—For 40 psf (1.92 kN/m²) live load.
Limited to span in inches (mm) divided by 360.
Strength—Live load of 40 psf (1.92 kN/m²) plus dead load of 10 psf (0.48 kN/m²) determines the required bending design value.

Joist Size (in) ×25.4 for mm	Spacing (in)	Modulus of Elasticity, E, in 1,000,000 psi ×0.00689 for N/mm²																
		0.8	0.9	1.0	1.1	1.2	1.3	1.4	1.5	1.6	1.7	1.8	1.9	2.0	2.1	2.2	2.3	2.4
2×6	12.0	8-6	8-10	9-2	9-6	9-9	10-0	10-3	10-6	10-9	10-11	11-2	11-4	11-7	11-9	11-11	12-1	12-3
	16.0	7-9	8-0	8-4	8-7	8-10	9-1	9-4	9-6	9-9	9-11	10-2	10-4	10-6	10-8	10-10	11-0	11-2
	19.2	7-3	7-7	7-10	8-1	8-4	8-7	8-9	9-0	9-2	9-4	9-6	9-8	9-10	10-0	10-2	10-4	10-6
	24.0	6-9	7-0	7-3	7-6	7-9	7-11	8-2	8-4	8-6	8-8	8-10	9-0	9-2	9-4	9-6	9-7	9-9
2×8	12.0	11-3	11-8	12-1	12-6	12-10	13-2	13-6	13-10	14-2	14-5	14-8	15-0	15-3	15-6	15-9	15-11	16-2
	16.0	10-2	10-7	11-0	11-4	11-8	12-0	12-3	12-7	12-10	13-1	13-4	13-7	13-10	14-1	14-3	14-6	14-8
	19.2	9-7	10-0	10-4	10-8	11-0	11-3	11-7	11-10	12-1	12-4	12-7	12-10	13-0	13-3	13-5	13-8	13-10
	24.0	8-11	9-3	9-7	9-11	10-2	10-6	10-9	11-0	11-3	11-5	11-8	11-11	12-1	12-3	12-6	12-8	12-10
2×10	12.0	14-4	14-11	15-5	15-11	16-5	16-10	17-3	17-8	18-0	18-5	18-9	19-1	19-5	19-9	20-1	20-4	20-8
	16.0	13-0	13-6	14-0	14-6	14-11	15-3	15-8	16-0	16-5	16-9	17-0	17-4	17-8	17-11	18-3	18-6	18-9
	19.2	12-3	12-9	13-2	13-7	14-0	14-5	14-9	15-1	15-5	15-9	16-0	16-4	16-7	16-11	17-2	17-5	17-8
	24.0	11-4	11-10	12-3	12-8	13-0	13-4	13-8	14-0	14-4	14-7	14-11	15-2	15-5	15-8	15-11	16-2	16-5
2×12	12.0	17-5	18-1	18-9	19-4	19-11	20-6	21-0	21-6	21-11	22-5	22-10	23-3	23-7	24-0	24-5	24-9	25-1
	16.0	15-10	16-5	17-0	17-7	18-1	18-7	19-1	19-6	19-11	20-4	20-9	21-1	21-6	21-10	22-2	22-6	22-10
	19.2	14-11	15-6	16-0	16-7	17-0	17-6	17-11	18-4	18-9	19-2	19-6	19-10	20-2	20-6	20-10	21-2	21-6
	24.0	13-10	14-4	14-11	15-4	15-10	16-3	16-8	17-0	17-5	17-9	18-1	18-5	18-9	19-1	19-4	19-8	19-11
Fb	12.0	718	777	833	888	941	993	1,043	1,092	1,140	1,187	1,233	1,278	1,323	1,367	1,410	1,452	1,494
	16.0	790	855	917	977	1,036	1,093	1,148	1,202	1,255	1,306	1,357	1,407	1,456	1,504	1,551	1,598	1,644
	19.2	840	909	975	1,039	1,101	1,161	1,220	1,277	1,333	1,388	1,442	1,495	1,547	1,598	1,649	1,698	1,747
	24.0	905	979	1,050	1,119	1,186	1,251	1,314	1,376	1,436	1,496	1,554	1,611	1,667	1,722	1,776	1,829	1,882

FIGURE 5–4
Joist Tables. Courtesy Uniform Building code, ICBO.

1994 DWELLING CONSTRUCTION UNDER THE U.B.C.

TABLE 23-I-V-J-3—CEILING JOISTS WITH *L/240* DEFLECTION LIMITS

The allowable bending stress (*Fb*) and modulus of elasticity (*E*) used in this table shall be from Tables 23-I-X-1 and 23-I-X-2 only.

DESIGN CRITERIA:
Deflection—For 10 (0.48 kN/m²) psf live load.
Limited to span in inches (mm) divided by 240.
Strength—Live load of 10 psf (0.48 kN/mm²) plus dead load of 5 psf (0.24 kN/mm²) determines the required fiber stress value.

Joist Size (in)	Spacing (in) ×25.4 for mm	Modulus of Elasticity, E, in 1,000,000 psi ×0.00689 for N/mm²																
		0.8	0.9	1.0	1.1	1.2	1.3	1.4	1.5	1.6	1.7	1.8	1.9	2.0	2.1	2.2	2.3	2.4
2×4	12.0	9-10	10-3	10-7	10-11	11-3	11-7	11-10	12-2	12-5	12-8	12-11	13-2	13-4	13-7	13-9	14-0	14-2
	16.0	8-11	9-4	9-8	9-11	10-3	10-6	10-9	11-0	11-3	11-6	11-9	11-11	12-2	12-4	12-6	12-9	12-11
	19.2	8-5	8-9	9-1	9-4	9-8	9-11	10-2	10-4	10-7	10-10	11-0	11-3	11-5	11-7	11-9	12-0	12-2
	24.0	7-10	8-1	8-5	8-8	8-11	9-2	9-5	9-8	9-10	10-0	10-3	10-5	10-7	10-9	10-11	11-1	11-3
2×6	12.0	15-6	16-1	16-8	17-2	17-8	18-2	18-8	19-1	19-6	19-11	20-3	20-8	21-0	21-4	21-8	22-0	22-4
	16.0	14-1	14-7	15-2	15-7	16-1	16-6	16-11	17-4	17-8	18-1	18-5	18-9	19-1	19-5	19-8	20-0	20-3
	19.2	13-3	13-9	14-3	14-8	15-2	15-7	15-11	16-4	16-8	17-0	17-4	17-8	17-11	18-3	18-6	18-10	19-1
	24.0	12-3	12-9	13-3	13-8	14-1	14-5	14-9	15-2	15-6	15-9	16-1	16-4	16-8	16-11	17-2	17-5	17-8
2×8	12.0	20-5	21-2	21-11	22-8	23-4	24-0	24-7	25-2	25-8								
	16.0	18-6	19-3	19-11	20-7	21-2	21-9	22-4	22-10	23-4	23-10	24-3	24-8	25-2	25-7	25-11		
	19.2	17-5	18-1	18-9	19-5	19-11	20-6	21-0	21-6	21-11	22-5	22-10	23-3	23-8	24-0	24-5	24-9	25-2
	24.0	16-2	16-10	17-5	18-0	18-6	19-0	19-6	19-11	20-5	20-10	21-2	21-7	21-11	22-4	22-8	23-0	23-4
2×10	12.0	26-0																
	16.0	23-8	24-7	25-5														
	19.2	22-3	23-1	23-11	24-9	25-5												
	24.0	20-8	21-6	22-3	22-11	23-8	24-3	24-10	25-5	26-0								
Fb	12.0	711	769	825	880	932	983	1,033	1,082	1,129	1,176	1,221	1,266	1,310	1,354	1,396	1,438	1,480
	16.0	783	847	909	968	1,026	1,082	1,137	1,191	1,243	1,294	1,344	1,394	1,442	1,490	1,537	1,583	1,629
	19.2	832	900	965	1,029	1,090	1,150	1,208	1,265	1,321	1,375	1,429	1,481	1,533	1,583	1,633	1,682	1,731
	24.0	896	969	1,040	1,108	1,174	1,239	1,302	1,363	1,423	1,481	1,539	1,595	1,651	1,706	1,759	1,812	1,864

NOTE: The required bending design value, *Fb*, in pounds per square inch (0.00689 for N/mm2) is shown at the bottom of this table and is applicable to all lumber sizes shown. Spans are shown in feet-inches (1 foot = 304.8 mm, 1 inch = 25.4 mm) and are limited to 26 feet (7925 mm) and less.

FIGURE 5–4 *(continued)*
Joist Tables. Courtesy Uniform Building code, ICBO.

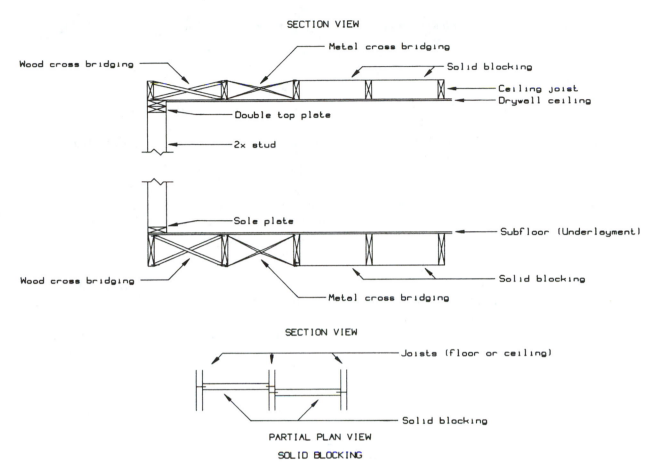

FIGURE 5–5
Joist Framing

Joists are placed utilizing the shortest practical span from bearing point to bearing point due to the allowable bending (fiber) stress, *Fb*, and the modulus of elasticity, *E*, the ability of the lumber to stretch. All code books include the structural capabilities of lumber and the maximum span allowable. For example, information found in the Uniform Building Code, the code book now used by 21 states, as established by the International Conference of Building Officials (ICBO), one of three construction regulation groups, has determined that floor and ceiling joists must meet the following criteria:

A 2 × 8 (5.08 cm x 20.32 cm) floor joist:

"2 × 8 floor joist @ 16" O/C may span 14'-8" (maximum)"
"*Fb* @ 16" O/C at maximum load = 1,629 psi bending stress value"

A 2 × 8 (5.08 cm x 20.32 cm) ceiling joist:

"2 × 8 ceiling joist @ 24" O/C may span 23'-4" (maximum)"
"*Fb* @ 24" O/C at maximum load = 1,864 psi bending stress value"

In metric measure the statements read as follows:
A 5.08 cm × 20.32 cm floor joist:

"5.08 cm × 20.32 cm floor joist @ 40.64 cm O/C may span 4.47 m (maximum)"

"*Fb* @ 60.96 cm O/C at maximum load = 738.9 kg/6.45 cm² bending stress value"

A 5.08 cm × 20.32 cm ceiling joist:

"5.08 cm × 20.32 cm floor joist @ 0.6 m O/C may span 7.11 m (maximum)"

"*Fb* @ 60.96 cm O/C at maximum load = 845.5 kg/6.45 cm² bending stress value"

The maximum span depends upon the installed or anticipated load and the joist spacing. For example, a floor joist may have a maximum 40 pounds per square foot (psf) (18.18 kg/0.0929 m²) live load and a 10 pound psf (4.55 kg/0.0929 m²) dead load, whereas a ceiling joist of the same size may have a maximum 10 psf (4.55 kg/0.0929 m²) live load and a 5 psf (2.27 kg/0.0929 m²) dead load. A **live load** is any load that is moveable, such as a person or furniture not affixed to the structure (chair, table, desk, and so on). A **dead load** is any load that is fixed to the structure such as cabinetry, plumbing fixtures, or HVAC units, as well as the weight of the structure itself.

There is one additional load included in a roof structure, the **wind lift.** It deals with wind resistance. The engineer designing the structural roof support must also include this where strong winds such as gales, hurricanes, and the like are of concern.

A double joist must be installed parallel to, and under, a bearing wall. Double joists must also be installed perpendicular to walls running the other direction. For example, joists installed in a north-south direction for one room may change to an east-west direction at an adjoining room, requiring a double joist at the direction change. Additional joists may be required where the load placed upon them, such as under kitchens and bathrooms, is greater than normal.

Header Joists. The header joist, also known as the rim joist, is a continuing member the same size as the floor or ceiling joist extending end-to-end (out-to-out) along the perimeter of a wall. It is placed on the sill plate so the outside face of the header matches the outside edge of the sill plate. It is used to hide, protect, and stiffen the ends of the interior joists abutting it. The lengths of these members may be all the same or in random lengths.

Bridging. *Refer to figure 4–4.* Bridging may or may not be indicated on the plans. Most building code requirements state that bridging must be installed for all joists where the span is greater than 8'–0" (2.44 m). The purpose of the bridging is to provide more strength and rigidity to the floor or ceiling structure, thus offering a shorter span upon which to apply load from above. The bridging may be a *solid* member (the same size as the joist) cut to fit between joists, 2× (5.08 cm ×) wood cross, or pre-fabricated metal cross bridging.

Laminated Beams

See figure 5–6. Alternates to the standard 2× (5.08 cm ×) joists are the Microllam® or Parallam® beams and joists (manufactured by Trus-Joist/MacMillan), and truss joists (solid or open web). The beams and joists are prefabricated and shipped to the site ready for installation. Maximum lengths are prescribed by code in the same manner as a 2× (5.08 cm ×) joist member.

FIGURE 5–6
Beam Joists. Permission Trus Joist MacMillan.

Microllam®. The Microllam® beam/joist is manufactured from several layers of plywood, glued and compressed into a beam in sizes from 10″ (25.40 cm) to 12″ (30.48 cm) in width, 2″ (5.08 cm) to 6″ (15.24 cm) thick, and up to 20′–0″ (6.10 m) in length in regular lumber increments of 2′–0″ (0.61 m). They may also be ordered in specific lengths as required. The Microllam® beam may be used for floor joists, ceiling joists, or lintel (header) beams over framed wall openings, such as a garage door header beam.

Parallam®. One of the more recent beams to be manufactured is the Parallam® beam. This beam is manufactured from compressed and glued wood fragments and fibers to form framing members for use as joists or beams similar to the Microllam®. They may also be installed as exposed architectural and/or structural support beams or lintels (headers) over framed wall openings.

Glue-Laminated Beams. *See figure 5–7.* Another more common and larger beam is known as the **glue-laminated beam** (glu-lam or GLB). Glu-lams may be used solely for architectural aesthetics, for structural support, or both. They may be used as a girder beam for floor support, as a hip or ridge beam for roof support, or as a buttress support for wall structures where both aesthetics and structural design criteria are desired (such as church construction). The architectural beam is finished with a varnish, lacquer, or paint for appearance. The structural beam is used where no finishing is necessary, or, in some cases, where a paint finish may be required.

The glu-lam is manufactured from multiple layers of milled select lumber. The lumber is glued on the wide side under compression and heat, milled for a smooth finish, and wrapped in plastic (heavy-gauge polyethylene sheets) when totally dried. The milling reduces the size of the lumber even more than the original milling. The nominal 2 × 4 (5.08 cm × 10.16 cm) size is reduced to a 1½″ × 3⅛″ (3.81 cm × 7.94 cm) and is ordered by its finish size.

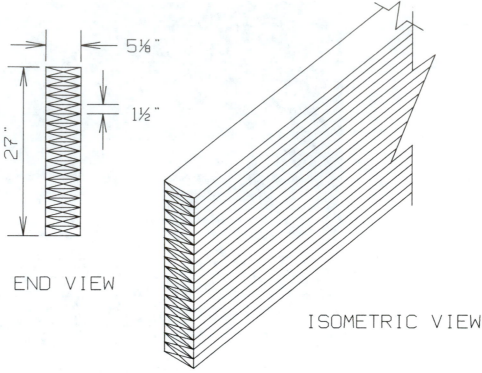

FIGURE 5–7
$5^1/8'' \times 27''$ Glue-Laminated Beam

For example, the drawing in figure 5–7 shows a glu-lam beam produced from 2×6 (5.08 cm $\times$ 15.24 cm) lumber. The milled lumber is $1\frac{1}{2}'' \times 5\frac{1}{8}''$. The beam is 27″ (68.58 cm) deep. The quantity of lumber necessary to make a 27″ (68.58 cm) deep beam is determined as follows:

$27'' \div 1\frac{1}{2}'' =$

$27'' \div 1.5'' = 18$ pc

or, in metric calculation:

68.58 cm $\div 3.81$ cm $= 18$ pc

The beam is identified as a $5\frac{1}{8}'' \times 27''$ (13.02 cm $\times$ 68.58 cm) beam. GLBs are manufactured on special order and prepared in specific lengths as required.

The Truss Joist

Refer to figure 5–6. Truss joists are manufactured with one or two $2 \times$ (5.08 cm $\times$) top and bottom *chords* with several layers of plywood fastened edgewise between, or may be manufactured using a tubular metal or $2 \times$ wood webbing in diagonal design, extending the full length of the truss. As with glue-laminated beams, open-web trusses are prefabricated to prescribed lengths on special order.

Subflooring

Refer to figures 5–3 and 5–4. Subflooring, or underlayment, is normally installed by gluing and nailing ¾″ (1.91 cm) or 1″ (2.54 cm) CDX, 5-ply, $4' \times 8'$

(1.22 m × 2.44 m) plywood sheets over the floor joists. The subfloor adds stability to the floor structure as well as backing for the finish floor materials. The letters CDX identify the type of plywood to be used as established by the American Plywood Association (APA). The letters *"C"* and *"D"* identify the exterior layers of plywood. C is a smooth, finished face with few knot holes. D is slightly less smooth with some knot holes exposed. The designation *5-ply* means that there are five layers of laminated plywood. The grain of each layer is always at right angles to the previous layer and glued on both sides, except for the exposed layers, which are glued on one side only. Plywood is always produced in an odd number of layers (three and five layers). The *"X"* is the abbreviation for "exterior grade." Therefore, CDX is an exterior grade plywood with a layer of C and D classifications exposed. Subflooring is available with plain butts (straight ends), tongue-and-groove (T&G) joints, or shiplap joints. The T&G and shiplap board offers better control of the installation of the board.

An alternate subfloor is the Oriented Strand Board® (OSB®) installed in the same manner as the plywood. OSB® is made from the same basic materials as the Parallam® beam. The compressed and glued chips and fragments are mixed with fibrous strands (vegetable and/or mineral) and formed into sheet sizes similar to plywood.

Wall Framing

See figure 5–8. Wall framing includes top and bottom (sill or sole) plates, studs, and window and door lintels (headers). The walls may be either bearing walls or partition walls (non-bearing walls). All exterior walls supporting the structure above are bearing walls. There may also be interior bearing walls installed as part of the structural support system. Exterior and interior bearing walls in residential construction are normally framed with minimum 2 × 6 (5.08 cm × 15.24 cm) studs at a maximum 16" (40.64 cm) O/C. Stud sizes equal to, or larger than, 2 × 6 (5.08 cm × 15.24 cm), such as 3 × 4 (7.62 cm × 10.16 cm), 2 × 8 (5.08 cm × 20.32 cm), 2 × 10 (5.08 cm × 25.40 cm), and so on, may be installed if necessary or desired. Studs larger than 2 × 6 (5.08 cm × 15.24 cm) may be spaced at 20" (50.80 cm) or 24" (60.96 cm) O/C, depending upon the structural load requirements. Some codes allow 2 × 4 (5.08 cm × 10.16 cm) studs, at 16" (40.64 cm) O/C, for exterior and interior bearing walls in one-story residences. Interior partition (non-bearing) plumbing walls are also normally framed with 2 × 6 (5.08 cm × 15.24 cm) studs spaced at 24" (60.96 cm) O/C with 2 × 6 (5.08 cm × 15.24 cm) top and bottom plates. The plumbing wall may also be 2 × 4 (5.08 cm × 10.16 cm) studs installed on 2 × 6 (5.08 cm × 15.24 cm) or 2 × 8 (5.08 cm × 20.32 cm) top and bottom plates at 24" (60.96 cm) O/C, staggered. The remaining non-bearing partition walls are usually framed with 2 × 4 (5.08 cm × 10.16 cm) studs at 24" (60.96 cm) O/C.

Studs are graded as DF, construction grade (CG) or HF, #3 common. Both grades are available in precut sizes from $92^{1}/8''$ to $92^{5}/8''$ (2.339 m to 2.353 m) for standard 8'-1" (2.46 m) high walls, or can be obtained in even 2'-0" (60.96 cm) increments for shorter or longer wall heights. The standard wall height is identified from the precut $92^{1}/2''$ (2.349 m) studs and the top and bottom plates (using actual thicknesses or lengths) as follows:

$1^{1}/2''$ sill or sole plate + $92^{1}/2''$ stud + 3" ($1^{1}/2'' \times 2$) double top plate = 97" or 8'-1"

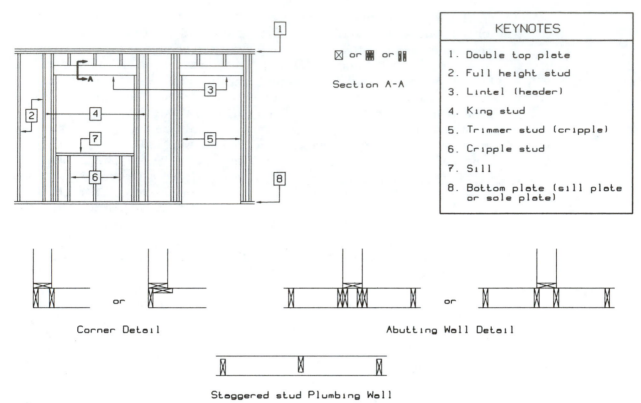

FIGURE 5–8
Miscellaneous Wall Framing—Wood

In metric calculation, the stud is identified as follows:

3.5 cm sole plate + 235 cm (2.35 m) stud + 7.62 cm double top plate = 246.43 cm or 2.46 m

Lintels (Headers). *Refer to figure 5–8, section A–A.* The lintel (or header) is installed over an opening in the wall framing to replace the load support for the structure above the opening. It may be made from double or triple lengths of 2 × (5.08 cm ×) structural members or a beam of the proper wall thickness. The lintel gets larger by at least one size (length) as the opening gets wider. A rule of thumb for a structural member over a window or door opening states that the lintel should be one size larger than the wall opening and is at least 8″ (20.32 cm) longer than the opening (4″ [10.16 cm] on each end). For example, the member required for a 4′-0″ (1.22 m) wide opening in a 2 × 6 (5.08 cm × 15.24 cm) bearing wall should have a minimum of two 2 × 6 (5.08 cm × 15.24 cm) framing members placed flush with the exterior and interior faces of the stud wall, or three 2 × 6 (5.08 cm × 15.24 cm) framing members back-to-back, or a 6 × 6 (15.24 cm × 15.24 cm) framing member. The framing members should be DF, #1 or #2, or equal.

Specifications may require even larger sizes, depending upon the load the header supports. For example, in a balloon frame wall 20′-0″ (6.10 m) to 24′-0″ (7.32 m) high, the member required over a 6′-0″ (1.83 m) window on the lower level may be as large as three 2 × 12 (5.08 cm × 30.48 cm) or a 6 × 12 (15.24 cm × 30.48 cm), DF #1. These spans are determined by engineering calculations in the same manner as joists. Lintels over openings in non-bearing partitions may be a flat single member the size of the stud, or a double stud placed on end.

King and Trimmer Studs. *Refer to figure 5–8.* Wherever an opening in a wall occurs there are two king studs, one on each side of the opening. The king stud is the full-height stud immediately adjacent to an opening and abutting the header over the opening. There are two trimmer studs, one on each side of the opening inside the king studs The trimmer stud, also referred to as a cripple stud, is cut to fit under both ends of the header for its support. The opening between the trimmers should be no less than ⅛″ (0.32 cm) nor more than ¼″ (0.64 cm) larger than the required opening for the door or window that is to be installed.

Cripple Walls. *Refer to figure 5–8.* Wall framing above an opening is supported by the lintel (header) and extends to the top plate above a door or window. This is called a cripple wall. A cripple wall also extends from the sole or sill plate to the sill frame below a window opening. The stud spacing of a cripple wall is the same as the full-height wall framing in which the opening exists.

Diagonal Bracing or Shear Wall. *See figure 5–9.* The purpose of **diagonal bracing** or **shear paneling** is to give additional structural strength, seismic stability, and lateral wind load protection to a structure, as well as to maintain a true and straight alignment of the walls. *Seismic stability* refers to the ability of a structure to resist violent fluctuations and vibrations (such as earthquake). Lateral **wind load** refers to the ability of the structure to resist wind pressure exerted on the walls. The seismic and lateral wind requirements vary with the location of the construction.

Diagonal, or let-in, bracing may be 1 × 4 (2.54 cm × 5.08 cm), HF, utility, or DF, common, notched into the studs and nailed to each stud in which the embedment is made. The standard metal let-in brace may be used instead of the wood let-in brace and should also be notched into the studs. A diagonal brace is installed in both directions at each exterior corner at an angle of 60° (maximum) from horizontal. Additional bracing is installed in the same manner at intervals of 25′–0″ (7.62 m) clear wall space (no openings) along any exterior wall.

Wind and seismic codes, to provide for lateral loads imposed by wind and violent vibration, respectively, require that a shear panel, ⅜″ (0.95 cm), 3-ply, or ½″ (1.27 cm), 5-ply, plywood, or equivalent OSB®, must be installed

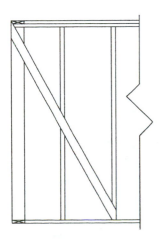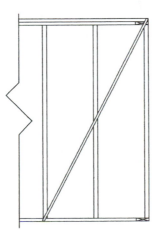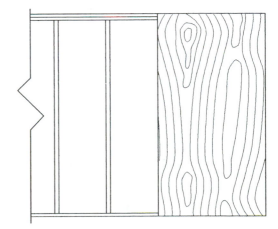

1x4 Let-in Brace   Let-in Strap   Shear Panel

FIGURE 5–9

Diagonal Bracing and Shear Wall Construction

vertically from bottom plate to top plate on both sides of the exterior corner in lieu of the let-in bracing. Code may require that the panels be installed both inside and outside of the exterior bearing walls. Such paneling may serve a dual purpose by installing the shear panels completely around the face of the structure to use as the back-up sheathing for exterior veneers or sidings as well as for shear wall.

Platform Framing vs. Balloon Framing

See figure 5–10. Until this section, the materials required for platform framing are all included in the previous sections. **Platform,** or *western,* **framing** is the more common framing system used today. This type of construction is more conducive to structural support requirements. The system is constructed using joists and subflooring between floors of a multistory structure. The first floor framing may include girders and joists over a foundation with a sill plate, subflooring, sole plate, wall framing, and double top plate. Where on-grade slab construction is performed, the girders, joists, and subflooring are eliminated. The upper floors use the same procedure to the roof structure with the exception of the sill plate and girders. The walls are usually 8'-1" high on all levels in tract or standard home construction. They may extend to 10'-0" or 12'-0" in some areas for larger custom residences and commercial office construction. Some variation of balloon framing may be incorporated into a western framing pattern as explained in the following paragraphs.

Refer to figure 5–10. Wall framing extending continuously from the sill or sole plate at grade level to the roof structure in structures of more than one story is **balloon frame construction.** Balloon framing was used extensively in the

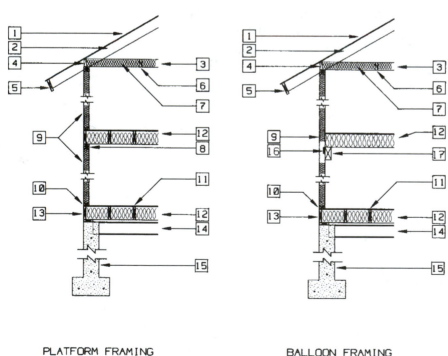

KEYNOTES

1. Roof sheathing
2. Rafter
3. Ceiling joist
4. Frieze blocking
5. Fascia
6. Blocking (typ)
7. Insulation (typ)
8. Double top plate
9. Exterior stud
10. Sole plate (typ)
11. Subfloor (typ)
12. Floor/Ceiling joist
13. Header (rim) joist
14. Steel girder beam
15. Foundation wall and footing
16. 1x4 ribbon
17. Ledger

PLATFORM FRAMING

BALLOON FRAMING

FIGURE 5–10
Platform vs. Balloon Framing

eastern parts of the country. The practice has been generally stopped by code regulations because of the structural weaknesses in this type of framing.

The exterior, balloon-framed bearing walls for two-story structures may extend as high as 24'–0" (7.32 m) A.F.F. These walls require a **ribbon** (a 1 × 4 [2.54 cm × 5.08 cm]) notched perpendicular (horizontally) to the studs at a level just below the upper level floor joists. The ribbon is installed to help maintain rigidity in the walls in the same manner as the let-in brace is used for corner support. A **ledger** is another structural horizontal member installed on the interior side of the balloon framing to support those upper level floor joists. Interior partition walls may extend as high as 10'–0" (3.05 m) A.F.F.

See figure 5–11. The only area of balloon framing still allowed by code is found mixed in with the platform framing in today's construction where *vaulted* or *cathedral* ceilings are designed. A vaulted ceiling is one that slopes in only one direction. A cathedral ceiling is one that slopes in two directions forming a gable-like appearance on the interior of the residence. This type of construction is used to provide smaller rooms in a residence with the aesthetic feeling of larger, more spacious rooms.

Fire-Blocking or Fire-Stopping. Building codes may require installation of **fire-blocking** (horizontal framing components) at every 4'–0" (1.22 m) vertically between all exterior and interior bearing studs where the top plate is above 8'–0" (2.44 m). The purpose of the blocking is to reduce air space through which a fire may spread within a wall. The same size lumber as used for the wall stud must be installed for fire-blocking. The waste lumber from the wall framing, the braces which support the walls until joists, roof structure or trusses are installed, and/or plate stock (except PTMS sill plate) may be used for the blocking.

Conventional Roof Framing

See figure 5–12. There are a variety of roof shapes, such as flat, hip, gable, shed, and mansard or combinations of them, that are common to residential construction. Each roof design requires special care as to the materials and structural requirements necessary for a properly constructed roof. Sloped roofs require totally different construction considerations than do flat roofs. The

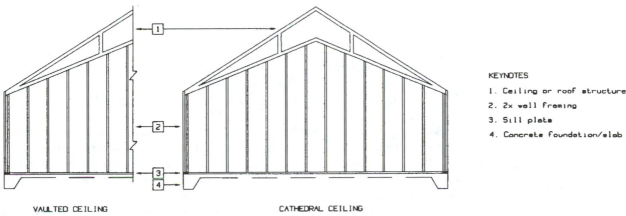

KEYNOTES

1. Ceiling or roof structure
2. 2x wall framing
3. Sill plate
4. Concrete foundation/slab

VAULTED CEILING   CATHEDRAL CEILING

FIGURE 5–11
Vaulted and Cathedral Ceilings (Balloon Framing)

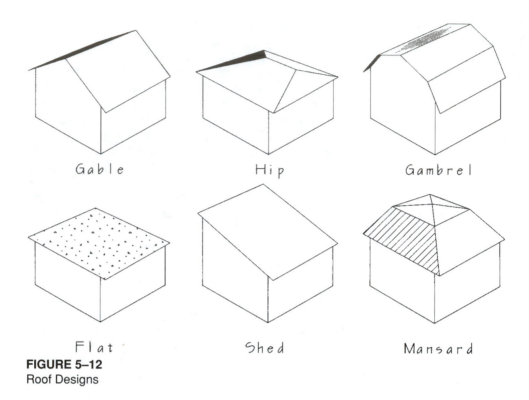

FIGURE 5–12
Roof Designs

ceiling joist and rafter in flat roof construction are often one and the same framing member when the slope is ½" (1.27 cm) per lineal foot or less. All styles sloped more steeply than this may require separate ceiling joist and roof rafter members for the roof construction.

Ceiling Joists. *Refer to figures 5–4 and 5–9. Ceiling joists* are horizontal framing members that may be considered part of the wall construction or part of the roof construction. Where there is more than one story to a structure, the floor joist for the floor above is also the ceiling joist for the lower floor. Ceiling joists are also considered the base of the roof structure in sloped-roof construction. Most residential and light commercial construction may have a minimum 2 × 4 (5.08 cm × 10.16 cm), DF #2, or better (one-story construction), or a 2 × 6 (5.08 cm × 15.24 cm), DF #2, or better (multistory), for a ceiling joist. The spacing of a ceiling joist is determined by the required structural support for the finished ceiling materials, the walls below, and the roof above. Spacing usually is at 16" (40.64 cm) O/C or 24" (60.96 cm) O/C, and, like the floor joist, the shortest practical span is utilized. Bridging must also be applied where spans exceed the 8'–0" (2.44 m) limit. A rim joist or rim blocking may be installed at the exterior ends of the ceiling joists.

Frieze-Blocking. Another system, called *frieze-blocking*, or *vent-blocking*, common to some of the southern areas of the United States, is installed to aid air circulation in attic spaces. If used, the quantity is determined by the number of spaces between the rafters. The block is usually installed in every second or third space between rafter tails similar to the rim joist or rim joist blocking. A frieze-block may be manufactured in 1 × or 2 × (2.54 cm × or 5.08 cm ×) thick common stock, OSB®, or 1" (2.54 cm) plywood, with two or three screened holes cut into the member to provide the necessary air circulation.

The screens are placed over the openings to prevent insulation from falling from the attic space and to keep birds and rodents from nesting in the attic. Rim blocking is installed in the remaining spaces.

Rafters. Rafters—framing members that form the roof shapes shown in figure 5–12—are also DF #2 or better. The rafter size and spacing is governed by the load that is to be placed upon them. For example, a sloped roof using a tile roofing system requires more strength than one with composition shingles. In another example, the load applied to a flat roof (3″ [7.62 cm] per foot or less slope) with several pieces of heavy air-handling equipment installed requires heavier and/or closer spaced rafters than one with only a small single air-handling unit. The loads are determined in the same way as those for joists are determined, by live load, dead load, and wind lift requirements.

See figure 5–13. The drawing notes the comparative size of a ridge beam to a rafter connection in conventional roof framing. A practical rule of thumb is that a ridge beam should be at least 2″ (5.05 cm) deeper than the rafter to be attached to it. As the slope in a pitched roof gets steeper the size ridge beam must be larger so as to accommodate the end cut of the rafter. The drawing notes this necessity by indicating the ridge size comparisons. On the left side of the drawing the pitch and slope are indicated. The ridge and rafter drawings are horizontally aligned to match the left-hand symbols. For example, the ridge beam in the center drawing is a 2 × 6 (5.08 cm × 15.24 cm). This beam is sufficiently wide to accommodate a 2 × 6 (5.08 cm × 15.24 cm) rafter at 3:12, but the ridge beam is too small for the cut of the 2 × 6 (5.08 cm × 15.24 cm) rafter at the 6:12 slope. The ridge beam for the 4:12 slope could be used but it is also better to be enlarged because of the depth of the rafter.

The two types of rafters installed in a sloped roof structure are the common rafter and the jack rafter. A **common rafter** extends from the ridge (the highest point on the roof) to the top plate at the exterior bearing wall

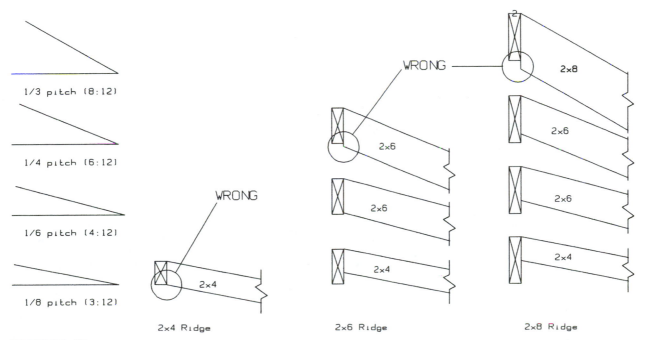

FIGURE 5–13
Rafter-to-Ridge Connections

without interruption. A rafter that is interrupted somewhere between the ridge and the top plate, for example, by a chimney, dormer, or hip beam is called a **jack rafter**.

Ridge, Hip, and Valley. *See figure 5–14.* The final portion of a conventional structural roof frame may include both hips and ridge. As previously mentioned, the hips and ridge are a minimum one size larger than the rafters. For example, a 2 × 6 (5.08 cm × 15.24 cm) raftered roof should have a single or double 2 × 8 (5.08 cm × 20.32 cm), or a single timber member of similar size. The ridge is the topmost framing member of all sloped roofs. A hip, if used, slopes from the ridge in any direction to a junction point with the bearing walls at the top plate. A valley is the inverse of a hip. For example, where a building is L shaped, with a sloped roof structure, the connecting members at the intersection of the two slopes is the valley. The valley may be a single timber member or may be a double smaller member similar to the hip.

Additional Structural Roof Members and Accessories. Additional members that may be used to support the roof structure in conventional framing include *king posts, purlins,* and *bracing.* **King posts** are structural members used to support the ridge and/or hip beam, are placed directly under the beam, and are spaced equidistant under the roof structure at a maximum 4′–0″ (1.22 m) O/C. The king posts may be double- or triple-stacked studs or a single structural member sufficiently large enough to support the roof structure above (such as three 2 × 6 [three 5.08 cm × 15.24 cm] or a 6 × 6 [15.24 cm × 15.24 cm]). Vertical bracing is centered between the king post and the top plate parallel to, and on both sides of, the ridge beam. Horizontal bracing, called a **collar tie,** is fastened to the rafters and the vertical bracing. Continuous horizontal members perpendicular to, and directly under, the collar ties and fastened to the vertical braces and collar ties are the **purlins.** Where such construction is required, the king posts are placed on double ceiling joists for support.

Other framing accessories include the installation of straps, clips, and hangers for strengthening and providing additional support to the framing

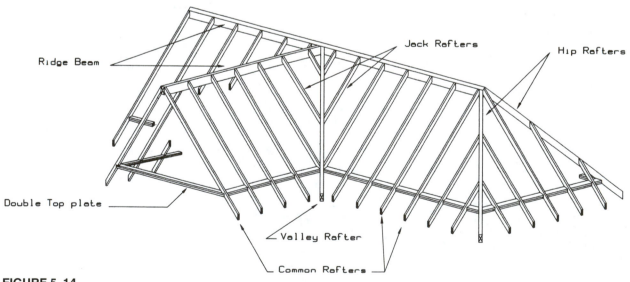

FIGURE 5–14
Roof Structure

members. The clips, referred to as *hurricane clips* (Simpson A34 or A35, or equal), are installed at the junction of the rafters and ceiling joists. Hangers are used to tie the rafters, hips, valleys, and ridges together. Straps are used between floors to tie plates and joists together on multistory structures.

Roof Sheathing. Roof sheathing is normally specified as a 4′ × 8′ × ½″ (1.22m × 2.44 m × 1.27 cm) CDX, 5-ply, plywood. CCX may be used where the underside of the roof is exposed, such as along the eave line, for appearance and the CDX is installed on the remainder of the roof. An alternate to the plywood is the use of a minimum ⅝″ (1.59 cm) OSB®.

Roof Trusses

Alternate installations use pre-fabricated trusses for sloped roof structures replacing both the ceiling joists and roof raftering. The most common trusses for residential construction use 2 × 4 (5.08 cm × 10.16 cm) bottom chords (the equivalent of the ceiling joists), with either 2 × 4 or 2 × 6 (5.08 cm × 15.24 cm) top chords (the equivalent of the sloped rafters). The structural members that are built into them replace the conventional framing members mentioned above.

Fireplaces

See figure 5–15. Fireplaces require special construction treatment. All masonry fireplaces require specially constructed footing pads at least 1′–0″ (30.48 cm) deep with reinforcement spaced at 8″ (20.32 cm) to 12″ (30.48 cm) O/C each way in the footing. The masonry required may be a double wythe brick, or CMU interior and face brick exterior, or all CMU exposed in single wythe. A

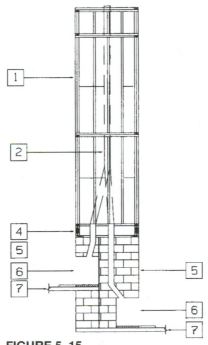

KEYNOTES

1. 2x6 chimney framing w/ ⅝″ "X" drywall interior (per code) and 3C-8 face brick veneer on exterior

2. 2-6″ DIA metal flue stacks per code (shown side elevation only)

3. Not used

4. 2x10 floor joists and ¾″ or 1″ underlayment o/2x sill plate

5. Masonry retaining wall w/ 3C-8 face brick over at fireplace only – GWB and furring at all other areas

6. 3′-8″x2′-8″x2′-0″ opening for metal firebox

7. 4″ concrete slab

FIGURE 5–15
Fireplace Construction

terra cotta flue liner and steel damper must be installed by the mason. A fire brick floor and walls must be installed for exposed wood or gas burning fireboxes. A clean-out pit must also be included and located at the lowest possible point on the structure. All floor and roof framing surrounding the masonry must be spaced a minimum 2″ from the masonry and connected for structural strength and support by steel connectors (straps) embedded in the masonry and bolted to the framing on all sides.

Fireplaces constructed for metal firebox modules may be all wood frame. The extra-deep footing is not required, although an additional 4″ (5.08 cm) to 8″ (10.16 cm) thickened concrete pad may be placed under the firebox area. The framing is installed using 2 × 6 (5.08 cm × 15.24 cm) lumber with single or double ⅝″ (1.59 cm) X (fire-retardant) drywall on the inside and outside. The number of layers is dependent upon the local codes. The flue is made in sections of 4″ (5.08 cm) or 6″ (15.24 cm) DIA GI (galvanized iron). A minimum 26-gauge (ga) GI fire stop must be installed, completely surrounding the flue and attached to the drywall and framing inside the chimney stack at maximum 8′–0″ (2.44 m) intervals.

Carpentry Accessories

All framing requires special connectors to assist in keeping a building structurally sound. Some accessories have been mentioned previously but most have not been discussed. The accessories may include the following:

1. Anchor bolts: ½″ (1.27 cm) or ⅝″ (1.59 cm) bent bolts placed in concrete with the threaded end exposed for anchoring steel or wood members to the concrete.
2. Hold-down anchors: A formed GI metal anchor fastened to the bottom plate and studs and anchored into the concrete.
3. Powder actuated shot-and-pin: Used in lieu of anchor bolts, to hold any framing member to concrete, masonry, or steel.
4. Rafter and joist anchor clips: Installed to aid in maintaining proper spacing and support to the framing member when fastened at the plate. Commonly used with truss installations.
5. Rafter and joist hangers: GI formed metal units in the widths and thickness of standard lumber—2 × 6, 2 × 8, 2 × 10 (5.08 cm × 15.24 cm, 5.08 cm × 20.32 cm, 5.08 cm × 25.40 cm), and so on—into which the joist or rafter is inserted and fastened.
6. GI straps: For supplying additional rigidity and strength between lower and upper levels of a structure. Installed vertically from lower level top plate to upper level bottom plate.

THERMAL INSULATION

Thermal protection includes products offering resistance to heat such as mineral wool (a by-product of soft coal/coke), fibrous materials (paper and wood), minerals (perlite and vermiculite), fiberglass, cementitious mixtures, and plastics such as polystyrene, polyester, or combinations of some of these products. The insulation materials may be formed into rigid board, foam, loose fill, batt, and blanket products.

The thermal insulation rating for resistance to heat and cold is called the **R-factor.** The most commonly installed insulations are rated at R–7, R–9, R–11, R–19, and R–30. The most recent energy requirements in most areas of the country include R–19 in exterior walls and under floors and R–30 in ceilings or on roofs. The thickness of the insulation helps to determine the R-value; for example, a 4″ (10.16 cm) thick fiberglass batt is designated as an R–11, a 6″ (15.24 cm) batt is rated as an R–19, and so on.

Batt and Blanket Insulation

Batts and *blankets* are made from fiberglass or similar insulating materials, combined with building paper, kraft paper, or foil backing and applied directly to, or between, studs and floor or ceiling joists. Batts are sheets 8′-0″ (2.44 m) long and blankets are in rolls 24′-0″ (7.3 m) or more long. They are both available in 16″ (40.64 cm) or 24″ (60.96 cm) widths.

Loose-Fill Insulation. The four types of loose-fill insulation are *perlite, vermiculite, cellulose,* and *mineral wool.* Loose-fill insulations are available in bags and may be blown under pressure or poured into wall or ceiling cavities. These materials are best used for horizontal installations such as ceilings, although it is not uncommon to find perlite and vermiculite in masonry walls in some areas of the Southwest.

Rigid Insulation. Insulation manufactured into board-like shapes is referred to as a rigid insulator. The boards are combinations of any of the previously mentioned insulating materials that may be mixed together, compressed, and covered with surfacing materials. The most commonly used materials are fiberglass, polystyrene and cementitious composite boards. The composite boards are made from cement and perlite or vermiculite with a covering to help protect from, or aid in, the installation of various roofing materials over them.

Polyurethane Foam. This material is used for insulating existing and new roof applications as well as for masonry wall cavities. The foam is applied in a liquefied state under pressure. The cured foam, when used for roofing, must be coated with an acrylic elastomer for moisture and ultraviolet ray protection.

ROOFING

Roofing refers to the finish materials used for moisture protection of any roof structure. The many varieties of roofing include composition asphalt shingle, wood shingle, wood shake, tile (clay, concrete and combinations of cement-based and organic or inorganic materials), panelized and pre-formed plastic, panelized and pre-formed metal, standing seam and corrugated cold-rolled steel. All of these materials are used on sloped roofs that must have a minimum 3:12 slope ($^1/8$″ [0.3 cm] pitch). Slopes of 3:12 that are to have any of the above materials installed must include a built-up roof (BUR) underlayment. *See Roof Slope table in appendix II.*

There are two types of roof design incorporated into the roof structure for the Garland residence. The roof slopes indicated include a 5:12 slope on the gable-end portion of the roof and a 6:12 slope at the hip areas. The roofing materials required are a minimum 43 lb underlayment and medium wood shake roofing.

LIGHT-GAUGE METAL FRAMING

See figure 5–16 and appendix II, Light Gauge Metal Studs and Joists. Also see the Apartment Walls Floor Plan. Wherever wood frame construction is installed, an alternate *structural light-gauge* and *light-gauge metal framing* may be substituted. Structural light-gauge metal framing includes both studs and joists in 18 gauge to 14 gauge cold-rolled steel forms used primarily for exterior and interior bearing walls, floor and ceiling joists, and roof rafters. Most structural studs and joists are unpunched (no prefabricated holes in their lengths) and pre-painted with rust-resistant primer baked into the stud.

Standard structural studs and joists have a C-shaped cross-section. There are several other varieties of structural studs available for special construction. Included are E-shaped, H-shaped, and L-shaped studs used for installations such as elevator shafts, where rigidity and soundproofing are desired. These special studs may be installed with both drywall and rigid insulation as integral parts of the construction. Structural light-gauge metal framing requires the use of *stiffeners* at all connections. The stiffeners are angles similar to angle-iron clips, but are of the same gauge as, or slightly heavier than, the framing being installed. The stiffeners may be connected to the framing with screws, but all connections are always welded.

Light-gauge metal framing is available as studs only in 20 gauge, 22 gauge, 25 gauge, and 26 gauge galvanize-coated cold-rolled steel. The 20 gauge stud may be used in residential one-story, or light commercial, construction for bearing walls. The lighter studs are used for interior non-bearing

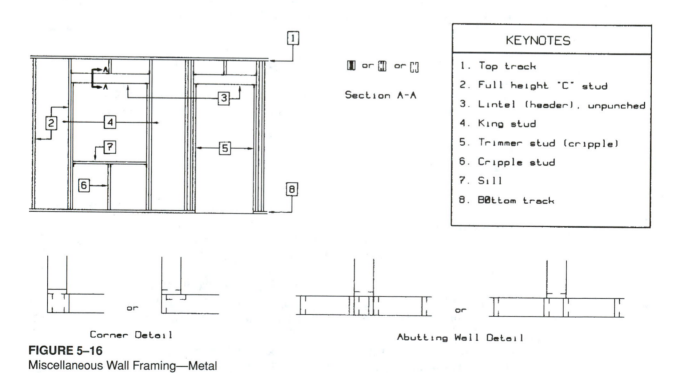

KEYNOTES
1. Top track
2. Full height "C" stud
3. Lintel (header), unpunched
4. King stud
5. Trimmer stud (cripple)
6. Cripple stud
7. Sill
8. Bottom track

Section A-A

Corner Detail

Abutting Wall Detail

FIGURE 5–16
Miscellaneous Wall Framing—Metal

partitions or other non-structural framing. The studs have either C-shaped or channel shaped cross-sections. The C-shaped stud offers more rigidity than the channel shapes. Light-gauge metal framing and accessories do not require stiffeners or welding. All connections for the stud and track are screwed to-gether with ¾" to 1¼" long case-hardened metal screws known best as Tek screws.

An unpunched channel-shaped metal member, called *track*, is used in lieu of the top, bottom, and sill plates for all metal stud framing. The gauge of the track may be the same gauge as, or a heavier gauge (never lighter) than, the stud gauge. A wood sill plate, although rarely required, may be necessary under certain circumstances beneath the bottom track when framing is in-stalled below grade.

Accessories used for metal soffit or suspended ceiling installations in-clude light-gauge angle iron (steel or structural aluminum), called *black metal* because of the black anodized finish applied to it, and ¾" to 1¼" wide GI channel, called *hat channel,* for finish applications such as drywall attachment at furred-down or suspended ceilings. Like the light-gauge metal frame, these materials are screwed together at all connections.

CHAPTER EXERCISES

True or False

T F   1. The geographical location of the source of lumber determines its quality classification.

T F   2. The sill plate is the horizontal framing member used to protect other framing members above from termite infestation.

T F   3. The sill plate and the sole plate are one and the same.

T F   4. A platform frame includes a ribbon and a ledger in the wall con-struction.

T F   5. The top plate may be either single or double thickness.

T F   6. A rafter is the horizontal member of a roof support system.

T F   7. A joist header is the framing member used to support a structure above a door or window opening.

T F   8. Sheathing may be used for both shear panel construction and as a roof underlayment.

T F   9. Three major concerns of a structural engineer include the necessity of determining dead load, live load, and wind lift.

T F   10. Conventional sloped roof framing is installed using prefabricated trusses.

T F   11. The material installed over the floor joists is called the sub-floor, or underlayment.

T F   12. The trimmer stud is used for support of a lintel (header) over a wall opening.

T F   13. A king post is the same as a king stud.

T F 14. Purlins are the vertical support members of a conventional roof structure.

T F 15. Studs are graded as DF, construction grade, or HF structural grade 3.

T F 16. All framing members are available in increments of 2'–0" unless special ordered.

T F 17. The structural classifications for rafters and joists determines the allowable span for the framing member.

T F 18. The term *laminated beam* includes glue-laminated 2x members as well as glue-laminated plywood for use as beams and trusses.

T F 19. Wall framing requires additional support at the corners using diagonal bracing or shear paneling.

T F 20. The term *header* is used for a perimeter joist and is also referred to as a *rim joist*.

Completion

1. The lowest framing member for exterior walls is called the _____ plate.

2. The connectors used for rafter and ceiling joist connections is referred to as a(n) _____ fastener.

3. The symbol *E* is a notation referring to the _____ of a framing member.

4. Most bearing walls in wood frame construction require a(n) _____ top plate.

5. The standard precut stud measures _____".

6. The work involving the structure itself is called the _____ work.

7. There is a bottom and top _____ used in light-gauge metal framing of a wall.

8. The vertical framing member, called a(n) _____, is used to support the ridge.

9. The walls over and under wall openings are referred to as _____ walls.

10. The lumber classifications are determined by the location of the _____ from a log.

11. Structural light-gauge framing includes cold-rolled steel from 18 gauge to _____ gauge.

12. The standard classification for a horizontal support member is _____ #2 or better.

13. Balloon framing is in use today only for _____ or cathedral ceiling installations.

14. Balloon framing, when used, may extend to _____' above finish floor (A.F.F.).

15. Western framing is also referred to as _____.

16. In wood frame floor construction the _____ plate is installed over the subflooring.

17. Underlayment used for floor construction may be 4′ × 8′ plywood sheets butted together, or may have tongue-and-groove (T&G) or _____ edges.

18. Nailing of double top plates where they lap at other than the corners calls for _____ 10d or 16d nails.

19. The sections for the Garland residence (figures 5–1 and 5–2) note that the trusses used over the living room area are called _____ trusses.

20. The header over a 6″ wide bearing wall opening better than 4′-0″ long may be a double 2 × 6, triple 2 × 6, or a(n) _____.

21. A glue-laminated beam, identified as a 5⅛″ × 27″, is produced from re-milled _____ lumber and requires _____ pieces.

22. Insulation may be used for both thermal and _____ protection.

23. Non-bearing partitions are usually placed at _____″ O/C.

24. The symbol *Fb* refers to the _____ of a structural member.

25. Wood frame fireplaces require a fire shield spaced at a maximum of _____′ apart, vertically.

Multiple Choice

_____ 1. The lower member of a wood frame floor is:
    a. The sole plate.
    b. The double top plate.
    c. The sill plate.
    d. None of the above.

_____ 2. The floor joists are:
    a. Larger in size than the ceiling joist in multistory structures at all times.
    b. Smaller in size than the ceiling joist in single-story structures.
    c. Larger than the ceiling joist in a single-story structure.
    d. Is interchangeable with the ceiling joist.

_____ 3. A conventionally framed roof structure includes:
    a. Rafters, purlins, braces, and king posts.
    b. Ceiling joists and sheathing only.
    c. None of the above.
    d. All of the above.

_____ 4. Thermal protection is provided by:
    a. Batt insulation, rigid insulation or foam insulation.
    b. Batt insulation and rigid insulation only.
    c. Rigid insulation and foam insulation only.
    d. Batt insulation only.

_____ 5. Light-gauge metal framing is:
   a. 25 gauge to 16 gauge cold-rolled steel forms.
   b. 18 gauge to 12 gauge cold-rolled steel forms.
   c. 25 gauge to 12 gauge cold-rolled steel forms.
   d. 25 gauge to 20 gauge cold-rolled steel forms.

_____ 6. The top and bottom plates of light-gauge metal are made from:
   a. The same gauge steel.
   b. The same or heavier gauge steel.
   c. Lighter gauge steel.
   d. The same or lighter gauge steel.

_____ 7. The bearing wall stud spacing for light-gauge metal framing is:
   a. Always the same as that for wood framing.
   b. May be spaced at 24" O/C for 6" bearing studs.
   c. Must be spaced at 24" O/C for 6" bearing studs.
   d. None of the above.

_____ 8. The difference between structural light-gauge and light-gauge metal stud framing is:
   a. The finish used on the cold-rolled metal.
   b. The structural light-gauge metal is from 18 gauge to 12 gauge metal.
   c. There is no difference.
   d. Light-gauge metal framing is used for bearing walls only.

_____ 9. In conventional roof framing a roof rafter:
   a. Is larger than the ridge or hip beam.
   b. Is normally at least one size smaller than the ridge or hip beam.
   c. It makes no difference in the sizes, it depends only on span requirements.
   d. Is trimmed to fit.

_____ 10. The subfloor is:
   a. Referred to as an underlayment.
   b. Usually ¾" or 1", 5-ply, plywood or equivalent OSB®.
   c. Both a and b.
   d. Neither a nor b.

_____ 11. Shear paneling or diagonal bracing:
   a. May be required at all wall construction corners.
   b. Is required where lateral wind pressure is a major problem.
   c. Is required for seismic stability.
   d. All of the above.

_____ 12. A perimeter joist used to protect floor joists is called a:
   a. Lintel.
   b. King stud.
   c. Trimmer.
   d. Header (rim) joist.

_____ 13. 6" wide lumber, or larger, used for structural joists, is classified as:
   a. Select structural.
   b. Stud grade.
   c. #1, #2, #3, or economy.
   d. Utility or common.

COMPLETE

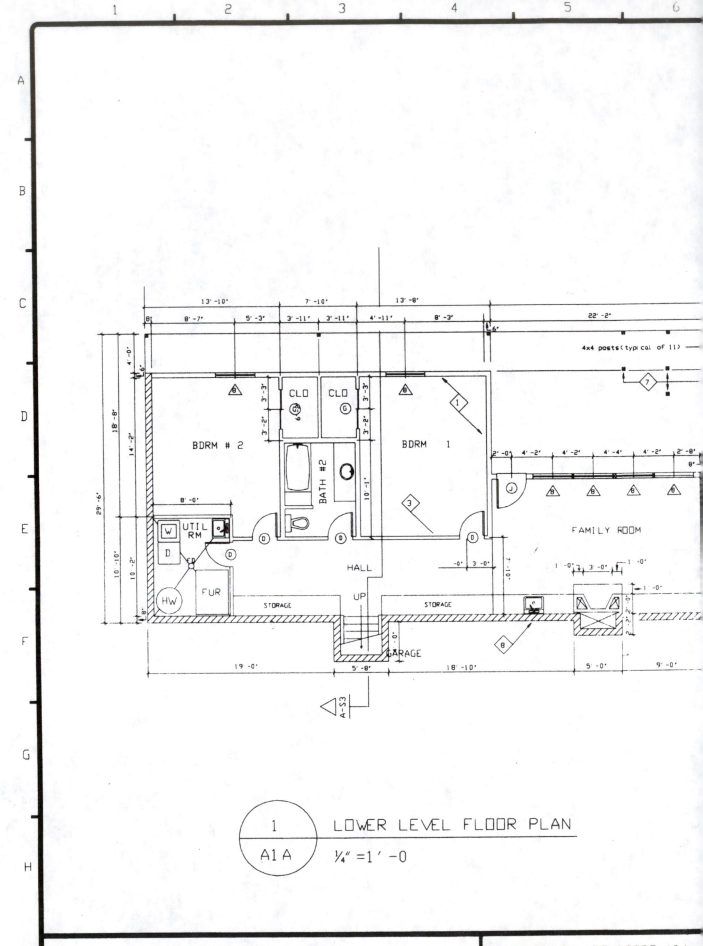

1 — LOWER LEVEL FLOOR PLAN
A1A   ¼" = 1' -0

GARY CLARK ARCHITECT AIA
12 RICHMOND DRIVE
ROANOKE, VIRGINIA 20000

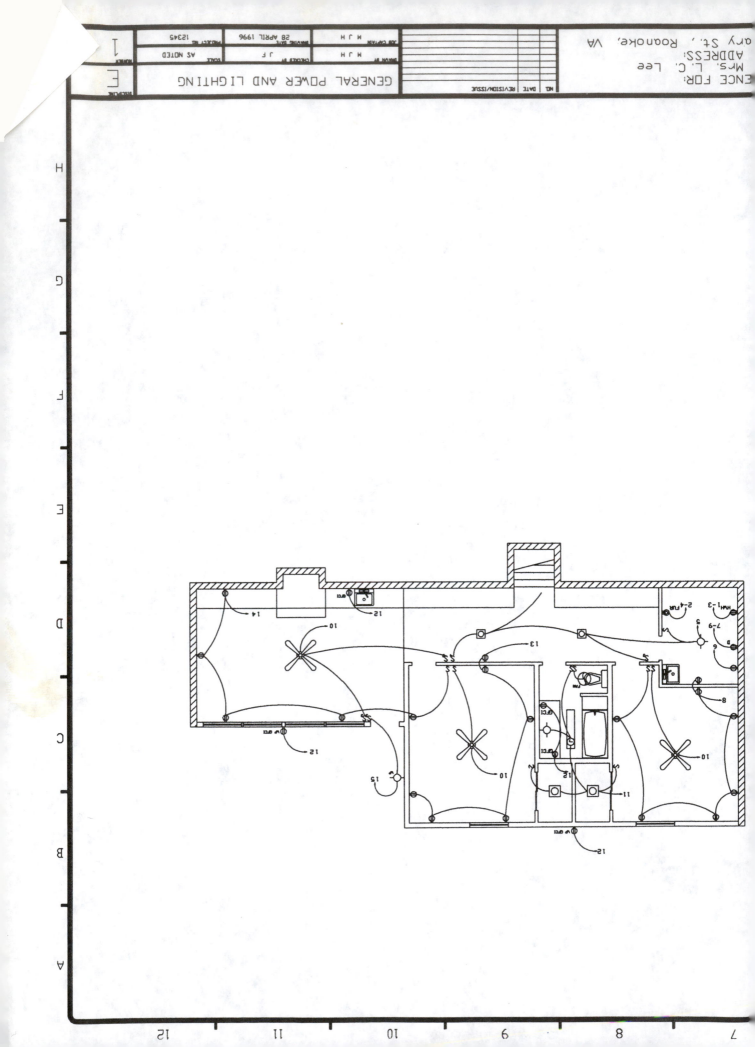

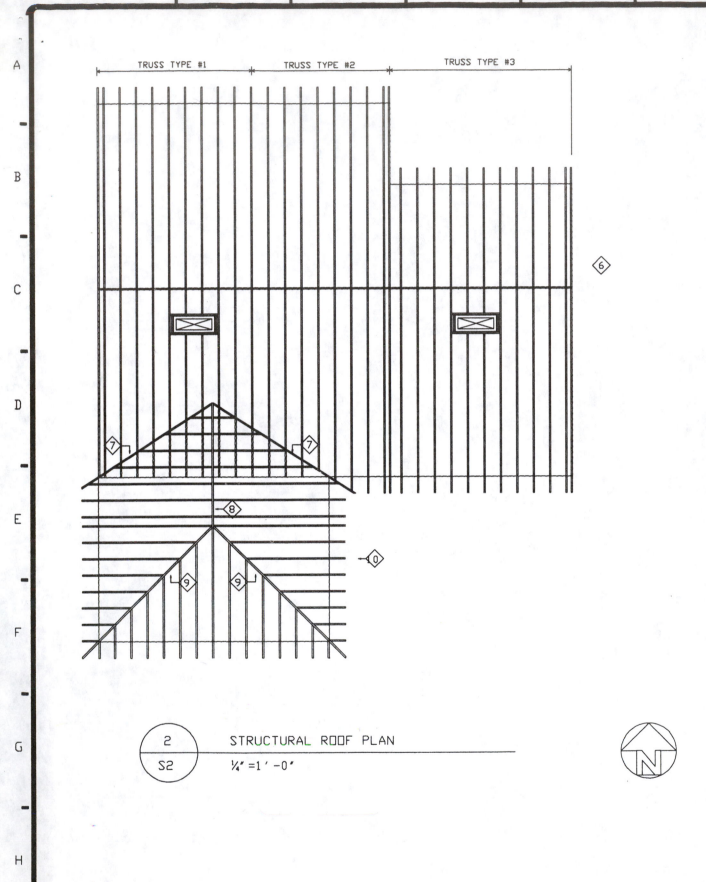

TRUSS TYPE #1   TRUSS TYPE #2   TRUSS TYPE #3

2	STRUCTURAL ROOF PLAN
S2	¼″ =1′ −0″

J. BROPHY, ENGINEERING, PE
12 RICHMOND DRIVE
ROANOKE, VIRGINIA 20000

RESID
Mr
PROJE
90

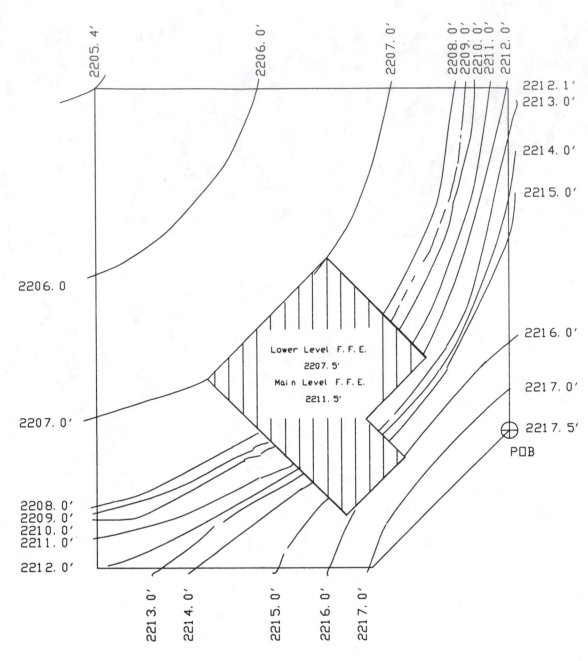

2205. 4' 2206. 0' 2207. 0' 2208. 0' 2209. 0' 2210. 0' 2211. 0' 2212. 0'

2212. 1'
2213. 0'
2214. 0'
2215. 0'

2206. 0

2216. 0'

Lower Level F.F.E.
2207. 5'

2217. 0'

Main Level F.F.E.

2211. 5'

2217. 5'

2207. 0'

POB

2208. 0'
2209. 0'
2210. 0'
2211. 0'

2212. 0'

2213. 0' 2214. 0' 2215. 0' 2216. 0' 2217. 0'

Nearest datum point to P

of Beginning (POB) is

SITE PLAN

at the intersection o

and New Streets - 117

GARY CLARK ARCHITECT AIA
12 RICHMOND DRIVE
ROANOKE, VIRGINIA 20000

RESI
Mr
PROJE
90

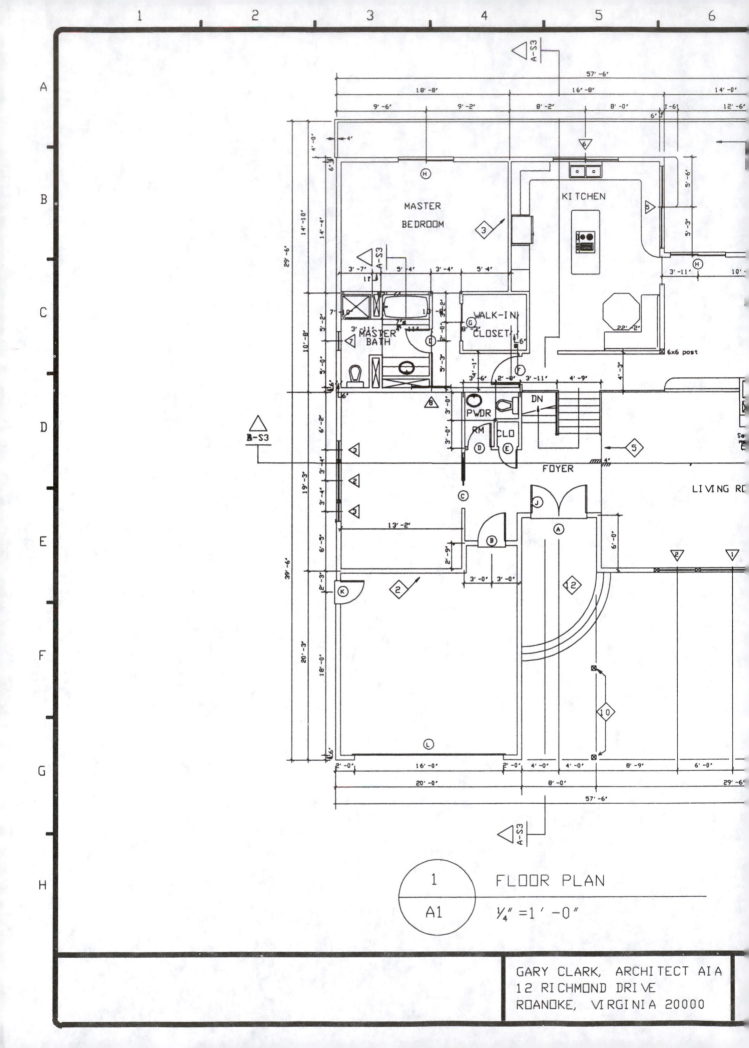

FLOOR PLAN

1
A1

$\frac{1}{4}" = 1'-0"$

MASTER
BEDROOM

KITCHEN

WALK-IN
CLOSET

MASTER
BATH

PWDR
RM

CLO

DN

FOYER

LIVING RO

6x6 post

GARY CLARK, ARCHITECT AIA
12 RICHMOND DRIVE
ROANOKE, VIRGINIA 20000

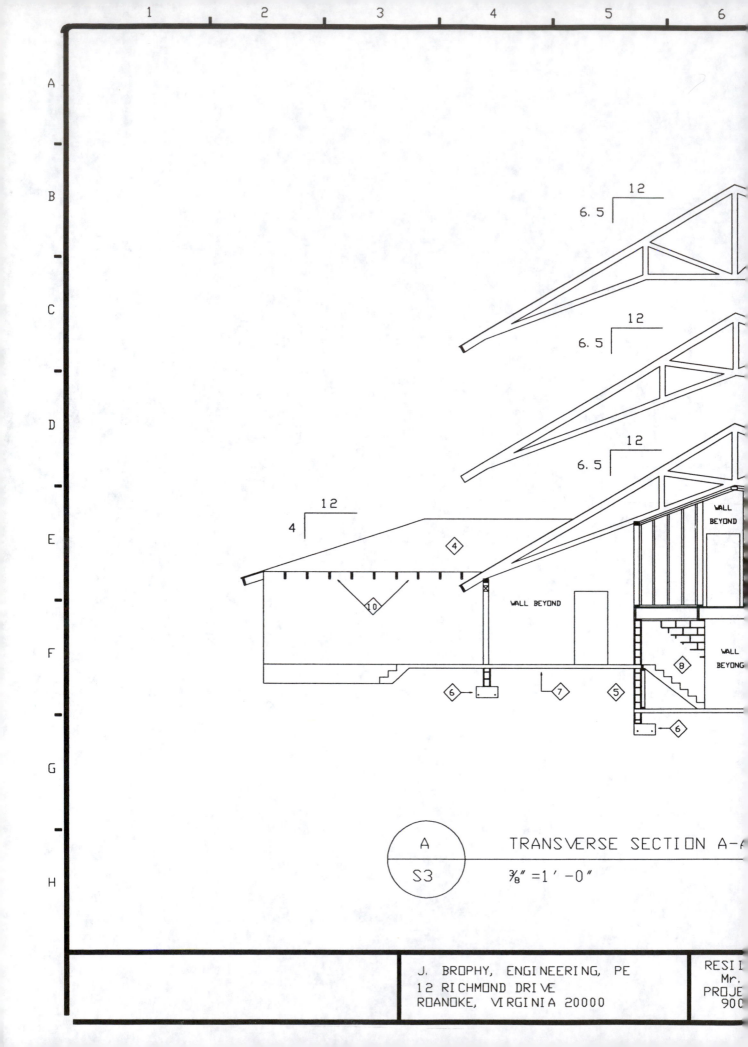

12
6.5

12
6.5

12
6.5

12
4

⟨4⟩

WALL
BEYOND

WALL BEYOND

⟨10⟩

WALL
BEYOND

WALL
BEYOND

⟨6⟩

⟨7⟩

⟨5⟩

⟨8⟩

⟨6⟩

A
S3

TRANSVERSE SECTION A-A

³⁄₈″ =1′ −0″

J. BROPHY, ENGINEERING, PE
12 RICHMOND DRIVE
ROANOKE, VIRGINIA 20000

RESI
Mr.
PROJE
900

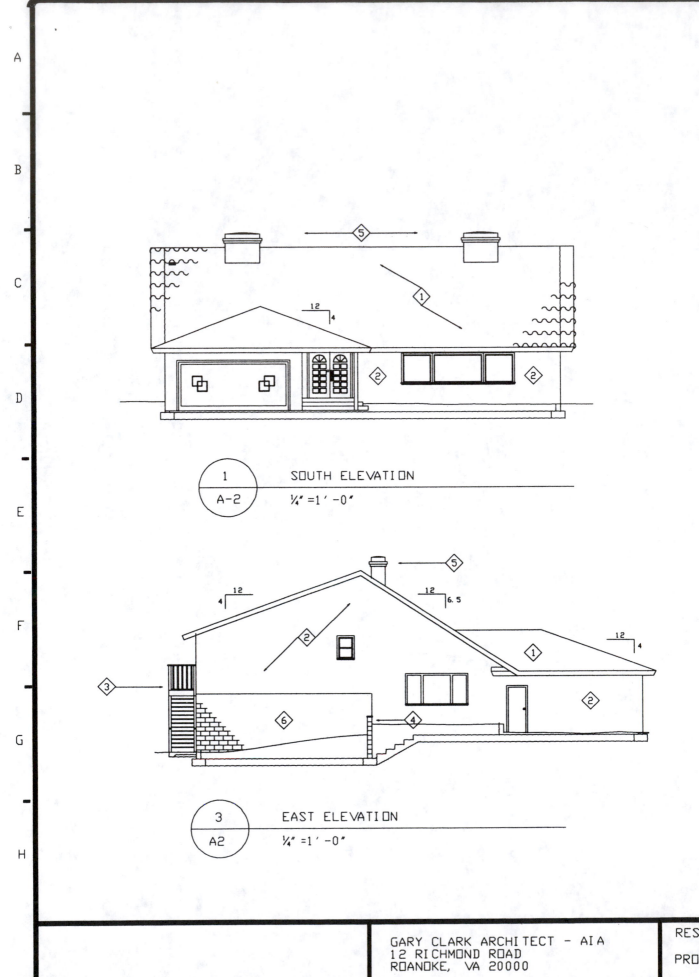

1 SOUTH ELEVATION
A-2 ¼" =1' -0"

3 EAST ELEVATION
A2 ¼" =1' -0"

GARY CLARK ARCHITECT - AIA
12 RICHMOND ROAD
ROANOKE, VA 20000

RESID
MR
PROJE
90

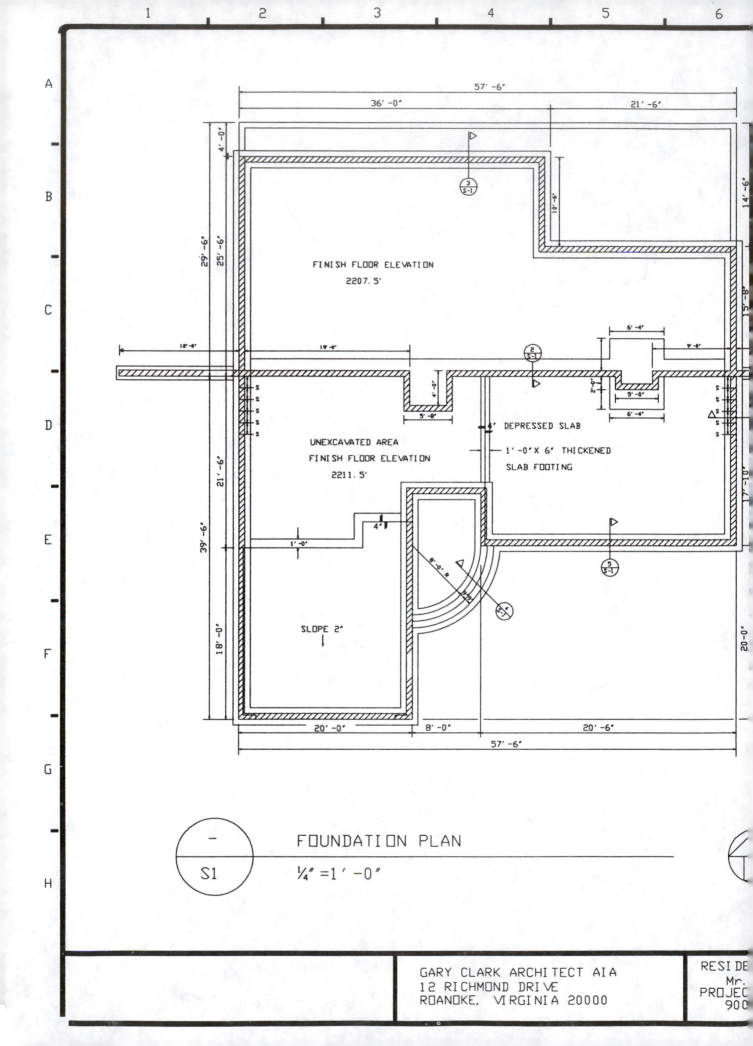

FINISH FLOOR ELEVATION
2207.5'

DEPRESSED SLAB

1'-0" X 6' THICKENED
SLAB FOOTING

UNEXCAVATED AREA
FINISH FLOOR ELEVATION
2211.5'

SLOPE 2"

FOUNDATION PLAN
¼" = 1' - 0"

57'-6"
36'-0"
21'-6"
4'-0"
29'-6"
25'-6"
10'-6"
14'-6"
15'-8"
6'-4"
9'-0"
2'-0"
5'-0"
6'-4"
17'-10"
12'-0"
19'-0"
4'-0"
5'-8"
21'-6"
39'-6"
1'-0"
4'
8'-0". R
18'-0"
20'-0"
8'-0"
20'-6"
57'-6"
20'-0"

S1

GARY CLARK ARCHITECT AIA
12 RICHMOND DRIVE
ROANOKE, VIRGINIA 20000

RESIDE
Mr.
PROJEC
900

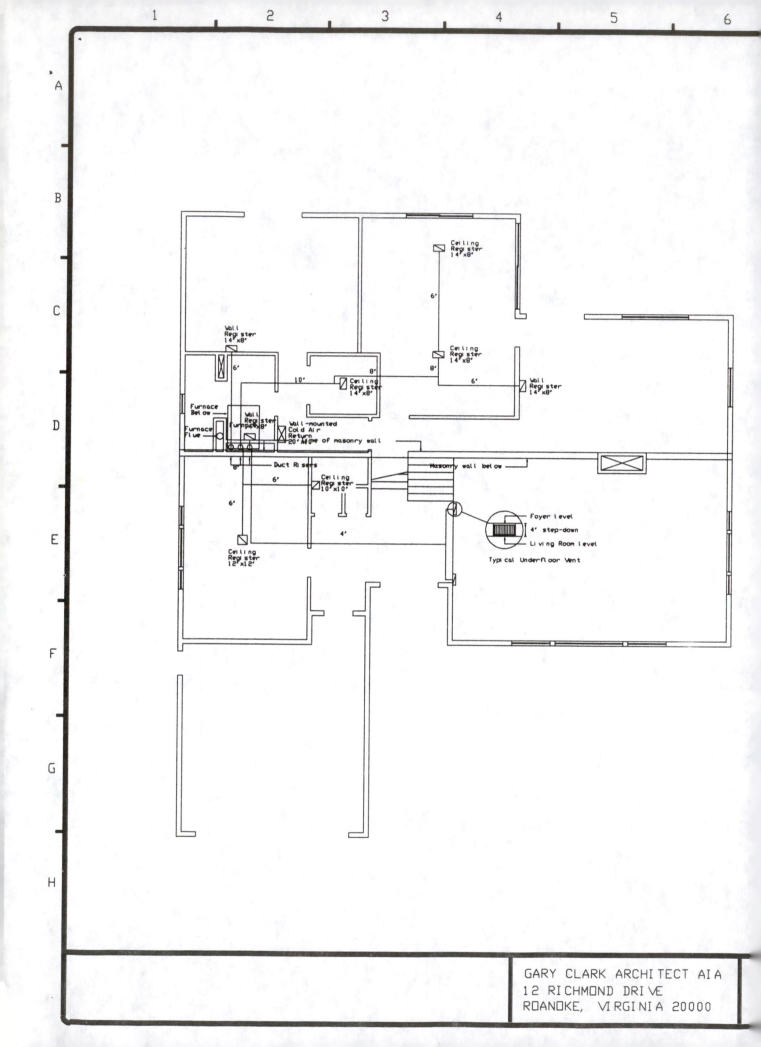

Ceiling
Register
14"x8"

6'

Ceiling
Register
14"x8"

Wall
Register
14"x8"

8'

10'

Ceiling
Register
14"x8"

6'

Wall
Register
14"x8"

Wall
Register
14"x8"

8'

Furnace
Below

Furnace
Flue

Wall
Register 8"

Furnace

Wall-mounted
Cold Air
Return

20' high of masonry wall

Masonry wall below

8'

Duct Risers

6'

Ceiling
Register
10"x10"

6'

Foyer level

4' step-down

Living Room level

6'

4'

Typical Underfloor Vent

Ceiling
Register
12"x12"

GARY CLARK ARCHITECT AIA
12 RICHMOND DRIVE
ROANOKE, VIRGINIA 20000

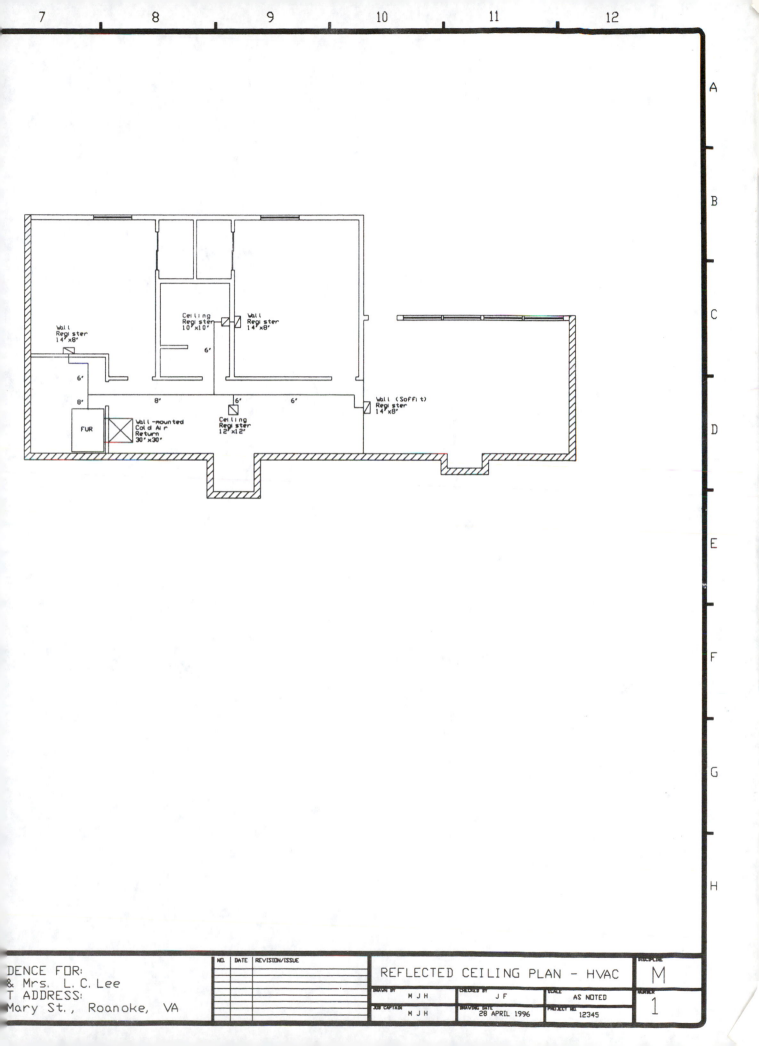

Wall
Register
14"x8"

Ceiling
Register
10"x10"

Wall
Register
14"x8"

6'

6'

6'

8'

8'

6'

6'

Wall (Soffit)
Register
14"x8"

FUR

Wall-mounted
Cold Air
Return
30"x30"

Ceiling
Register
12"x12"

DENCE FOR:
& Mrs. L.C. Lee
T ADDRESS:
Mary St., Roanoke, VA

NO.	DATE	REVISION/ISSUE

REFLECTED CEILING PLAN - HVAC

DISCIPLINE
M

DRAWN BY	CHECKED BY	SCALE
M J H	J F	AS NOTED

JOB CAPTAIN	DRAWING DATE	PROJECT NO.
M J H	28 APRIL 1996	12345

NUMBER
1

A

4" CONCRETE
SLAB

MAIN LEVEL

4" CONCRETE
SLAB

B

LOWER LEVEL

8" MASONRY
FOUNDATION
WALL (see
specs for reinf)

4" CONCRETE
SLAB

CONCRETE
FOOTING
w/2-#4 rebar
and #5 rebar dowel

C

STEPPED FOOTING

1 / S1 — STEP FOOTING @ FOUNDATION WALL — No Scale

2 / S1 — FOUNDATION WALL @ MAIN LEVEL — No scale

D

4" CONCRETE
SLAB

CONCRETE
TURNDOWN
w/#4 rebar

CONCRETE
SLAB

REINFORCEMENT
(#5 rebar)

CONCRETE
SIDEWALK

E

3 / S1 — MONOLITHIC SLAB @ PATIO — No Scale

4 / S1 — CONCRETE PORCH STEPS — No Scale

F

4" CONCRETE
SLAB

8" MASONRY
FOUNDATION
WALL

CONCRETE
FOOTING

G

5 / S1 — TYPICAL STEM WALL — No Scale

H

R:
L. C. Lee
ESS:
St., Roanoke, VA

NO.	DATE	REVISION/ISSUE

FOUNDATION PLAN

DISCIPLINE

S

DRAWN BY	M J H	CHECKED BY	J F	SCALE	AS NOTED	NUMBER
JOB CAPTAIN	M J H	DRAWING DATE	28 APRIL 1996	PROJECT NO.	12345	1

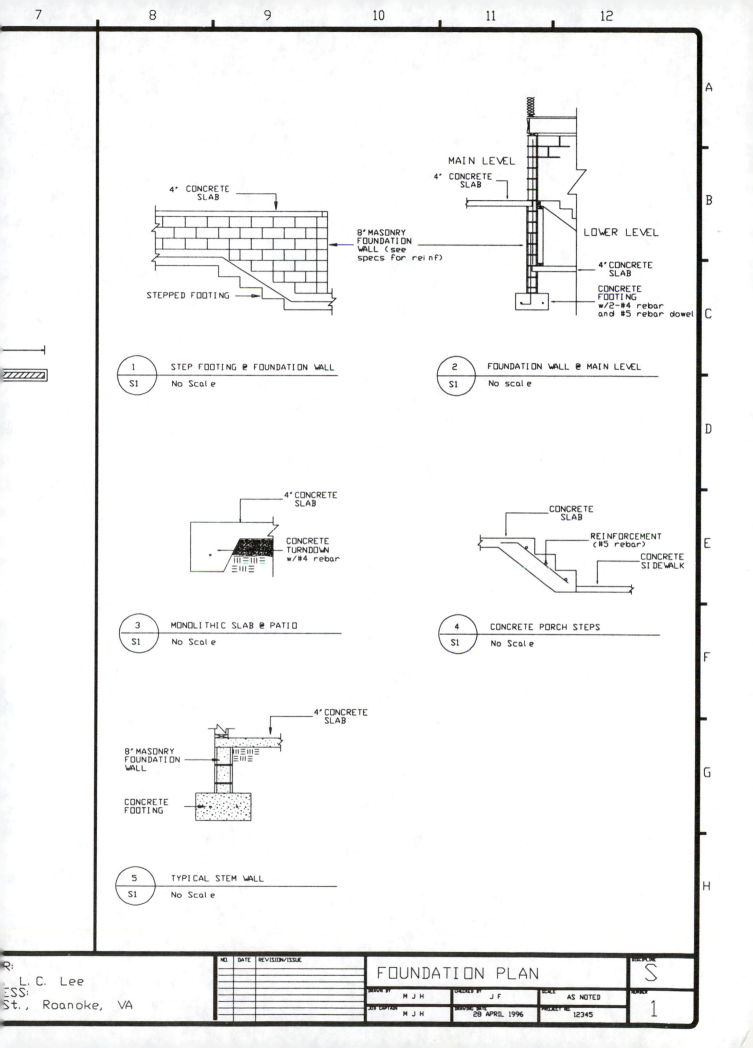

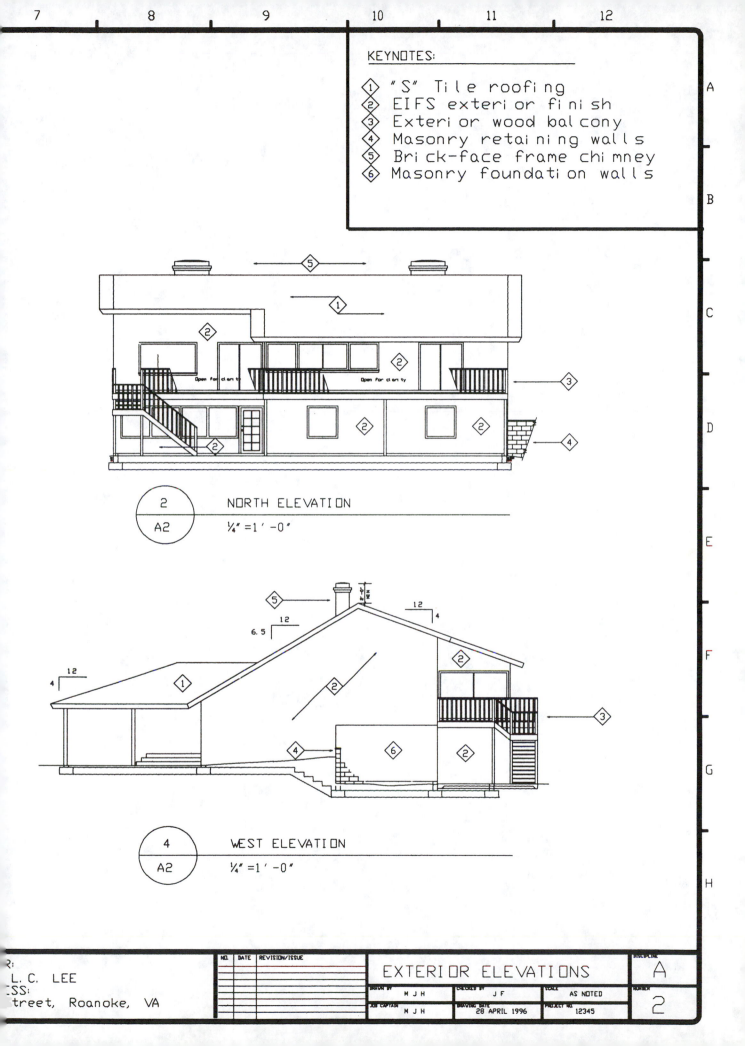

KEYNOTES:

1. "S" Tile roofing
2. EIFS exterior finish
3. Exterior wood balcony
4. Masonry retaining walls
5. Brick-face frame chimney
6. Masonry foundation walls

2	NORTH ELEVATION
A2	¼" =1' -0"

4	WEST ELEVATION
A2	¼" =1' -0"

Open for clarity

Open for clarity

12
6.5

12
4

12
4

R:
L. C. LEE
SS:
treet, Roanoke, VA

NO.	DATE	REVISION/ISSUE

EXTERIOR ELEVATIONS

DISCIPLINE
A

DRAWN BY	M J H	CHECKED BY	J F	SCALE	AS NOTED
JOB CAPTAIN	M J H	DRAWING DATE	28 APRIL 1996	PROJECT NO	12345

NUMBER
2

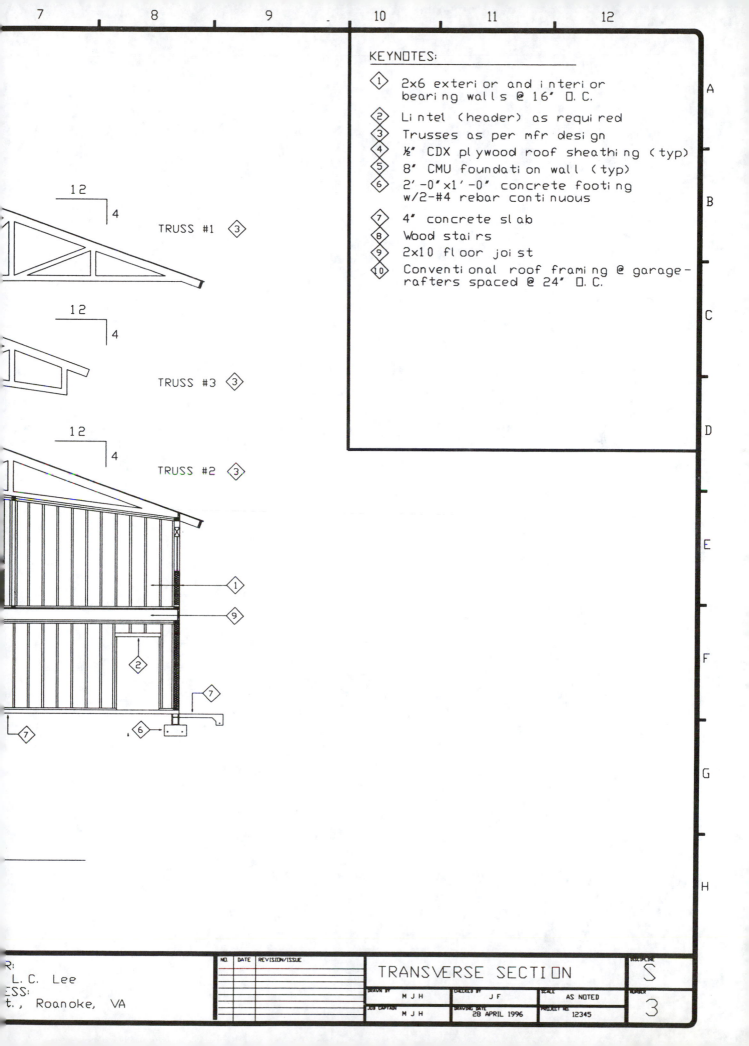

KEYNOTES:

1. 2x6 exterior and interior bearing walls @ 16" O.C.
2. Lintel (header) as required
3. Trusses as per mfr design
4. ½" CDX plywood roof sheathing (typ)
5. 8" CMU foundation wall (typ)
6. 2'-0"x1'-0" concrete footing w/2-#4 rebar continuous
7. 4" concrete slab
8. Wood stairs
9. 2x10 floor joist
10. Conventional roof framing @ garage-rafters spaced @ 24" O.C.

12
4
TRUSS #1 ⟨3⟩

12
4
TRUSS #3 ⟨3⟩

12
4
TRUSS #2 ⟨3⟩

R:
L. C. Lee
ESS:
t., Roanoke, VA

NO.	DATE	REVISION/ISSUE

TRANSVERSE SECTION

DRAWN BY	CHECKED BY	SCALE
M J H	J F	AS NOTED

JOB CAPTAIN	DRAWING DATE	PROJECT NO.
M J H	28 APRIL 1996	12345

DISCIPLINE
S

NUMBER
3

_____ 14. The milled finish of lumber is also classified. A piece of lumber that is smoothed on all sides only is classified as:
   a. S1S.
   b. R/S.
   c. S4S.
   d. S4S2E.

_____ 15. The typical roof sheathing is referred to as CDX plywood. The meaning of the classification is:
   a. Special exterior grade, structural II, glued.
   b. Marine grade, structural I, glued.
   c. Neither a nor b.
   d. Both a and b.

Matching

_____ 1. Truss

_____ 2. Sill plate

_____ 3. Balloon frame

_____ 4. Joist

_____ 5. Header

_____ 6. Frieze block

_____ 7. Sheathing

_____ 8. Trim

_____ 9. Sill frame

_____ 10. Trimmer

_____ 11. King post

_____ 12. Rafter

_____ 13. Conventional frame

_____ 14. Platform frame

_____ 15. Sole plate

_____ 16. King stud

_____ 17. Hip

_____ 18. Cripple

_____ 19. Top plate

_____ 20. Ridge

a. Blocking between rafter tails at top plate

b. System using ceiling joists and rafters

c. Support post for ridge beam

d. Framing member on concrete or masonry

e. Western framing system

f. Made with top and bottom chords

g. Full-height stud next to wall opening

h. A structural horizontal roof member

i. Bottom plate of wood frame structure

j. Horizontal structural wall member

k. Main sloped structural roof member

l. Stud framing system continuous from foundation to roof structure

m. Horizontal floor or ceiling structural member

n. Structural floor, wall or roof cover of plywood

o. Double or single member at top of wall frame

p. Stud above or below wall opening

q. Sloped member of a roof structure

r. Bottom member of window opening

s. Finish framing material

t. Stud used to support lintel (header)

6

The Structure, Part II–Finishes

Once the rough-in construction work is completed—foundation, framing, rough-in plumbing, and electrical—the trades used for the purpose of covering or completing their work, or installations necessary to provide an aesthetic appearance for a structure are called upon. These include finish carpentry, door and window installations, and those trades referred to as *Finishes*, Division 9, of the CSI format. Division 9 includes lath; other metal support systems, such as suspended ceilings and light-gauge metal stud framing (discussed in chapter 5); exterior and interior cement plaster and interior gypsum plaster; drywall (GWB, gypsum wall board); quarry and ceramic tile for floors and walls; floor coverings, such as carpeting, vinyl resilient floor covering (sheet and tile), and special wood flooring (parquet and the like); acoustical treatments, such as spray-on acoustical, acoustical directly adhered tiles, and suspended acoustical tile systems; painting; and wallcoverings.

See figure 6–1. All of the finish installations are identified and located on the finish schedule. The finish schedule indicates the location (room, office, and so on), as well as the materials or finishes to be installed to the floor, base, wall, and ceiling. The information on a finish schedule must be adhered to in the same way as the specifications. The schedule may be included in the drawings, in the specifications found in a project manual accompanying the set of plans, or both. The schedule is a specific part of the specifications. The finish schedule in figure 6–1 is for the Garland residence.

LOCATION	FLOOR	BASE	WALLS				CEILING	REMARKS
			N	S	E	W		
Living Room	1	1	a	a	a	a	1	vaulted ceiling
			b	b	b	b		
Dining Room	1	1	a	a	a	a	1	8'-0" ceiling
			b	b	b	b		
Kitchen	2	2	a	a	a	a	1	8'-0" ceiling
			a	a	a	a		
Bedroom	1	1	a	a	a	a	1	vaulted ceiling
			b	b	b	b		
Study	1	1	a	a	a	a	1	8'-0" ceiling
			b	b	b	b		
Laundry	3	3	a	a	a	a	1	8'-0" ceiling
			a	a	a	a		
Bathroom	2	2	a	a	a	a	1	8'-0" ceiling
			b	b	b	b		
			a	a	a	a		
Garage	4	-	a	a	a	a	2	8'-0" ceiling

FINISH SCHEDULE

KEYNOTES:

FLOOR:
1. Carpet w/pad
2. Quarry tile - 12" square
3. VCT - 8" square
4. Exposed concrete

BASE:
1. 4" oak base
2. Tile coving to match floor tile
3. VCT coving to match floor tile

WALLS:
a. 1/2" GWB orange peel texture
b. Flat latex paint - 2 coats
c. 5/8" "X" GWB both sides of wall. Textured one side only. Firetaped to underside of roof on garage side.

CEILINGS:
1. 1/2" GWB w/acoustical texture

FIGURE 6-1
Finish Schedule, Garland Residence

THE GARLAND RESIDENCE

See Sheets A–1 and A–2, Architectural Plans for the Garland Residence. The floor plan of the Garland residence provides several symbols that are used for identification of rooms, walls, and fixtures, as well as doors and windows. The following sections are written to supply general information regarding use of these symbols and schedules, which are an important part of a well-organized set of plans.

FINISH CARPENTRY

Finish carpentry includes the installation of all wood, plastic, and light-gauge metal finish materials used for both interior and exterior decorative trim. The same contractor may be involved with both the rough and finish carpentry, as well as the installation of all doors and windows. Cabinetry, both mass-produced (manufactured) and custom made, is also a part of finish carpentry. Manufactured cabinets are normally installed by the manufacturer or representatives of the supplier, whereas custom cabinetry is produced and installed by a custom cabinetmaker.

Interior Trim

Wood stairs, stair railings and newel posts, architectural woodwork (built-in bookcases and the like), cabinetry, interior window and door trim (not a part of a window or door package), baseboard, and moldings are all a part of the interior finish carpentry. Where no trim is included in the door and window package, the plans or finish schedule must indicate if, and where, such trim is to be installed. The areas that are of interest to the finish carpenter are all of the wood finishes, including pre-manufactured packages.

Exterior Trim

The amount and variety of materials necessary for exterior trim may also be noted on a finish schedule. Normally these materials are indicated on the exterior elevations or in the keynotes for the exterior elevations, which are a part of the drawings. Exterior trim includes items such as siding, plant-ons and exterior window and door trim not a part of a window or door package. Exterior trim may be installed prior to, or after, the installation of the finish siding. When exterior trim is installed after the siding or other exterior application (plaster, masonry, and so on) is completed, it is considered as a plant-on because the item is installed ("planted") over the exterior finish. Many windows and doors may be purchased that have no trim other than the jambs and casings, therefore the owner must select a trim to be added.

PLASTICS

The most common structural plastic fabrications include molded and laminated-surface countertops and molded fiberglass countertops, both used for kitchen and bath cabinet surfaces. Other structural plastics considered in finish construction are impact-resistant decorative items such as room divider screen walls, posts, shelving, atrium and patio roof covers, and plastic (vinyl) sheets and panels used for roofs and siding.

Also included in this category are some non-structural fabrications such as items made for decorative use in lieu of wood or concrete. These plastics are included with carpentry since, again, the carpenter or cabinet installer are usually responsible for the installation of siding, cabinetry, and roofing. Some of the plastics may be rigid molded units or may be Styrofoam® units used as forms for the decorative impressions or plant-ons.

DOORS AND WINDOWS

Doors

See figure 6–2. Door and window schedules may be included in the drawings, in the specifications found in a project manual accompanying the set of plans, or both. An identification number or letter on the floor plan identifies the door or window to be found on the schedule, referred to as the *mark*. When a number is used for the door mark, a letter is used for the window mark. The same number or letter is found in the first column of the schedule(s). In addition to the mark, door and window schedule formats have columns identifying the size of the unit, the style of the unit, the finish, and any other information necessary (remarks).

See figure 6–3. Doors are identified by the style of the unit. The door size may be indicated in either of two ways, the normal measurement in feet and inches (3'–0" × 6'–8" [0.91m × 2.03 m]), or by the numbers without foot and inch notations (3068). Both methods are in common use.

There are two main classifications of door styles, *panel* and *flush* (slab). All doors are fabricated in these two styles or combinations of them. They are manufactured from steel or wood, a combination of structural light-gauge, cold-rolled steel formed over wood, or a structural plastic molded over wood.

DOOR SCHEDULE

MK	SIZE	TYPE	MATERIAL	QA	REMARKS
1	3'-0" x 6'-8"	3-panel s/c	metal-clad	1	hdwre selected by owner
2	3'-0" x 6'-8"	Flush. s/c	birch	1	self-closer stain finish
3	3'-0" x 6'-8"	Flush. h/c	birch	1	stain finish
4	2'-6" x 6'-8"	Flush. h/c	luan	2	paint finish by owner
5	6'-0" x 6'-8"	Sliding glass	aluminum frame	1	anodized bronze finish
6	10'-0" x 7'-0"	garage door	steel	2	white baked enamel finish
7	8'-0" x 6'-8"			1	cased opening
8	4'-0" x 6'-8"			1	cased opening

WINDOW SCHEDULE

MK	SIZE	TYPE	MATERIAL	QA	REMARKS
A	1'-6"x6'-8"	sidelites	plastic	2	Wood frame - custom
B	4'-0"x4'-0"	Fixed	insulating	2	" " "
C	4'-0"x4'-0"	single hung	insulating	6	" " "
D	6'-0"x4'-0"	Fixed	insulating	3	" " "

FIGURE 6–2
Door and Window Schedules, Garland Residence

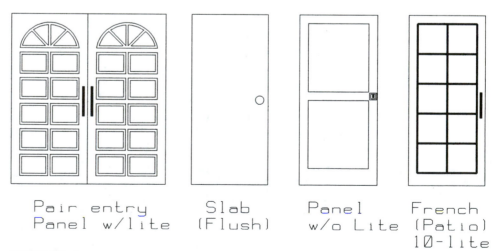

Pair entry
Panel w/lite

Slab
(Flush)

Panel
w/o Lite

French (Patio)
10-lite

FIGURE 6–3
Door Types

Combination metal-and-wood doors are referred to as *metal-clad wood doors;* wood-and-plastic door combinations are called *vinyl-clad wood doors.*

Many other designations, as shown in the schedule, are necessary to supply the proper door for the purpose and location desired. For example, exterior doors are 1¾″ (4.45 cm) thick while interior doors are 1⅜″ (3.49 cm) thick. The exterior flush doors may be both solid-core (*s/c*), units filled with wood blocking for strength and insulating material for sound attenuation, or panelized doors of hardwood materials, with or without glazing. Interior doors may also be both panelized or flush doors. Flush doors are normally hollow-core *(h/c),* lighter in weight and have little additional strengthening materials added. Insulating materials such as corrugated cardboard sound barriers may be installed within the door.

Panel doors are designed and manufactured in a variety combinations. The doors may have a minimum of just one panel to as many as ten panels. They may have glass (lites) installed, for example, a single lite, a half-moon lite, or multi-lites (the French door), or may be a solid glass lite with just the headers and stiles for support.

Doors are further designated as the following:

1. Inside swing: The door opens into the structure or room.
2. Outside swing: The door opens outward to a hall or to the outdoors.
3. Right-hand swing: The door is hinged on the right when facing the door from the inside of a room.
4. Reverse right-hand swing: The same as the right-hand swing, except it swings outward; used for exterior commercial or institutional installations.
5. Left-hand swing: The door is hinged on the left when facing the door from the inside of a room.
6. Reverse left-hand swing: The same as the left-hand swing except it swings outward; used for exterior commercial or institutional installations.
7. Double-swing: This door is hinged to swing both inward and outward, such as the connecting door to a restaurant kitchen and dining room.
8. Gate (Dutch): The door is halved in the middle so that the upper or lower sections can be opened separately; hinged in the same manner as a left-hand or right-hand swing; can also be latched together to be opened as a regular full door.
9. Sliding: A single or double door that moves horizontally on a track; such doors may be glass exterior doors or mirrored for closet doors.
10. Bi-fold: A double-leaf door hinged between leaves and at the attachment to the jamb; used primarily for multipurpose room construction in hotels and schools; also used for closet doors; may or may not include latches.
11. Accordion: This door has smaller leaves for folding together more tightly; also common in multipurpose room construction in hotels and schools; smaller versions may be used for closet doors.

Windows

See figure 6–4. Windows, like doors, are also available in a variety of materials, such as steel, aluminum, metal-clad wood, vinyl-clad wood, or wood. The steel and aluminum windows are normally manufactured without casings or jambs, installed in the walls and trimmed over with drywall or other trims

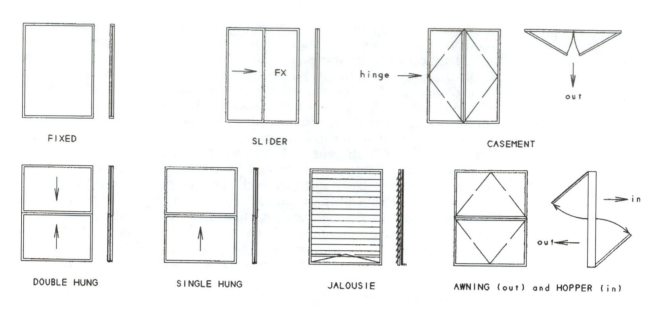

FIXED   SLIDER   CASEMENT

DOUBLE HUNG   SINGLE HUNG   JALOUSIE   AWNING (out) and HOPPER (in)

TYPICAL FACE AND SECTION VIEWS

FIGURE 6–4
Window Types

selected by the owner. Other styles, similar to the doors, are available in complete packages, including the casings, frames, and jambs.

Refer to figure 6–2. Schedules are also provided for windows. The window schedule is designed in the same format as the door using the mark, size, description, and remarks. There may be a section drawing for the windows included with the pictorials of the window sizes and types matching the schedule. The window sizes are often identified in the same way as the doors: a window may be sized as a 4′–0″ × 4′–0″ (1.22 m × 1.22 m), or as a 4040. There are designations (classifications) for windows, which include the following:

1. Fixed glass (FX): cannot be opened such as used for picture windows
2. Sliding glass (OX or XO): opens horizontally on a track assembly; the "X" identifies the fixed portion of the slider
3. Single-hung sash (SH): in two sections, one above the other; only the bottom half opens vertically
4. Double-hung sash (DH): Similar to single-hung; both halves may be opened vertically
5. Awning (AW): a top-hinged window that swings outward
6. Hopper (HO): a bottom-hinged window that swings inward
7. Casement: a single or double window that swings outward horizontally using a crank or lever to open.
8. Jalousie: used primarily for enclosed porch doors, windows, and screens and on mobile homes, motor homes, and trailers; is actually a multi-paneled awning operated by a crank or lever

Metal Doors and Door and Window Frames

Doors and door and window frames made of heavy-gauge (16 or 14 gauge) steel, with matching steel frames and casings, are known as *hollow-metal (HM)*. They are manufactured in standard sizes, but customized construction is available on special order. Such doors and frames are used primarily for commercial and institutional construction because of their strength and resistance to fire and vandalism.

A second type of steel frame, used for installations with wood, metal-clad wood, vinyl-clad wood, and plastic doors, is called a *knock-down hollow-metal (KDHM)*. It is manufactured from 18 gauge or 16 gauge cold-rolled steel. The purpose of the KDHM frame is to provide damage protection requiring minimal maintenance. They are used in exterior and interior door construction for multifamily housing, such as apartments, and for interior door installations for hotels, offices, and other commercial or institutional construction.

HARDWARE

All plans and/or specifications also have a hardware schedule included. The schedule may be included in the door and window schedules, as a separate schedule, or included as part of the specifications governing the plans. The hardware is identified by the manufacture, style, and type of door handles, latches, deadbolts, and hinges (butts).

Hinges are identified by the number required to be installed on a door. The quantity may be designated for two hinges as *2 hinges* or *1 pair of butts*. A door with three hinges may be designated as *3 hinges* or *1½ pair of butts*. Other special door and window hardware may include *no special knowledge* door fasteners, kick plates, non-latching handles, and emergency locks.

FINISHES

Plaster

The general term *plaster* includes both cement plaster, used primarily as an exterior wall covering, and gypsum plaster, applied on interior walls for a hard, smooth finish.

Exterior Cement Plaster. Cement plaster, also known as **stucco,** is a smooth concrete mix in a semi-liquid state that can be sprayed or troweled and textured on a surface. Cement plaster may be used as a surface coating for new structures or for rehabilitation of the exteriors of existing structures. The textures most commonly used for cement plaster include a sand (smooth) finish, a lace texture (slightly roughened), or a rough antique Spanish finish. Plaster is often pigmented (colored) to give a permanent color to the finish, eliminating the necessity for paint over the plaster.

Cement plaster may be etched or stamped to look like brick or stone. Many of the finishes found on the buildings in some of the major amusement parks—for example, the Disneyland and Disney World Main Street building facades—use a hard-coat cement plaster that is designed to look like brick or stone in lieu of real materials because it is more cost efficient, both in the materials required, the labor necessary for a completed finished product, and maintenance.

Cement plaster is applied in one, two, or three coats. The application procedures are as follows:

1. One-coat system: The base for this method is a Styrofoam board with 1"–20 gauge (2.54 cm – 20 gauge) wire lath. A fine clay-sand, hydrated lime, and cement mix is applied to the lath approximately ⅜" (0.95 cm) thick. When properly cured, a finish coat using a white (silicone) sand and cement, with or without integral color, is applied approximately ⅛" (0.32 cm) thick. This system is in common usage today in residential tract construction, particularly throughout the west and southwest areas of the country.

2. Two-coat system: This system is applied over masonry walls, primarily CMU, to provide an aesthetic finish as desired. The application is identical to the one-coat system without the lath.

3. Three-coat system: Although this is the more common exterior plaster system, it is losing popularity because of its weight requirements and tendency toward feathering and cracking as it cures and ages. The system uses the same base lath as the one-coat system with a base coat referred to as the scratch, a coarse clay-sand, cement mix applied approximately ⅜" (0.95 cm) thick over which the other two coats are applied after curing.

Exterior Insulation and Finish System (EIFS). *See figure 6–5.* A more recent trend in exterior plastering is the installation of the EIFS procedure. This system also uses an insulation board base the same as the one-coat system, but

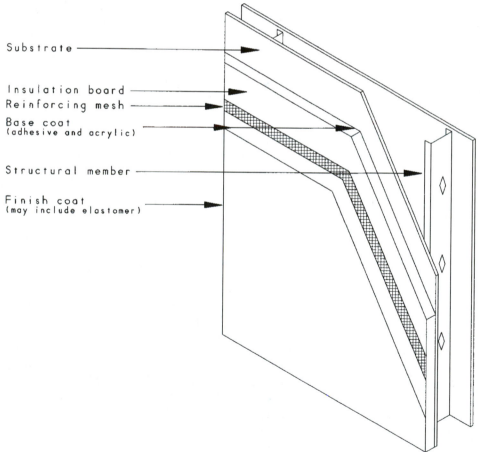

FIGURE 6–5
Exterior Insulation and Finish System

there the similarity ceases. A fiber mesh, such as nylon or polyester, is applied over the foam board with an adhesive. A skim coating of cement plaster (⅛″ [0.32 cm] thick) is applied over the fiber mesh. When cured, an acrylic color coating (20 to 60 mil thick) is applied, over which an elastomeric coating (60 mil thick) is installed. This system is especially popular in the desert areas of the country because it is both an insulating and weather protection.

Gypsum Plaster. Gypsum plaster is primarily an interior plaster system in use prior to the introduction of drywall. The original lath used was made from rough-sawn (R/S) 1 × 2, 1 × 3, or 1 × 4 (2.54 cm × 5.08 cm, 2.54 cm × 7.62 cm, or 2.54 cm × 10.16 cm) common or utility grade lumber spaced ½″ apart. Upon the introduction of metal lath products, expanded metal lath became popular and replaced the wood. Later, a gypsum board called Sheetrock®, a product of United States Gypsum Corporation (USG), became popular and replaced metal lath in many applications. Sheetrock® is still available in lengths from 4′–0″ (1.22 m) to 8′–0″ (2.44 m) long by 2′–0″ (0.61 m) wide. Originally, a dry spackle (plaster of Paris) mixed with water was used with Sheetrock® for the plaster.

Gypsum plaster is used as a fine, smooth wall finish in more expensive residential construction, especially custom homes, and commercial construction (offices and hotels, in particular). The cost is greater than a drywall and texture installation but is much more durable than drywall. Gypsum plaster is rarely, if ever, sprayed. It is hand applied with trowels and sanded smooth or textured as desired similar to cement plaster.

Lath. Included with both cement and gypsum plaster is the lath that is applied as a base for the plaster. Exterior lath applications may be installed using a wire mesh, classified as 1″–17 gauge or 1″ –20 gauge (2.54 cm-17 or –20 gauge) wire mesh, available in rolls up to 100 lf × 3 lf (30.48 m × 0.91 m). There are two types of 26 gauge GI lath: expanded metal lath and hi-rib lath. Both types are available in sheets from 8′–0″ to 10′–0″ × 3′–0″ (2.44 m to 3.05 m × 0.91 m. The 1″–17 or 2.54 cm–20 gauge (2.54 cm–17 or –20 gauge) wire mesh, similar in appearance to "chicken wire" fencing, is recommended for application on vertical walls only.

Expanded metal lath is smooth finished with punched holes similar to a grill-work or grating. This lath is also used primarily for wall applications. There are some applications where expanded metal laths may be used for horizontal surfaces in the same manner as hi-rib lath.

Hi-rib lath is similar in appearance and thickness to the expanded metal lath. The difference is that the hi-rib lath has ribs (small circular rods) staggered throughout the lath to give it more rigidity and to aid in gripping the plaster surrounding the holes. Hi-rib lath is primarily used for horizontal applications such as ceilings and soffits.

Lath is available without a moisture barrier (building paper, and so on), or with the moisture barrier as an integral part of the lath. Where moisture protection already exists, or sheathing has already been applied over a moisture barrier, the lath without the moisture barrier is used.

Gypsum Wall Board

Gypsum wall board (GWB), better known as **drywall,** is a product that is already finished to look like a smooth gypsum plastered wall. It has replaced most interior plaster systems because of its economy. The material needs no lath and is, therefore, applied directly to the rough framing. It is available in sizes from $4' \times 8'$ (1.2 m $\times$ 2.4 m) to $4' \times 12'$ (1.2 m $\times$ 3.7 m) sheets. GWB is also available in several thicknesses and fire-rated categories. *See figure 6–6.*

Drywall may be applied to any surface, wood or metal frame, and masonry or concrete. Drywall is nailed or screwed to the framing, directly adhered (glued) to masonry or concrete, or applied over special insulating wall systems. In all instances a pre-mix compound (prepared mix) or spackle (dry mix) must be applied to the drywall joints and over the nail or screw indentations. The joints must be taped with a paper tape or self-adhering nylon mesh tape, with the compound or prepared spackle sanded smooth and, if necessary, taped, coated, and sanded again to give a complete smooth wall finish.

Drywall may remain smooth to appear as plaster or may be textured. The most common textures are the "orange peel," a light roughened finish, usually sprayed on the wall or ceiling; "lace," hand-troweled and similar in appearance to the special plaster finish; or "knock-down," also hand-troweled to attain the look similar to the rough antique Spanish plaster. The pre-mixed compound used for taping is also used to achieve these textures.

Specialty drywall products, manufactured for purposes other than just a covering for rough framing, concrete, or masonry, include systems used for thermal insulation, sound attenuation, radiation shielding, and fire protection.

Other Special Drywall Applications

Radiation Protection. Another product, radiation shielding drywall, includes a leaded layer from $\frac{1}{32}$" (0.08 cm) to $\frac{1}{8}$" (0.32 cm) thick added to the GWB and

BOARD THICKNESS	BOARD SIZE				BOARD TYPES				
	8'	9'	10'	12'	Reg	MR**	WR***	*C**	*X**
1/4" GWB	×			×	×				
3/8" GWB	×			×	×	×	×		
1/2" GWB	×	×	×	×	×	×	×	×	×
5/8" GWB	×	×	×	×	×	×	×	×	×

REMARKS:

* Fire-resistant Gypsum Board – 1/2" "C" – 3/4 hr rating
  5/8" "X" – 1 hr rating
** MR Board – Moisture-resistant for exterior use.
*** WR Board – Water-resistant for interior wet area use.

Standard sizes available as indicated.
Other sizes may be obtained upon special order.

FIGURE 6–6
Gypsum Wallboard (GWB) Sizes and Types

installed as a single unit to prevent and/or reduce radiation exposure to other areas. This product is for use in X-ray and radiation laboratories, hospitals, other clinical applications, and in locations such as nuclear reactor control centers.

Thermal Insulation Systems. The thermal insulation referred to here is separate from the others mentioned previously only because it is a part of the drywall installation. One of the thermal insulation systems is called the "Styrostud" system, using either 26 gauge aluminum, or 26 gauge GI cold-rolled steel framing and Styrofoam board insulation. The studs are 1½" (3.81 cm) or 2" (5.08 cm) deep (Z-shaped or channel-shaped) in lengths of 8'–0", 9'–0," or 10'–0" (2.44 m, 2.74 m, or 3.05 m).

Where Z studs are used, they are screwed, nailed, or shot-and-pinned into the wall. The Styrofoam boards are 2 lf (0.61 m) wide, and 1½" (3.81 cm) or 2" (5.08 cm) thick to match the stud being used. The boards slip into the Z studs and are adhered to the wall with a panel glue.

The channel-shaped studs are placed over the Styrofoam panels with grooves matching the end return depth and width of the channel. The panels are adhered in the same manner and the channels are fastened in the same manner as the "Z" studs. The studs or channels are also used as the backing for fastening the drywall over the insulation system.

Sound Insulation. This section may be considered a part of acoustical treatment (see section on acoustical treatment) or drywall treatment. There are two classifications of sound insulation—*sound attenuation* and *sound enhancement.*

Sound Attenuation. Sound attenuation is the ability to reduce sound between areas. There are two types of sound attenuation systems applied in which GWB

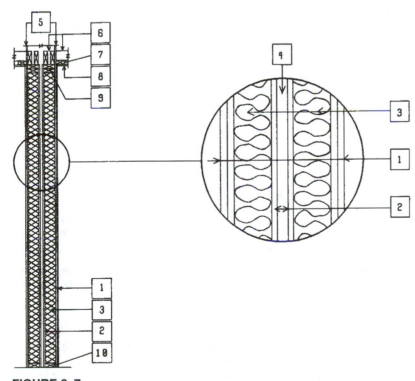

KEYNOTES:

1. Dbl 5/8" "X" GWB o/2x or steel frame
2. 1/2" sound (fiber) board.
3. Alternate batt imsulation.
4. 1" air space
5. 5/8" "X" GWB to underside of roof.
6. Ceiling joists.
7. Furring.
8. 5/8" "X" GWB on furring @ ceiling.
9. Dbl top plate.
10. Sole (bottom) or sill plate.

FIGURE 6–7
Sound Wall Insulation System

is included. One is the pre-fabricated sound attenuation panel with integral wall-coverings, padding and connection fittings affixed to wall framing. Many office complexes (especially for conference rooms), and schools (for music and rehearsal rooms) frequently use these panel systems.

See figure 6–7. The system commonly installed in multifamily (apartments, hotels, etc.) and commercial construction (offices, public restrooms, and so on) uses drywall with batt or board sound insulation built into the wall between the units. The drywall, in combination with the insulating materials provides this control.

Most areas allow a maximum sound (noise) level of eighty-five to ninety decibels (85 Db to 90 Db). This sound (noise) level may be attained for only a few hours without protection. Where such conditions exist, and the sound is to be retarded, special walls are constructed to prevent this level of sound from penetrating to other areas.

Sound Enhancement. Where it may be necessary to *increase sound* such as in concert halls, theaters, opera houses, and the like, the sound may be increased by sound enhancement. Special ceiling shapes and moveable ceiling panels, using drywall panels with acoustical additions, provide this ability to make and control the volume change and echo reduction.

Fire Protection. Fire protection may require special applications such as those used for elevator, hoist, and dumbwaiter shafts. Firewalls are constructed within residential and commercial structures to aid in the reduction of the spread of fire. These walls may be required to extend to the underside of a roof structure on one or both sides of a separation wall. In commercial construction such a wall is located between several areas. This depends upon the size of the project. In many areas of the United States, residential construction requires a firewall partition between an attached garage and the residence, extending the full width of the garage and to the underside of the roof structure.

The wall is constructed with ⅝" X (1.59 cm), GWB on both sides of the frame wall to ceiling height. The drywall on the garage side continues to the underside of the roof sheathing. Any installations, such as pipe, wire, HVAC duct, or conduit, that pass through a firewall must have fire-insulating wrap, and the wall must be sealed to maintain the fire-resistant rating and to meet the requirements of local and national fire codes. This type of installation is classified as a one-hour fire-rated drywall system.

Tile

Quarry Tile. Quarry tile, used primarily for floor covering, is a kiln-dried, clay-based (terra cotta) material available in sizes from 8" to 12" (10.16 cm to 30.48 cm) square. The tiles are normally installed in a bed of thinset cement approximately ½" (1.27 cm) thick with a maximum 1" (2.54 cm) wide gap between the tiles and grouted between the tiles to the level of the top edge of the tile so as to seal the joints for moisture protection. Tiles may also be vitrified and glazed to increase the moisture protection and appearance.

Ceramic Tile. Ceramic tile is a glazed, vitreous tile that may be used for either floor or wall tiles. The tiles may be clay-based or cement-based and are available in a variety of baked enamel plain colors or colorful designs. The sizes range from 1" (2.54 cm) square tiles (called mosaic tiles), 1" (2.54 cm) squares adhered to a 12" (30.48 cm) square base sheet, to larger tiles from 4" to 12"

(5.08 cm to 30.48 cm) square. The same application procedures are used for ceramic tiles as for quarry tiles. It may be necessary to install the tile with thinset mortar and grout over a lath when applied on walls for moisture protection.

Terrazzo. Terrazzo pavers, when used for interior floors, manufactured from thin, natural, or cut pieces of slate, stone, or granite, are also considered tiles. Another common form of the terrazzo paver tiles may be made from combinations of natural crushed rock, slate, or shale, crushed sea shells, nut shells and/or glass, or in combinations of any of the materials mentioned and mixed with concrete and formed into various sizes and designs.

Marble, although also a stone, is considered a tile because it can be cut into tile panels or into smaller sizes similar to the standard quarry and larger ceramic tiles.

Acoustical Treatment

Also see section on sound insulation above. Direct-adhered acoustical treatment includes either of two systems. One uses a pre-mixed compound and the other is a manufactured direct-adhered acoustical tile. The *pre-mixed compound* is more commonly used for residential, light commercial, and some office construction. Its appearance is produced by a mixture of pre-mixed drywall compound, with loose-grain perlite, vermiculite, or fiberglass, combined with moistened powdered gypsum and sprayed on the ceilings.

Direct-adhered acoustical tiles are manufactured from the same materials as used for composite board or fiberglass insulations but are compressed and formed into 8″ to 12″ (10.16 cm to 30.48 cm) squares from ⅛″ to ½″ (0.32 cm to 0.64 cm) thick. They may require an adhesive base or may be self-adhering. In either case, they are pressed directly onto walls and ceilings. These tiles are most commonly used in small areas where sound attenuation is required, such as the enclosures surrounding public telephones. Direct-adhered tiles may have the same appearance and texture as suspended acoustical tiles.

See figure 6–8. Although not common to residential construction, suspended acoustical ceiling tile (ACT) systems may be found in some locations such as kitchens, bathrooms, or garages. The system makes use of tie wires suspended from the roof or ceiling structure above with runners attached at the bottom end into which the acoustical tiles are placed. The runners (track) are flanged in a T shape to support the tiles and are fastened perpendicular to one another to form 2′ × 2′ (0.61 m × 0.61 m) or 2′ × 4′ (0.61 m × 1.22 m) spacings for the tile installation. The depth of the suspension system depends upon the height between the ceiling height desired and the structure above.

Finish Flooring and Floor Coverings

Finish flooring materials include wood plank, parquet, and special elastomeric and polymeric mixtures. The wood flooring may be installed over a subflooring or adhered directly to a concrete slab and can be set in many esthetic designs. Oak, walnut, cherry, or other hardwoods are used for such installations because of their durability and appearance.

Special materials and coatings such as asphalt planking (similar to roof pads), plastic laminated floor coverings, and epoxy-based semi-liquid mixes (such as crushed gravel mixed with elastomeric-based or resin-based coatings) are especially popular for use as a finish for decks, exterior balconies,

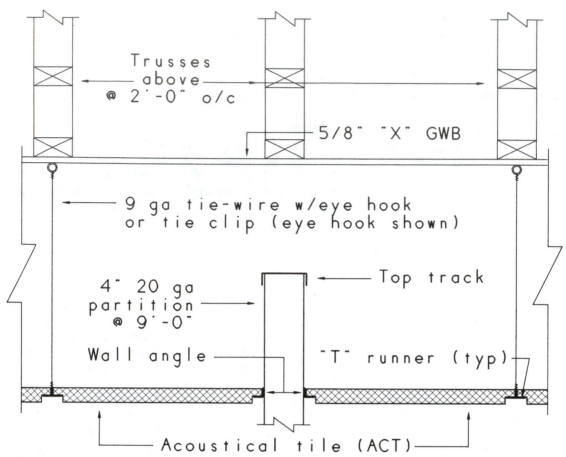

FIGURE 6–8
Acoustical Ceiling Tile (ACT) System

and arcades. These polymers are applied by spray, roll, or brush over a moisture barrier (asphalt felt, polyester sheets, or polyethylene sheets). Asphalt planking is installed over the same type of moisture barrier but uses a hot-mop application (hot bitumen) or cold-applied emulsion-based adhesive. Floor coverings include resilient vinyl composition sheet, vinyl composition tile (VCT), and carpeting for interiors.

Resilient vinyl sheet and vinyl tile floor coverings are manufactured with a pre-printed design (floral, symmetric, and so on) vinyl sheet in combination with bitumen-based mixtures and epoxy cements compressed in a calender mill under heat and moisture, and slowly dried. The vinyl sheet material is obtained in 12'–0" (3.66 m) wide rolls up to 100'–0" (30.48 m) in length.

The vinyl composition tiles (VCT) are compressed even more than the sheet materials to give more strength to them. Having completed the pass through the calender, they are passed through a shear mill and cut into the sizes desired. The sizes normally range from 8" to 12" (10.16 cm to 30.48 cm) square. These floor coverings are applied with a base adhesive.

Carpeting is classified as a floor covering that is installed from wall to wall in all directions. The materials are available in residential or commercial quality with many textures and designs. The complete carpet system includes a padding, a rubber-based mixture with fine scraps of carpeting for softness, which is partially adhered to the substrate (underlayment or slab), webbing, a nylon or other clothlike mesh available in rolls 4" (10.16 cm) to 6" (15.24 cm) wide up to 100' (30.48 m) long, for joining carpet edges and tack strips for use along the perimeter (walls) of a room. Rugs and mats are not considered carpeting, but instead are classified as specialty items included in Division 12, Furnishings.

Painting and Wall Coverings

Paints are coatings such as epoxies, acrylics, latexes, lacquers, varnishes, and stains used for exterior and interior finishes for walls, ceilings, exposed wood, or other back-up material specified to be weather protected or to have added aesthetic coloring and design. Paints are installed in two-coat or three-coat applications, using a base paint, or a sealer, with the finish coats in oil-based or latex mixtures. Both types may be used for interior or exterior applications. Oil-based paints include a linseed oil base, while latex paints are produced from a rubber or synthetic rubber base mixed with polymers or acrylics. Paints may be applied over concrete, masonry, steel, wood, or drywall. Lacquers, varnishes, and stains are applied to wood surfaces only for appearance and/or durable gloss finish. Epoxies are also a synthetic material that are mixed with some of the other materials mentioned in this section to produce a hard and durable surface. Such applications may include marine deck or concrete slab protection.

Any material applied to interior walls other than plaster or paint is considered a wall covering. Wallpaper includes paper, vinyl, cloth, or other woven materials, applied directly to the wall surface. Wall coverings also include decorative wood and paneling. In new construction, where wall coverings are applied, the drywall backing must be smooth and clean for wallpaper applications. The applicator cleans and prepares the wall with sizing when making preparations for wallpaper installation. The wallpaper (or cloth) is applied using a water-soluble paste mixture. Other wall coverings are applied using glue and/or nails or screws. Most wall covering installations other than wallpaper are applied by a finish carpenter.

CHAPTER EXERCISES

The following questions refer to the Garland residence.

Multiple Choice

_____   1. The main entry door is:
    a. Metal-clad wood.
    b. A panel door with "half-moon" lites.
    c. Two 3'–0" × 6'–8" (0.9 m × 2.03 m) doors.
    d. All of the above.

_____   2. The windows are:
    a. All custom made.
    b. All metal frame.
    c. Neither A nor B.
    d. Both A and B.

_____ 3. The door and window trim:
   a. Match the baseboard.
   b. Is customized and packaged with the doors and windows.
   c. May not be a part of the door and window package.
   d. Is pre-stained.

_____ 4. Exterior trim includes:
   a. All window and door trim and fascia board.
   b. Door trim only.
   c. Window trim only.
   d. Fascia board only.

_____ 5. The exterior finish is:
   a. CMU and ship-lap wood siding.
   b. Concrete plaster and exposed CMU.
   c. Brick veneer, exposed CMU, and metal siding.
   d. Exterior Insulation and Finish System.

_____ 6. The sheathing for the roof underlayments:
   a. Are $3/8''$ (0.95 cm) Masonite panels.
   b. Are either $5/8''$ (1.58 cm) OSB® or $1/2''$ (1.27 cm) CDX.
   c. Include $3/8''$ (0.95 cm) CDX shear panels over the sheathing.
   d. Are used with 34lb (15.45 kg) building paper.

_____ 7. The roofing is:
   a. A one-piece S tile application.
   b. A wood shake roofing material.
   c. Asphalt composition shingles.
   d. A panelized metal roof system.

_____ 8. All roof penetrations shall include:
   a. No protection.
   b. Galvanized iron or aluminum flashings.
   c. Galvanized iron or aluminum flashings with collar.
   d. None of the above.

_____ 9. The roof slope is:
   a. 4:12 and 8:12.
   b. 5:12 and 8:12.
   c. 5:12 and 6:12.
   d. 4:12 and 6:12.

General Information

_____ 10. The materials included in Finishes are:
   a. Painting and wallcoverings.
   b. Floor coverings and lath and plaster.
   c. Both a and b.
   d. Neither a nor b.

_____ 11. Gypsum wall board is available:
   a. In 5'×10' (1.52 m × 3.05 m) sheets.
   b. In $3/4''$ (1.91 cm) thickness.
   c. As Sheetrock or firecoded.
   d. With finish compound and tape already attached.

_____ 12. Cement plaster:
   a. Is installed in one-coat, two-coat, and three-coat applications.
   b. Is a synthetic system.
   c. Does not require a moisture barrier.
   d. Must be trowel applied only.

_____ 13. Light-gauge metal framing is:
   a. Available by special order only.
   b. Available in sizes from 1½" (3.82 cm) to 6" (15.24 cm) wide.
   c. For use with wood framing installations.
   d. Used for commercial construction only.

_____ 14. The metal bottom and top plates are:
   a. Usually the same gauge as the studs.
   b. Called tracks.
   c. Often used as headers and sills for partition openings.
   d. All of the above.

_____ 15. Quarry tile:
   a. Is available in sizes from 8" (20.32 cm) to 12" (30.48 cm) square.
   b. Is used for wall tiles.
   c. Must be self adhering.
   d. Is produced from quarry stone.

_____ 16. Ceramic tiles:
   a. May be used only for kitchen floors.
   b. Are kiln baked and glazed.
   c. May be used for both floor and wall finishes.
   d. None of the above.

_____ 17. Resilient flooring:
   a. Is produced in the same manner as vitreous tile.
   b. Is always adhered with a cement-based material.
   c. Is tacked to the substrate.
   d. Is available in sheets and tiles.

_____ 18. Painting includes:
   a. Wallcoverings and sealants.
   b. Integral coloring of cement plaster.
   c. Latex, lacquer, varnish, epoxy and oil-based materials used for covering interior and exterior surfaces.
   d. Plastic coatings for below-grade moisture protection.

_____ 19. Exterior plaster systems include:
   a. Metal lath with moisture barrier.
   b. Cement-based and gypsum-based plaster materials.
   c. Synthetic plaster systems with nylon or other polyester mesh for lath.
   d. All of the above.

_____ 20. Lath for plaster coatings:
   a. May be 1" (2.54 cm)–20 gauge wire mesh, expanded metal or hi-rib lath.
   b. May require a foam board backing.
   c. Neither a nor b.
   d. Both a and b.

_____ 21. Also included in Finishes are:
 a. Carpeting.
 b. Special wood flooring such as parquet.
 c. Wall paneling (not specified in Wood and Plastics).
 d. All of the above.

_____ 22. Drywall classifications include:
 a. Moisture-resistant (MR) and water-resistant (WR) sheets.
 b. A finish plaster requirement for all surfaces.
 c. Only fire-resistant material.
 d. None of the above.

_____ 23. Wallpapering is adhered by using:
 a. A cement base.
 b. An all-purpose glue.
 c. Spackle.
 d. A wheat paste.

_____ 24. Wallcoverings:
 a. Are a variety of paper materials.
 b. Include paper, cloth, and wood materials.
 c. Are all paint materials.
 d. None of the above.

True or False

T F 1. Lath is used for drywall applications.

T F 2. Light-gauge metal stud framing is installed basically in the same manner as wood stud framing.

T F 3. Suspended ceiling systems for plaster or drywall finishes are similarly installed.

T F 4. Acoustical ceiling tile (ACT) systems include track and angle iron.

T F 5. A three-coat cement plaster is applied with two brown coats and a scratch coat.

T F 6. A synthetic plaster system may be a panelized system applied over a polystyrene foam board.

T F 7. Carpeting normally includes the edge-tack strips, padding, webbing, and the carpet.

T F 8. Latex paint may be used for both interior and exterior surfaces.

T F 9. When used for exterior surfaces, the paint specifications require a primer.

T F 10. Light-gauge metal framing includes materials made from 26 gauge to 20 gauge galvanized metal.

T F 11. Floor tile is made only from quarry tile.

T F 12. Tiles may be glazed and vitrified with designs and multiple colors.

T F 13. All tiles are made from a cement-base material.

T F 14. Tiles may be applied with a self-adhering adhesive base or a thin-set concrete.

T F 15. Acoustical treatment infers the installation of a suspended ACT ceiling only.

T F 16. Special lead-backed drywall sheets are used for radiation protection.

T F 17. A common system for drywall installation over masonry includes the installation of wood 1" × 2" (2.54 cm × 5.08 cm) or 1" × 4" (2.54 cm × 10.16 cm) furring strips applied directly to the masonry and the drywall fastened to the strips.

T F 18. Hi-rib lath, when used, is applied on the underside of any area referred to as a *lid,* such as soffits, overhangs, or ceilings.

T F 19. A track is installed so that the light-gauge metal materials may be more quickly supplied to the installers.

T F 20. GWB is available in ¼", ⅜", ½", and ⅝" (0.64 cm, 0.95 cm, 1.27 cm, and 1.59 cm) thicknesses.

T F 21. Sloped roof systems may include only composition shingle or tile.

T F 22. Tile roof systems include an asphaltic or pitch felt underlayment.

T F 23. Wood framed chimney construction requires ⅝" X (1.59 cm) GWB installed completely around the interior and exterior framing.

Completion

1. The _____ wire mesh is the cheapest and most common lath used for cement plaster.

2. A(n) _____ application is most common for cement plaster over a masonry surface.

3. Synthetic plaster systems use a(n) _____ surface material over cement plaster and polystyrene foam board.

4. _____ protection is required under all exterior plaster systems.

5. A ⅞" (2.22 cm), three-coat cement plaster system requires a ⅜" (0.95 cm) scratch coat, a _____" (_____cm) coat, and a ⅛" (0.32 cm) finish coat.

6. Drywall, when installed for a fire-rated wall system, is usually a single or double layer of _____" (_____cm), type X board.

7. To complete a drywall system, screws or nails, _____, and tape are required.

8. _____ may be used to repair existing gypsum plaster or drywall.

9. A(n) _____ system may be required in lieu of wood framing in any structure, especially in commercial construction.

10. Carpeting is applied using _____, webbing, pads, and the finish carpet.

11. The _____ contractor is responsible for all trim work.

Refer to the schedules for the Garland residence to answer the following questions.

12. Window type "Mark D" is a _____.

13. Door "Mark _____" is a 3'–0" × 6'–8" (0.9 m × 2.0 m) panel door.

14. The exterior walls have _____" wide R–19 insulation.

15. A(n) _____ underlayment is installed over the ½" (1.27 cm) CDX plywood roof sheathing for moisture protection.

16. 26 gauge galvanized iron, aluminum, or _____ may be used for flashings at pipe penetrations.

7

Plumbing, Mechanical, and Electrical (On-Site)

As with the off-sites and site improvements, all of the on-site mechanical, plumbing, and electrical work must be coordinated with all of the other trades. The rough-in work by these trades include any sleeving, pipe, and/or conduit, which must be installed prior to, or during, the placement of concrete or masonry so that the stub-outs are in the proper locations. A *stub-out* is the exposed plumbing, piping, or electrical conduit installed from the off-sites extending into the structure and exposed above the concrete slab or wood floor so that future crews can complete the construction as the work progresses.

Coordination must continue because the same contractors, having installed the off-sites and site improvements, must also install plumbing, piping, conduit and/or wiring, and the mechanical ductwork in the floors, walls, and ceilings during the concrete, masonry, and framing installations, making certain that all openings are properly located prior to closure by the finish trades (refer to chapter 6). When the framing and drywall work is completed, the plumbing crews return to install the plumbing fixtures and connections; the mechanical crews return to install the HVAC grilles and registers; and the electricians return to install the electrical fixtures, switches, outlets, and protective covers. The water and waste pipes, and gas lines with appropriate angle stops (a shut-off valve at a fixture), and electrical outlets must also be in place for the cabinet and appliance installers.

Other common installations included in on-site plumbing are fire-protection systems such as fire-sprinkler systems; automatic chemical spray systems (foam or CO_2); gas and fuel-oil heating systems; and liquid-transfer heating and cooling systems associated with HVAC. All information, regulations, and codes are based upon the recommendations of the American National Specifications

Institute (ANSI) and/or the National Fire Protection Association (NFPA). There are some areas now requiring sprinkler systems installed as part of the standard residential, as well as commercial, codes and ordinances.

PLUMBING AND PIPING

See figures 7–1 and 7–2. The drawings shown are for the Garland residence. An isometric plan or pictorial section of the plumbing and piping installations may be used for residential or small commercial structures. The isometric diagram is used for most commercial construction projects. The drawings include a layout of the materials necessary for a complete installation with the exception of the fixtures. The fixtures are indicated on the architectural floor plan or on the floor plan layout within the plumbing drawings. Specifications include the material and installation procedures so that all codes are noted and properly followed. Schedules are used to indicate the fixture required, manufacturer of the fixture, and the fixture manufacturer's identification code.

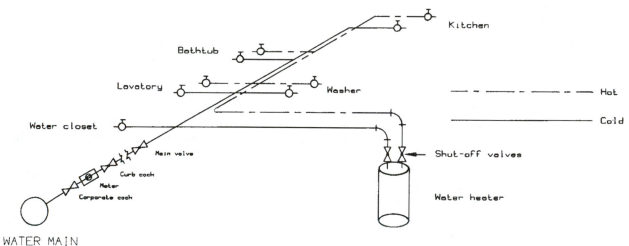

FIGURE 7–1
Isometric Piping Diagram, Garland Residence

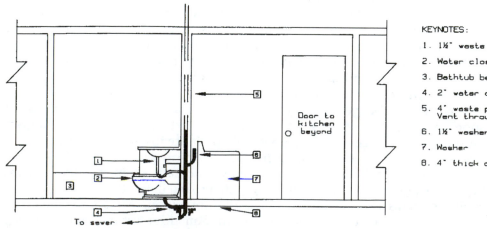

KEYNOTES:

1. 1½" waste pipe and P-trap @ lavatory
2. Water closet
3. Bathtub beyond
4. 2" water closet waste pipe
5. 4" waste pipe and vent – Vent through roof
6. 1½" washer drain
7. Washer
8. 4" thick concrete slab

FIGURE 7–2
Pictorial Plumbing Section, Garland Residence

One or all of the above must note the material types to be used. If no information exists, the contractor must have engineering requirements provided so that the system is installed in accordance with all codes and ordinances and in accordance with the standards of the trade.

MECHANICAL

See figure 7–3. Mechanical specifications and drawings include all *Heating, Ventilation* and *Air-Conditioning* (HVAC). All pertinent information regarding the type of unit, such as a combination furnace/air-conditioner, a roof-top air-conditioner, a gas-fired or oil-fired furnace, or a heat pump, as well as the necessary accessories (piping, ductwork, supply registers and return grilles, and so on), are a part of the mechanical system.

Heating and air-conditioning units are rated in British thermal units (Btu). A Btu is the amount of heat—1 calorie—required to raise the temperature of 1 pound of water 1° Fahrenheit. This rate is determined on the basis of

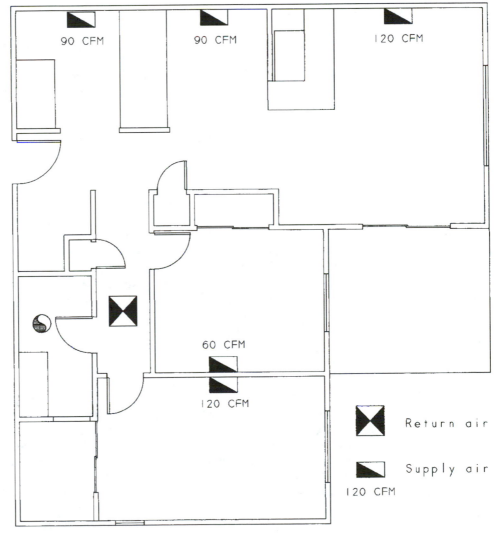

FIGURE 7–3
HVAC Reflected Ceiling Plan, Apartment

the maximum density of water at 39° Fahrenheit (approximately 22° Centigrade or Celsius). There is more energy expended for cooling; therefore, the amount of Btu required for cooling is greater than for heating. It is for this reason that furnaces, used in areas where heating more than cooling is necessary, are designated rather than air conditioners. In addition, air-conditioning units are in "tons of cooling" capacity, where one ton is equal to 12,000 Btu.

HVAC piping or ductwork installations are divided into two categories; supply and return. *Supply* includes all parts of an installation, excluding the unit, required to move the heated or cooled water or air into the structure. *Return* includes all parts, excluding the unit, used to remove the heating or cooling from the piping or the air, and re-circulate it to the unit for re-heating or re-cooling. The unit is the third part of the system and is separated from the supply and return definitions since it is involved with both the supply and re-circulation.

Where space is available, such as a basement or utility room, either an air-conditioning unit or furnace may be used. Furnace systems may include forced-air heating, hot water heating, or steam heating. The supply system for heating is installed utilizing the most efficient placement of the ducts or plumbing to maximize the output.

Hot water and steam heating systems include circulating pumps to force the water or steam through the supply piping as quickly as possible. These systems are less efficient than forced air because a return is piped back to the boiler from each radiator or radiant heater supplied so as to bypass the heating supply lines. The units farthest from the heating unit will receive less heat as a result. Forced-air systems have a circulating motor and fan that forces the air to the areas supplied as efficiently as possible. There are fewer return air lines since the cooled air can be drawn directly from a general area (more than one room) back to the furnace for reheating.

The warmer climates making use of air conditioning will normally install combination units, heat pumps or air-conditioning units, and/or swamp coolers. The "rule-of-thumb" for sizing an air-conditioning unit is one ton (12,000 Btu) per every 400 sq ft to 500 sq ft of area. Therefore, the average residence of 1800 sq ft to 2000 sq ft usually requires no more than a four- or five-ton unit. Unless a combination unit is installed, utility space is unnecessary. Self-contained units are frequently placed on roofs or in attic spaces. A split unit (the compressor is separated from the heating/cooling unit) may be placed in an attic space or the garage with the compressor placed outdoors on a concrete pad next to the structure in the vicinity of the unit. For larger structures (2500 square feet or more), it is necessary to install larger units, such as five- to ten-ton sizes, or multiple units equaling the same capacity.

This unit installed for the apartment is a three-ton unit, or the equivalent of 36,000 BTU. The apartment reflected ceiling plan identifies the locations of all HVAC supply and return equipment. A schedule is supplied with a set of HVAC plans showing the size of the A/C unit, the size(s) of the supply duct(s), the supply registers (diffusers), and the return grilles and duct(s). The units for each apartment are placed on the apartment roof for convenience of maintenance and protection from vandalism. The duct used may be flexible insulated duct common to residential installations, or sheet metal insulated ductwork. All supply and return ducts are installed in the walls of the unit (as in the apartment drawing in figure 7–3), or in an attic space to and from the unit supplying the apartment.

THE HVAC AND ELECTRICAL TRADES RELATIONSHIP

There are times when the responsibilities of mechanical and electrical contractors may be required to interact. In most instances the agreement is specified in a manner similar to the following instructions:

1. The installation and maintenance of all wiring and conduit from the power supply to the disconnect controlling the HVAC unit is the responsibility of the electrical contractor.
2. The conduit installation for the thermostat cable is the responsibility of the electrical contractor.
3. The supply, installation and maintenance of the units and internal controls and wiring, including the thermostat cable from the unit, is the responsibility of the HVAC contractor.

ELECTRICAL

Electrical systems include all materials and equipment installed from the power source to the smallest outlets within a structure. The on-site construction includes everything electrical from the service entrance equipment (residential) or switchgear equipment (commercial/industrial) to the finished interior product, excluding the appliances unless they are included in the contract. The service entrance equipment includes the meter, main circuit breaker, and branch circuit breakers located in a metal enclosure on the exterior of a residence (garage, utility, or basement wall). Again, the work must be coordinated with the other trades to complete the rough-in and, later, return to complete the electrical finish installation. *See figure 7–4.*

The power source is a step-down transformer located near or on the property. For commercial and industrial installations, a small substation may be installed to supply the power necessary to run machinery. The

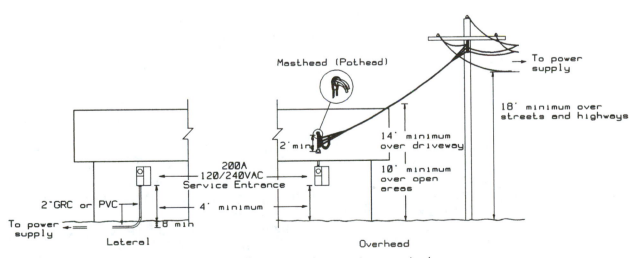

FIGURE 7–4
Electrical Service Entrance Systems, Apartment

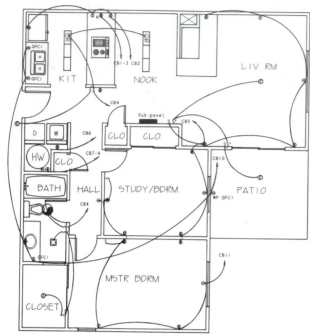

FIGURE 7–5
General Power/Lighting, Apartment

The sub-panel schedule from the figure:

SUB-PANEL

Main CB 150A

CB1 Range/oven -50A	CB2 Kitchen appliance circuit -20A	
CB3	CB4 Kitchen/Nook lighting -15A	
CB5 Liv Rm Recept -20A	CB6 Washer/Dryer circuit -20A	
CB7 Water heater -30A	CB8 Bath lighting/fan -15A	
CB9	CB10 GFCI circuit -20A	
CB11 Bdrm Recept -20A	CB12 Air conditioner (not shown) -30A	
	CB14	

power is supplied from the transformer to switchgear equipment located in an enclosure next to the exterior wall or within the substation established for security around the equipment. The power for such supply is referred to as the voltage (V), an alternating current (AC) supply usually reduced from 4160VAC to 480VAC, 240VAC or 208VAC, and 120VAC. Residential and small commercial projects (strip centers, and so on) require only the 240VAC and 120VAC. The current (the flow of electricity forced over a wire by the voltage) is rated in amperes (A). For example, the standard duplex receptacle (convenience outlet) is rated at a maximum 240VAC and 20A, whereas a standard light switch is normally rated at a maximum 125VAC and 15A.

Electrical requirements are established by an electrical engineer in much the same manner as the mechanical requirements. All calculations are completed by the engineer to determine the size of the wire necessary to supply power to the completed project, as well as the size of the service entrance equipment to a residence or switchgear requirements to a commercial or industrial project. The National Electric Code (NEC) establishes the minimum requirements for all these calculations and for the materials to be used within a structure. If none have been supplied by an engineer, the electrical contractor may be required to determine the load calculations to ascertain the proper equipment necessary for the dwelling.

See figure 7–5. The general lighting and power layout for the apartment shows the placement of the convenience outlets, light switches, lights, and circuitry. The apartment has its own individual service equipment supplied from a central source. A schedule is also provided showing the circuit breakdown for the unit.

CHAPTER EXERCISES

True or False

T F 1. The plumbing vent pipe in figure 7–2 is 6″ (15.24 cm) DIA.

T F 2. Plumbing, in the general meaning, refers to all water, sewer, and gas work.

T F 3. Normally, the electrician is responsible for maintaining all wiring to and including the HVAC unit.

T F 4. There are eight hot and cold water connections within the Garland residence (see figure 7–1).

T F 5. The HVAC compressor is always located on a pad outside of a structure.

T F 6. All supply air ducts are to have grilles installed.

T F 7. The connection used to reduce the size of a duct is called a transistor.

T F 8. The air output capacity of a HVAC system is referred to as the CFM.

T F 9. The service entrance equipment for a residence is rated at 120/240VAC.

T F 10. Smoke detectors are part of an electrical alarm system.

T F 11. At least one convenience outlet in the living room, master bedroom, and study/bedroom in the apartment (figure 7–5) is partially energized by a switch.

T F 12. There is a combination ceiling fan/light in the apartment living room (figure 7–5).

T F 13. The apartment bathroom (figure 7–5) has a combination heat/vent/light installed in the ceiling.

Multiple Choice

_____ 1. A stub-out is:
a. The end of pipe or conduit installed in the concrete slab.
b. A short fixture connection.
c. The same as a clean-out.
d. Any framing member cut longer than necessary.

_____ 2. The electrical and mechanical contractors normally contract:
a. For the electrical power supply to be installed by the electrical contractor.
b. For the mechanical contractor to install the power supply.
c. For the electrical contractor to maintain the complete unit.
d. None of the above.

_____ 3. The unit used to change size from one duct to another is called:
a. A collar.
b. A sleeve.
c. A transition.
d. A diffuser.

_____ 4. The type of air-conditioning/heating duct installed in the apartment is:
    a. 20 gauge galvanized prefabricated metal duct.
    b. Flexible insulated fiber and plastic duct.
    c. Flexible non-insulated fiber and plastic duct.
    d. 26 gauge galvanized prefabricated metal duct.

_____ 5. The plumber's responsibility includes:
    a. Installation of all piping and plumbing including fixtures.
    b. Installation of natural gas supply from the meter to the appliances.
    c. Installation of the hot water heater and its controls.
    d. All of the above.

_____ 6. The cold and hot water piping to be installed is:
    a. Copper ½" (1.27 cm) ID and ¾" (1.91 cm) ID.
    b. ½" (1.27 cm) ID and ¾" (1.91 cm) ID PVC cold water and CPVC hot water.
    c. Both a and b.
    d. Neither a nor b.

Completion

1. A(n) _____ is installed wherever HVAC duct changes size.

2. The electrician is responsible for connections to the _____ for the air-conditioning unit U.N.O.

3. The mechanical contractor installs the _____ for regulating heating and cooling.

4. The installation of materials and equipment that are a part of the potable water supply is called _____.

5. The _____ engineer is responsible for the design of all plumbing and heating/cooling equipment installations.

6. The electric service for the apartment has a maximum capacity of _____ A.

7. There is (are) _____ convenience outlet(s) installed on the exterior of the apartment.

8. A telephone jack is located in the _____.

9. The Btu rating of the apartment A/C unit is _____.

10. The hot water heater is connected to the _____ service.

11. The closet lights are operated with a _____ switch.

8

The Lee Residence Plans and Specifications

Most contracts in residential construction are negotiated between the owner and a contractor. Sometimes there may be a request for competitive bids by briefly advertising for contractors in local construction periodicals or the local newspaper, or the owner may take the responsibility to become an *owner-builder* where the law allows, or where no regulations governing such action exist. Other documents, such as those found in commercial negotiations, are used sparingly. In the case of an owner-builder, construction becomes the owner's responsibility from the building permit to the certificate of occupancy, and liability falls directly on the owner. The owner may hire crews directly. If the owner chooses to hire a contractor to build the structure, the contractor becomes liable for the permits and certifications.

GENERAL INFORMATION

Residential plans may have specifications indicated in one or more ways. Most pertinent information is included on the individual drawings or in additional sheets in the set of plans referred to as general architectural and/or structural notes. The materials to be used may be specified as follows:

1. Directly on the plans (floor plan, elevation, section, or detail) by use of the abbreviations, symbols, and keynotes
2. By a combination of a Description of Materials and the plans
3. By a combination of plans and a simplified Specification for each of the CSI divisions in paragraph form offering very basic information

Other documents, such as those found in commercial negotiations, are not usually found in residential legal documents. The basic legal documents in residential construction include a Description of Materials form, which is supplied by banks, and a proposal/contract.

DESCRIPTION OF MATERIALS

See figure 8–1. The Description of Materials is a combination specification and estimate initially filed for the purpose of determining costs of a residential project to enable the owner to apply for a construction loan.

SPECIFICATIONS

See figure 8–2 and the General Notes for the Lee Residence. As stated, the specifications given are minimum statements as to the work to be performed and the procedures to be followed. The specifications are written in this manner on the premise that the owner's representative and/or the contractors will follow, as repeated previously, the "best standards of the trade"; "shall include, but not be limited to" the information in the specifications; "and all materials, labor and/or equipment necessary to produce a complete installation"; or the installations shall be "in accordance with all local codes and ordinances." These statements added to any specification alert the contractor that all requirements must be met without going into the details of materials, equipment, or installation procedures to complete the work. There may be no specifications whatsoever if the dwelling is constructed under the owner-builder concept. All work in this case is in accordance with all of the above statements without any details.

CODES AND ORDINANCES

In most areas a specific set of rules are established for construction. These rules and regulations are referred to as the *codes*. Some are national, some are regional, others are local. National codes include such regulations as established by the National Electric Code (NEC), the American National Standards Institute (ANSI), the American Fire Protection Agency (AFPA), the Office of Safety and Health Administration (OSHA), the American Society of Heating, Refrigeration, and Air-Conditioning Engineers (ASHRAE), and others. A list of many of the organizations enlisted to help establish the codes are found in the Project Manual, chapter 10, for the construction of a commercial building called the Frontier Manufacturing Company.

The regional codes are established by the several building code organizations such as the International Conference of Building Officials (ICBO), the Building Officials Conference of America (BOCA), and so on. Many city, county, and rural areas also have established rules and regulations, referred to as the *local codes and ordinances*. Many manufacturers provide specifications for the products they make for construction to comply with the codes. Where such codes and regulations exist, although not defined in a specification, they are often included by inference. The quoted phrases above are inference statements.

NORTH RIVER BANK
DESCRIPTION OF MATERIALS

No. 101030

☒ Proposed Construction

☐ Under Construction

Property Address __900 South Mary Street__   City __Roanoke__   State __Virginia__

Borrower __Mr. & Mrs. L. C. Lee__   101 No State Street, Roanoke, Va
                    (Name)   (Address)

Contractor or Builder __ABC General Contracting__   4500 East 21st Street, Roanoke, Va
                          (Name)   (Address)

Legal Description

Lots 36 through 39, tract 1, Mountain Township, County of _____, State of

Virginia.

---

1. EXCAVATION:

Bearing soil. type __6'-2" high masonry wall over 2'-0" x 1'-0" footing__

---

2. FOUNDATIONS:

Footings: Concrete mix __1:2:5__   Strength (psi) __3,000__   Reinforcing __rebar__

Foundation wall: Material __8x8x16 CMU__   Strength (psi) __2,000__   Reinforcing __rebar__

Interior foundation wall: Material __same__   Party foundation wall __n/a__

Columns: Material and size __n/a__   Piers: Material and reinforcing __n/a__

Girders: Material and sizes __n/a__   Sills: Material __2x8 mudsill top of walls__

Basement entrance areaway __n/a__   Window areaways __n/a__

Waterproofing __dituthene w/protection__   Footing drains __yes__

Termite protection __yes (standard)__

Basementless space: Ground cover __n/a__   Insulation __n/a__   Foundation vents _____

Special Foundations __n/a__

---

3. CHIMNEYS:

Material __masonry, wood frame/brick veneer__ Prefabricated (make and size) _____

Flue lining: Material __metal flue liner__   Heater flue size __4"__   Fireplace flue size __6"__

Vents (material and size): Gas or oil heater __6" ⌀__   Water heater __2" ⌀__

---

4. FIREPLACES:

Type: ☐ Solid fuel: ☒ gas-burning: ☐ circulator (make and size) _____   Ash dump & cleanout _____

Fireplace: Facing __brick veneer__ lining __metal box__; hearth __brick veneer__; mantle __n/a__

---

5. EXTERIOR WALLS:

Wood frame: Grade and species __DF#2 or better, construction__ ☒ Corner bracing: ☒ Building paper: weight ____ lb __Tyvek__

Sub-sheathing __n/a__; thickness __n/a__ width __n/a__; ☐ solid: ☐ spaced ____ o.c.: diagonal __n/a__

Siding __n/a__; grade __n/a__; type __n/a__; size __n/a__; exposure ____; fastening _____

Shingles __n/a__; grade __n/a__; type __n/a__; size __n/a__; exposure ____; fastening _____

Masonry: Solid __CMU__; facing __n/a__; thickness __8__; type bond __running (common)__

Door sills __n/a__; Window sills __n/a__; Lintels __n/a__

Interior surfaces: Dampproofing. coats of __n/a__; furring __1x4 or 2x4 @ drywall__

Masonry veneer __n/a__; Sills __n/a__; Lintels __n/a__

FIGURE 8–1
Description of Materials–Lee Residence

DESCRIPTION OF MATERIALS
(Continued)

5. EXTERIOR WALLS (Continued):

Exterior painting: Material __exterior latex (walls), Olympic stain (trim)__; No. of coats __1 + 2__

Gable wall construction: ☑ same as main walls: ☐ other _____

6. FLOORING:

Concrete slab: ☑ Basement Floor: ☑ First Floor: ☑ ground supported: ☐ self-supporting: mix __1:2:5__; thickness __4__.

Reinforcing __rebar and WWF__; insulation __none__; membrane __20 mil polyethylene__

Fill under slab: Material __Type 2, compacted__; thickness __4__.

__fill compacted to 95% over virgin soil__

FLOOR FRAMING:

Joists: Wood. grade and species __DF#1__; other _____; bridging __mtl.cross__; anchors __n/a__

7. SUBFLOORING: *(Describe underflooring for special floors under item 22.)*

Material: Grade and species __CDX or OSB__; size __3/4"__; type _____

Laid: ☐ first floor: ☑ second floor: ☐ attic _____ sqft: ☐ diagonal: ☑ right angles _____

8. FINISH FLOORING: *(Describe kitchen and bath[s] under item 22)*

Location	Material	Size	Thickness	Area	Grade	Building paper	Underlayment
Basement							
First floor	carpet	n/a	1/2"	951 sf	#1	7 lb felt	3/4" CDX or OSB
Second Floor							

9. PARTITION FRAMING:

Studs: Wood. grade and species __HF construction__; size and spacing __2x4 @ 24"__; other __plumbing walls - 2x6__

10. CEILING FRAMING:

Joists: Wood. grade and species __n/a__; other __trusses__; bridging __n/a__

11. ROOF FRAMING:

Rafters: Wood. grade and species __n/a__; roof trusses (see detail) grade and species __see specs__

12. ROOFING:

Sheathing: grade and species __plywood Str 2__; size __4'x8' x 1/2"__; type __CDX__; ☑ solid: ☐ spaced _____ o.c.

Roofing __"S" tile__; grade __n/a__; weight and thickness __88#/sq__; size __n/a__; fastening __wire tie__

Stain or paint __n/a__; underlayment __43# felt__

Built-up roofing __n/a__; number of plies __n/a__; surfacing material __n/a__

Flashing: Material __lead/aluminum__; gauge or weight __3# or 26 ga__; ☐ gravel stop: ☐ snow guards

13. GUTTERS and DOWNSPOUTS:

Gutters: Material __PVC__; gauge or weight __n/a__; size __3"__; shape __"U"__

Downspouts: Material __PVC__; gauge or weight __n/a__; size __3"__; shape __round__; number __4__

Downspouts connected to: ☐ storm sewer: ☐ sanitary sewer: ☐ dry well: ☑ splash block: Material and size __2'x4' conc__

14. LATH and PLASTER:

Lath: ☐ walls: ☐ ceilings: Material __n/a__; weight or thickness __n/a__

Cement plaster: Type (1-. 2-. 3-coat) __n/a__; finish __sand/integral color__

Exterior Insulation and Finish System (EIFS): Manufacturer: __Dryvit, Stowe or equal__

15. DRYWALL (GWB):

Drywall: ☑ walls: ☑ ceilings: Material __UFS or equal__; thickness __1/2__; Finish __orange peel__; joint treatment __match finish tape__

11

FIGURE 8–1 *(continued)*
Description of Materials–Lee Residence

DESCRIPTION OF MATERIALS
(Continued)

16. DECORATING: *(Paint, wallpaper, etc.)*

Room	Wall Finish Material and Application	Ceiling Material and Application
Kitchen	semi-gloss latex – 2 coats	same as walls
Bath	semi-gloss paint/tile	semi-gloss paint – match walls
Other *Bedrooms*	wallpaper	acoustical spray finish (white)
Living room	paint – flat latex	same as bedroom
Family room	same as living room	same

17. INTERIOR DOORS and TRIM:

Doors: Type _flush_ : material _luan_ : thickness _13/8_

Door trim: Type _package_ : material _select pine_

Finish: Doors _oak veneer_ : trim _oak veneer_

Base: Type _Slimline_ : material _oak veneer_ : size _2"_

Other trim *(item, type, and location)* _n/a_

18. WINDOWS:

Windows: Type _vary_ : make _custom_ : material _pine_ : sash thickness _1/2"_

Glass: Grade _see plans_ : ☐ sash weights; ☑ balances: type _____ : head flashing _____

Trim: Type _match doors_ : material _match doors_ : paint, type and number of coats _none_

Weatherstripping: Type _3/8"_ : material _rubber_ : storm sash, number _n/a_

Screens: ☐ full; ☐ half: type _n/a_ : number _n/a_ : screen material _n/a_

Basement windows: Type _fixed_ : material _wood_ : ☐ screens, number _____ : storm sash, number _n/a_

Special windows: _____

19. ENTRANCES and EXTERIOR DETAIL:

Main entrance door: Material _oak_ : width _6_ : thickness _13/4_ : Frame material _oak_ : thickness _1/2_

Other entrance doors: Material _birch_ : width _3_ : thickness _13/4_ : Frame material _oak_ : thickness _1/2_

Head Flashing: _____ : weatherstripping: type _rubber_ : saddles _n/a_

Screen doors: Thickness _____ : number _____ : screen material _n/a_ : storm doors, number _____

Combination storm and screen doors: Thickness _____ : number _____ : screen material _n/a_

Shutter: ☐ hinged; ☐ fixed: railings _n/a_ : louvers _n/a_

Exterior millwork: Grade and species _n/a_ : paint type and number of coats _n/a_

20. CABINETS and INTERIOR DETAIL:

Kitchen cabinets, wall units: Material _oak_ : lineal feet – shelves _20_ : shelf width _12_

Base units: Material _oak_ : countertop _corian_ : edging _round_

Backsplash ☑ : endsplash ☑ : cabinet finish _oak_ : number of coats _15_

Medicine cabinets: Make _none_

Other cabinets and built-in furnishing: _storage and wet bar – oak/corian/58'_

21. STAIRS:

Stair	Treads Material	Treads Thickness	Risers Material	Risers Thickness	Stringers Material	Stringers Size	Handrail Material	Handrail Size	Balusters Material	Balusters Size
Basement	select	1"	select	1"			oak	2x4	wrought iron	see plan
Main	select	1"	select	1"	DF #2	2x14	oak	2x4		
Attic										

Disappearing: Make and model number _n/a_

FIGURE 8–1 (continued)
Description of Materials–Lee Residence

DESCRIPTION OF MATERIALS
(Continued)

22. SPECIAL FLOORS and WAINSCOAT:

	Location	Material. Color. Border. Size. Gauge. etc.	Threshold	Base	Underlayment
Floors	Kitchen	quarry tile, 12", cove base	yes	metal	as required
	Bath	VCT tiles, 8", cove base	yes	metal	as required

	Location	Material. Color. Border. Size. Gauge. etc.	Height	Height at Tub	Height at Shower
Wainscot	Bath	ceramic tile, 4", variegated	6'	full	full

Bathroom accessories: ☐ recessed: material _____ ; quantity _____: ☐ attached: material _____: quantity _____

23. PLUMBING:

Fixture	Number	Location	Make	Mfr. Fixture I.D. No.	Size	Color
Sink	1	kitchen	Elkay (double)	EK42-D	42"	stainless
Lavatory	3	Pdr rm/bath	custom		18"	marble
Bathtub	2	1 each bath	custom		5'-0"	gold
Shower over tub*	1	lower bath	custom			gold
Stall shower**	1	mstr bath	custom		3'-0"	custom
Laundry trays	1	utility rm	Elkay	EKLS 3020	30"	stainless
Wet bar	1	family room	Elkay	EKWB-2020	20"	stainless

*☐ Curtain rod:** ☑ Door _____

Water supply: ☑ public: ☐ community system: ☐ individual (private) system ✡

Sewage disposal: ☑ public: ☐ community system: ☐ individual (private) system ✡ _____

✡ *Show and describe individual system in complete detail in separate drawings and specifications*

according to requirements.

House drain (inside): ☐ cast iron: ☐ tile: ☑ ABS: ☐ other _____

House drain (outside): ☐ cast iron: ☐ tile: ☑ ABS: ☐ other _____

Water piping: ☐ galvanized: ☑ copper: ☑ PVC: ☐ other _____ : sill cocks. quantity _____

Domestic water heater: Type _electric_____ : make and model _Ruud SL50_

recovery __10__ gph. 100° rise. Storage tank: material _n/a_____ : capacity _n/a_ gallons

Gas service: ☑ utility company: ☐ liquid petroleum gas (LPG): ☐ other _____ : gas piping: ☐ cooking: ☑ heating

Footing drains connected to: ☑ storm sewer: ☐ sanitary sewer: ☐ dry well: ☐ sump pump _____

24. HEATING:

☐ hot water: ☐ steam: ☐ vapor: ☐ one-pipe system: ☐ two-pipe system

☐ radiators: ☐ convectors: ☐ baseboard radiation. Make and model _____n/a_____

Radiant panel: ☐ floor: ☐ wall: ☐ ceiling. Panel coil: Material ____n/a_____

☐ circulator: ☐ return pump. Make and model ____n/a____ : capacity _____ gpm

Boiler: make and model ____n/a_____ : output _____ Btuh: net rating _____ Btuh

Warm air: ☐ gravity: ☑ forced air. Type of system: _____self-contained_____

Duct material: supply _flexible_ : return _flexible_ : insulation _yes_ : thickness ___": ☐ outside air intake

Furnace: make and model _Lennox #-----_ : input _18000_ Btuh: output _18000_ Btuh

☐ space heater: ☐ floor furnace: ☐ wall heater : input _____ Btuh: output _____ Btuh: number of units _____

Make and model _____n/a_____

FIGURE 8-1 *(continued)*
Description of Materials–Lee Residence

DESCRIPTION OF MATERIALS
(Continued)

Controls: make and type(s) _Honeywell — energy saver — thermostat (manual and automatic)_

Fuel: ☐ coal; ☐ oil; ☒ gas; ☐ liquid petroleum gas (LPG); ☐ electric; ☐ other _____: storage capacity _____

Firing equipment furnished separately: _____ _n/a_

☐ gas burner, conversion type; ☐ stoker; ☐ hopper feed; ☐ bin feed; ☐ oil burner; ☐ pressure atomizing; ☐ vaporizing

Make and model _____ _n/a_ _____: control _____ _n/a_

Electric heating system: type _____ _n/a_ _____: input _____ watts; **0** _____ volts; output _____ Btuh

Ventilating equipment: Attic Fan, make and model: _____: capacity _____ CFM

Kitchen exhaust Fan: make and model _Braun_ _____: capacity _120_ _____ CFM

Other heating, ventilating or cooling equipment _____ _n/a_

25. ELECTRIC WIRING:

Service: ☐ overhead; ☒ underground (lateral) _____

Panel: ☒ fuse box; ☒ circuit breaker _____: number of circuits _____ _30 available_

Wiring: ☒ conduit; ☐ armored cable; ☒ non-metallic cable; ☐ knob and tube; ☐ other _____

Special outlets: ☒ range; ☒ water heater; ☐ other _wall oven_

☐ door bell; ☒ chimes; push-button location _front entry_

26. LIGHTING FIXTURES:

Total number of fixtures _____. Total allowance for fixtures, typical installation _$ 2500.⁰⁰_

·   ·   ·   ·non-typical installation $ _750.⁰⁰_

27. INSULATION:

Location	Thickness	Material, Type and Method of Installation	Vapor Barrier
Roof	2"	Owen/Corning fiberglass — screw/mop	43# underlayment
Ceiling	R-30	batts — 16: and 24" wide as required	n/a
Wall	R-19	batts — 16" exterior; 24" interior	n/a
Floor	R-19	batts — 16" or 24" as required	n/a

28. MISCELLANEOUS:

(Describe any main dwelling materials, equipment, or construction items not shown elsewhere)
Exterior deck — 2x4 self-spaced with matching railing, stairs and stringers — redwood or weather-treated construction grade DF or HF #3.

29. HARDWARE: (make, material and finish) _Schlage — antique brass for all window, door and cabinetry._

v

FIGURE 8–1 *(continued)*
Description of Materials–Lee Residence

DESCRIPTION OF MATERIALS
(Continued)

30. SPECIAL EQUIPMENT:

☑ Built-in range: make _Thermador_ model _#———_

☑ Built-in oven : make _Thermador_ model _#———_

☑ Dishwasher : make _Maytag_ model _#———_

☑ Hood and Fan : make _Thermador_ model _#———_

☐ Drop-in range and oven: make _____ model _____

☑ Garbage disposal unit: make _Kitchen-Aid_ model _#———_

☐ Barbeque : make _____ model _____

☐ Other : make _____ model _____

31. PORCHES:

32. TERRACES:

33. GARAGES:

Attached - 2-car. Drywalled w/5/8" "X" firecode all walls and ceiling

Firewall of same material to be installed at wall adjoining residence

34. WALKS and DRIVEWAYS:

Driveway: width _20'_ : base material _sand_ : thickness _10_ : surfacing material _concrete_ : thickness _4_ .

Front walk: width _3'_ : material _concrete_ : thickness _4_ .

Steps: material _concrete_ : treads _9_ : risers _7_ : cheek walls _____

Service walk: width _____ :material _n/a_ : thickness _____

35. OTHER ON-SITE IMPROVEMENTS:

(Specify all exterior improvements not described elsewhere including items such as unusual grading, drainage structures, retaining walls, fence, railings, and accessory structures.)

12' x 8'-2" retaining wall each side of residence w/16" x 8" concrete footing and

8x8x16 CMU and cap.

36. LANDSCAPING, PLANTING, and FINISH GRADING:

Topsoil _4_ : thick: ☑ front yard: ☑ side yards: ☑ rear yard to _____ feet behind main building _full property_

Lawns: (seeded): ☑ front yard _____ : ☑ side yards _____ : ☑ rear yard _26,563 sq ft (total)_

Date _____   Borrower _____

    Borrower _____

    Builder _____

vi

FIGURE 8–1 (continued)
Description of Materials–Lee Residence

GENERAL NOTES

1. All work shall be in accordance with all national, state and local codes and ordinances. All work shall also be completed in accordance with the best standards of the trade.

2. Owner reserves the right to refuse any and all bids. Bids shall be submitted in lump sum values only.

Alternates, if any, shall be submitted as an add or deduct amount without changing the base bid.

Alternatives will be permitted upon approval 14 days prior to bid date.

Division 2

Demolition, clearing and grubbing shall be done prior to construction. Hazardous materials shall be removed. Existing conduits, pipes, ducts, etc. shall be properly removed and/or capped as required by law.

All earthwork shall be done only after notification from "Call Before You Dig," 1/800-___-___ that all is clear.

All mass excavation earth is to be removed from the site.

Division 3

Concrete shall be 2500 psi. 2-#4 rebar shall be laid horizontally in all footings. 1-#5 rebar dowel shall be placed @ 6'-0" O/C (UNO) for masonry walls. Concrete contractor shall be responsible for concrete steel reinforcement only.

Any formwork required shall be installed by concrete layout carpenter.

Division 4

All masonry shall be be light-weight 8"x8"x16" CMU with necessary accessories for a complete installation.

Masonry contractor shall supply and install all rebar required for masonry.

Mortar and grout shall meet the minimum requirements of 1800 psi for mortar and 2000 psi for grout.

Division 6

All rough framing shall be as per plans. All lumber shall bear the approvals of the various organizations governing wood and wood products.

All materials bearing a specific manufacturer shall be supplied by said manufacturer. Acceptable manufacturer(s) for roof joists and trusses are:
Trus-Joist MacMillan for joists, beams, etc.
Valley Manufacturing for roof trusses.

Finish carpentry shall be as per finish schedule.

Doors and windows shall be supplied by:
Doors - Thomas Door Company
Windows - Andersen Windows, Inc.

All hardware shall be Schlage.

Division 7

Below-grade moisture protection shall be an elastomeric polymer @ 60 mil dry thickness with a protection board installed prior to backfilling.

Exterior building wrap shall be "Tyvek" by DuPont. To be installed over framing and sheathing prior to exterior siding installation.

Insulation shall be as follows:
R-19 batt for exterior walls
R-11 batt for under floors and in ceilings
R-30 batt in attic spaces
R-30 rigid roof insulation (if required)

Roofing shall be 1-piece clay "S" tile as manufactured by _____.

Division 9

All finishes shall be as per finish schedule. Colors and styles are to be confirmed by owner.

All work is to be performed in accordance with plans, finish schedule and these specifications.

Division 15 and 16

All work to be accomplished per plans and schematics.

Plumbing fixtures by American Standard, or equal.

HVAC equipment to be Lennox, or equal.

Electrical fixtures selected by owner.

Architectural dimensions on drawings take precedence over all other dimensions.

DO NOT SCALE DRAWINGS

Christle and Associates
Architects and Engineers

Owner J & M Lee	Drawn by JF
Project Residence	Checked by JdM
Date 1/27/96	Rev

SCALE No Scale   SHEET 1

FIGURE 8–2
Typical General Notes Plan Sheet

SCHEDULES

See figures 8–3, 8–4, and 8–5, Finish, Door, and Window Schedules for the Lee Residence. Schedules, like abbreviations, symbols, and keynotes, are used to assist in detailing information of importance without cluttering the plans. Schedules may also be noted in any Specifications or General Notes. The schedules

Room	Floors				Walls			Ceilings			Remarks
	Exposed Concrete	Tile	Carpet	Base	GWB 1/2	GWB 5/8	Wall Finish	GWB 1/2	GWB 5/8	Paint	Acoustical Treatment	
Dining Room			+	2	+		3	+			+	Vaulted ceiling
Kitchen		+		1	+		2	+		+		Ceiling 7'-0" A.F.F. Paint to match walls
Mstr Bedroom			+	2	+		1	+			+	Ceiling 8'-0"
Mstr Bath		+		3	+	4/2		+		+		Ceiling 8'-0" Finish 2 Tile to 6'-0"
Mstr Closet			+	2	+		2	+			+	Ceiling 8'-0"
Living Room			+	2	+		3	+			+	Vaulted ceiling
Den			+	2	⊠ ⊠		5	+			+	Install book shelves w/ paneling. Ceiling 8'-0"
Foyer		+		3	⊠ ⊠		2	+			+	Vaulted ceiling
Pwdr Rm/Clo			+	3	+	1/3		+		+		Ceiling 8'-0" Finish 2
Family Room			+	2	+		3	+			+	Ceiling 8'-0"
Bedroom #1			+	2	+		1	+			+	Ceiling 8'-0"
Bdrm #1 Clo			+	2	+		1	+			+	Ceiling 8'-0"
Bedroom #2			+	2	+		1	+			+	Ceiling 8'-0"
Bdrm #2 Clo			+	2	+		1	+			+	Ceiling 8'-0"
Bath #2		+		3	+	4/2		+		+		see note Master Bath
Utility Room	+			4	+		2	+		+		Ceiling 8'-0" Finish 2
Hall		+		3	+		3	+			+	Ceiling 8'-0"
Garage	+			3	⊠ ⊠		3		+	+		Ceiling 9'-0" Match wall finish

FIGURE 8–3
Finish Schedule–Lee Residence

FINISH NOTES:

BASE:

1. 4" oak – match cabinets
2. 2" "Slimline", oak veneer
3. Coved tile – match floor and wall tiles
4. 4" rubber cove base – brown

WALLS:

1. Wallpaper
2. Semi-gloss latex paint
3. Flat latex paint
4. 4" ceramic tile
5. Wood panel, light oak, full height

CEILINGS:

As noted. match paint

NOTE:

All materials selected by owner

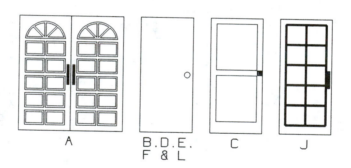

A   B.D.E. F & L   C   J

MARK	SIZE	DESCRIPTION	REMARKS
A	pr 3'-0"x6'-8"	1¾" panel stained	w/½ moon lites. custom
B	3'-0"x6'-8"	1¾" flush s/c paint	w/self closer
C	3'-0"x6'-8"	1⅜" pocket panel stained	
D	2'-6"x6'-8"	1⅜" flush h/c paint	stained @ powder room
E	2'-0"x6'-8"	1⅜" flush h/c stained	
F	3'-0"x6'-8"	1⅜" flush h/c paint	stained @ Mstr bedroom
G	4'-0"x6'-8"	Bi-pass closet w/mirror	
H	6'-0"x6'-8"	Wood frame sliding glass	custom design
J	3'-0"x6'-8"	Wood 10 lite patio	custom design
K	16'-0"x7'-8"	Wood garage door w/opener	custom design
L	2'-6"x6'-8"	1¾" panel stained	

FIGURE 8–4
Door Schedule

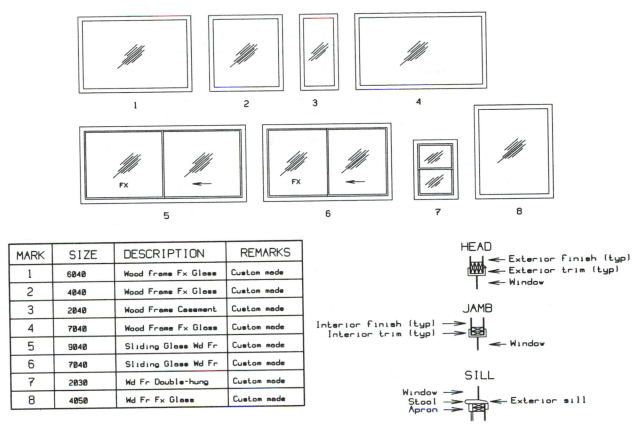

MARK	SIZE	DESCRIPTION	REMARKS
1	6040	Wood frame Fx Glass	Custom made
2	4040	Wood Frame Fx Glass	Custom made
3	2040	Wood Frame Casement	Custom made
4	7040	Wood Frame Fx Glass	Custom made
5	9040	Sliding Glass Wd Fr	Custom made
6	7040	Sliding Glass Wd Fr	Custom made
7	2030	Wd Fr Double-hung	Custom made
8	4050	Wd Fr Fx Glass	Custom made

FIGURE 8–5
Window Schedule

for doors, windows, and finishes (see chapter 5) are examples of the types of schedules typically found in a set of plans. Other schedules, such as for identifying the plumbing and electrical fixtures, may also be located on plans or in the Specifications. One or more schedules may be included for each of the six major plan groups as follows:

1. Civil schedules may include:
   a. Types of earth required for the areas of excavation or grading
   b. Grade elevations

2. Architectural schedules may include:
   a. Door and window schedules
      (1) Identifying letters or numbers at the window locations
      (2) Identifying letters or numbers at the door openings
   b. Finish schedule
      (1) Specific materials (GWB, paint, wallpaper) to be used in certain areas

3. Structural schedules may include:
   a. Foundation footing schedule
   b. Reinforcement schedule
   c. Beam, column girders, girts, etc. (commercial/industrial only)
   d. Framing schedules (types and sizes of materials required)

4. Plumbing schedules may include:
   a. Fixture schedule

5. Mechanical schedules may include:
   a. Equipment schedule (HVAC)
   b. Power supply schedule
6. Electrical schedules may include:
   a. Power and lighting schedule
      (1) Entrance panel circuit-breaker placement

The schedules listed above are more likely to be included in commercial plans. The door and window schedules and the finish schedule, along with an electrical fixture schedule, are usually the only schedules included in residential plans.

Refer to the Plot Plan C–1, the Lee Residence. The plot plan for the Lee Residence indicates no curb or gutter at the street. Although not noted, the street has an asphalt surface. All utilities are available along the street, or the right-of-way parallel to the street, outside of the property lines. The distance maintained for the separation of site improvements and on-site construction at the Lee Residence is 5'–0" (1.5 m) on all sides.

SITEWORK

The Lee residence requires excavating and grading to change the location and height of some of the earth on the property. There is also some mass excavation required for the lower level foundation. Special formwork is necessary to hold back the earth and align the foundation and foundation walls for installation of concrete and/or masonry construction. A sufficient quantity of earth is removed for installation of the drain at the walls and maneuvering about the work area. The completed work includes the back-fill necessary upon completion of all other below-grade installations. No landscaping, other than a few trees is specified. This indicates that there is a separate landscape plan or the owner is considering doing his or her own work.

If the utilities terminate some distance away from the project, the utility extensions from the termination to a location near the property are installed at the owner's expense. Any additional repairs to the street resulting from the extensions are also at the owner's expense.

The edge of the street nearest the Lee Residence is 10'–0" (3.05 m) from the property line. This area is for future sidewalks, curbs, and gutters not required at this time. The street is 26'–0" (7.92 m) wide. The plumber and electrician must make the taps at the street, trench and lay the necessary materials, install the metering, and so on, for installation into the residence. This work is all covered in the off-site work. Any repairs necessary to the street are included in the contract for the off-sites. All of the work at the street (metering, etc.) must be per local codes and utility requirements or under the jurisdiction of the area or national building codes. Specifications, schedules, and/or plans must also note the type of materials to be used.

Plumbing

Refer to Plan P–1, the Lee Residence. The plumbing includes all pipe (galvanized iron, copper, or plastic ABS) with the respective connections, accessories, and fixtures necessary to dispose of all liquid waste, and the installation of fuel lines (gas). The sewer location, if too low for the sewer main, must have a sump pump added to force the waste disposal from the residence to the main.

The sewer main is 8 feet (2.44 m) below the street surface. The lowest point at the Lee Residence is approximately 4 feet (1.22 m) higher; therefore, no pump is required. The location of the water and sewer mains, the taps, trenching, installation of lines to the structure, back-filling and any metering devices necessary are all a part of the off-site plumbing installation. The gas utility company is responsible for the installation to the gas meter, usually located immediately adjacent to a structure. The plumber may be required to install the service but does not make the taps or meter installation. The plot plan indicates supply from the street to the Lee Residence for water, sewer, and gas connections to the west side of the residence, entering or exiting at the utility room.

Piping

Refer to Plan P-2, the Lee Residence. The piping includes all pipe (galvanized iron, copper, or PVC) with the respective connections, accessories, and fixtures necessary to install the water supply lines. Galvanized iron pipe may still be in use in some areas, but copper and plastic pipes are most commonly used today because of their ability to withstand corrosion and reduce health hazards.

Electricity

Refer to C–2, Plot Plan, the Lee Residence. Electricity for the Lee Residence must extend laterally from the transformer supply on the south side of the street, under the street and into the property, to a convenient location for the service entrance. The plot plan indicates the electric service entrance is located on the southwest side of the garage. All site-improvement and off-site work must be included for the completion of the service. This includes street repair, trenching, conduit, and wire installation.

STRUCTURAL FOUNDATION PLANS

See Sheets S–1, Lower Level, and S–2, Main Level. Both the masonry foundation wall, with the concrete footing, and the monolithic slab construction are required for the lower-level foundation and patio slabs. A short masonry stem wall and footing is used along the north wall of the lower level and around the unexcavated areas (main level) on the south, east, and west sides with a slab-on-grade over these walls. The footing is expanded for the fireplace area at both the lower and main levels and for the stairwell at the lower level. An additional footing is noted along the depressed slab at the living room and for the garage separation wall. These footings are known as *thickened slab footings*. They are an additional 4" (10.16 cm) deep and 1'-0" (30.48 cm) wide. All slabs are 4" (10.16 cm) thick except the garage. The garage has a 6" (15.24 cm) high concrete curb on three sides. The slab starts at 6" (15.24 cm) thick at the north end (adjacent to the residence) and slopes 2" (5.08 cm) southward to a thickness of 4" (10.16 cm) at the garage entrance. The footing and foundation wall at the entrance may be replaced by a grade beam, if necessary. A grade beam is an enlarged footing separate from the slab with additional reinforcement and underpinning. This would only be necessary where soil and/or structure conditions may warrant such a change.

The walls on three sides (south, east, and west) of the lower level are constructed of 8" (20.32 cm) CMU a full 8'-0" (2.44 m) above finish floor (A.F.F.).

The walls are also constructed around three sides of the stairwell and the fireplace. Because the walls are below grade and are supporting the structure above, they are solid grouted. As previously mentioned, these walls may be solid concrete in lieu of the masonry.

MOISTURE PROTECTION

The foundation wall is protected from moisture penetration by a cementitious polymer with a protection board. This protection is to be applied to the structure masonry walls as well as the retaining walls extending to the east and west from the sides of the residence. The installation procedure is referred to as **parging** where the material is troweled onto the walls to a thickness of approximately 60 mils. A perforated, sloped tile drain is installed parallel to the dwelling walls through each retaining wall and beyond the patio slab to assist in drainage away from the dwelling.

FRAMING

Refer to both the Architectural and Structural Plans for the Lee Residence. The structural framing includes the upper-level floor structure, the north exterior wall on the lower level, all walls on the main and upper levels, two chimney stacks, and the roof structure.

The exterior walls for the lower level are framed with 2 × 6 (5.08 cm × 15.24 cm) PTMS sill plate on the north wall at slab level, and the south, east, and west walls of the main level and the garage. A 2 × 8 (5.08 cm × 20.32 cm) sill plate is installed on the masonry walls. The bottom of the upper-level floor joist is a nominal 8′–2″ (2.49 m) A.F.F. due to the height of the masonry walls (8′–0″ [2.44 m] above the lower-level slab). The exterior framing includes 2 × 6 (5.08 cm × 15.24 cm) studs with double top plate. The studs may be 92½″ (2.35 m) with three top plates instead of the normal double top plate. Another method of installation of the wall framing is to use 10′ (3.05 m) studs cut to the proper height using the double top plate.

On the east and west exterior walls, 2 × 6 (5.08 cm × 15.24 cm) balloon-framing is installed to accommodate the vaulted and/or cathedral ceilings. The interior bearing walls are also 2 × 6 (5.08 cm × 15.24 cm) balloon-framed (see floor plan and sections). All partition walls on the lower level are also 8′–2″ (2.49 m). All main-level and upper-level partitions are 8′–1″ (2.46 m) U.N.O. The fireplaces and the flue stacks are framed with 2 × 4 (5.08 cm × 10.24 cm) and 2 × 6 (5.08 cm × 15.24 cm) lumber, as shown on the plans or as required by local codes and ordinances.

The main roof structure is constructed with three variations of scissors trusses that give the exterior roof slope and provide for the interior vaulted and cathedral ceilings. The trusses are manufactured with a 2 × 8 (5.08 cm × 20.32 cm) top chord and 2 × 6 (5.08 cm × 15.24 cm) bottom chord. The structural garage roof may be constructed using conventional framing or gable trusses. The end trusses at the east and west exterior walls and the extended wall between the kitchen and dining room along the upper patio (balcony) are all gable-end trusses.

The Finish Schedule indicates the rooms that are to be trimmed with wood and the location of wood paneling to be installed. The keynotes on the floor plan and/or section(s) also indicate wood stairwells and railings, balusters, and newel posts. The door and window schedules identify the type and location of each item to be installed in the residence. The column identified as *Mark* gives a number or letter corresponding with identifying marks within a circle, square, or triangle located on the floor plan, which indicates the location of that particular style of door or window. One geometric symbol is used for the doors and another for the windows. The doors and windows may be identified with a manufacturer's numbering system.

See figure 8–6. The frame wall structure uses a Tyvek® plastic wrapper, a product developed for use in the same manner as building paper, which is applied over the framing or sheathing (if used) prior to the installation of siding. This material is considered moisture protection because it will allow moisture changes to escape to the outside but will not allow moisture to penetrate inward.

The exterior walls have R–19 fiberglass batt insulation installed between studs from foundation to roof structure. The floor and ceiling joists are to have R–30 fiberglass roll insulation. Rigid fiberglass insulation, 1½″ (3.81 cm) thick, is installed over structural roof and sheathing. The roofing material to be installed over the insulation is a one-piece, clay S tile over a 43 lb (19.55 kg) asphalt felt underlayment.

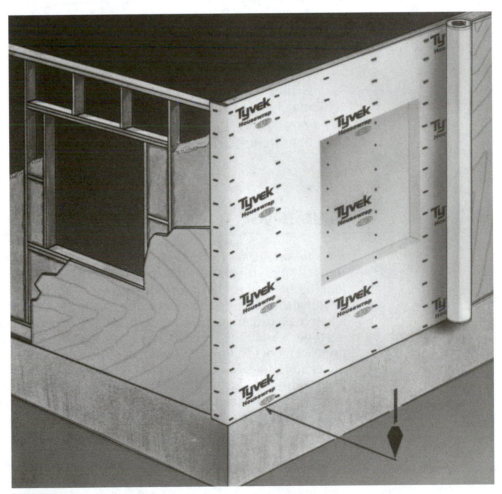

FIGURE 8–6
Tyvek® Housewrap, Lee Residence. Permission of DuPont, Tyvek Housewrap.

Refer to the General Notes, Architectural Plans, and the Finish Schedule. The Finish Schedule supplies information regarding the materials required to finish each room in the house at all levels. In addition, the General Notes specify information that may not be indicated in the schedule. The primary notation on these notes to be aware of is any statement referring to "all local codes and ordinances," "standards of the trade," and "to supply a complete installation." These statements infer that any information not specifically stated are to be included as part of the contract requirements. The Finish Schedule is divided into three areas:

1. Floor and base section, identifying the material(s) to be installed on the floor and at the base of the walls.
2. Walls section, identifying the drywall types, painting, and wall coverings
3. Ceilings section, identifying ceiling heights and the finishes to be installed on them (if any)

For example, per the Finish Schedule, the kitchen finish requirements are as follows:

Floor: Quarry tile for floor to be selected by owner

Base: 4" (10.2 cm) wood base to match color of cabinets

Walls: All exposed walls to be covered with wood paneling to be selected by owner except at breakfast nook area; breakfast nook walls to be padded to match seat coverings (kitchen side only)

Ceiling: Off-white semi-gloss latex paint inside light fixture recess with matching color for exposed ceiling areas

Remarks: Ceiling height to be 7'–0" (2.1 m) A.F.F. except at recess for light fixture; recess to be 7'–6" (2.3 m) A.F.F.

PLUMBING

Refer to the Architectural Plans. The plumber uses the floor plan fixture locations along with the isometric drawings to determine the types, sizes, and lengths of material necessary for the water and waste system installations. Reading the blueprint using both the floor plans and the isometrics allows for a better picture of items and locations. The isometric plumbing drawing, for example, shows the complete waste disposal system including all off-site, site improvement, and on-site parts from the farthest fixture location in the residence to the sewer main. The isometric drawing further shows the three floor levels. Pipe sizes are indicated for the plumbing contractor. The fixtures are excluded from the diagram but the location is noted on the floor plans and the General Notes specify the fixtures and fixture manufacturer. The piping isometric offers the same comparisons with the floor plans. The location of each fixture is noted and can be identified on the floor plans. The hot and cold water lines, with sizes, are also given on the drawing.

To further assist in identifying materials and locations, interior elevations (details), such as the master bathroom elevations in figure 8–3, are provided so that the plumbing contractor can coordinate the work with a cabinet installer.

Wherever plumbing, piping, and cabinetry are associated, an interior elevation is drawn. By identifying the type of cabinet and the location of the fixture, and by making use of the isometric drawings, the piping and plumbing can be properly located to prevent conflict with the cabinet installation.

HVAC

See the HVAC plans for the Lee Residence. The plans indicate a heating unit (furnace) in the utility room. The specifications in the General Notes indicate that the unit is a combination heating/cooling system with a built-in humidifier and a separate compressor unit for cooling located on the outside of the wall next to the utility room. The ductwork for the upper level is located in the trusses or soffitted ceilings. Duct and air-supply registers are located in a soffit in the master bath, in the master bedroom walls, in the master closet ceiling, the kitchen ceiling, and on the wall of the dining room on the upper level. The ducts and supply registers for the main level are located in the den and powder room ceilings. The living room is supplied through underfloor ducts embedded in, or beneath, the main floor slab with the registers exposed at the step-down from the foyer into the living room. The lower level is supplied from ductwork in the floor joists or in soffits above (ceilings) with the registers located in the walls of bedrooms #2 and #3, bath #2 ceiling, the hall ceiling, and the family room wall. The cubic feet per minute (CFM) is noted at each supply air register. The quantity of air required for each room is calculated by a mechanical engineer. These calculations aid in determining the size of duct and supply register required for each location.

One return air duct with return register is located in the floor of the entry hall to the master bedroom and one return register is located in the base of the partition wall separating the hall from the utility room at the air plenum on the lower level. The stairwell into the lower level is a satisfactory return for the air from the dining room and main levels and none is required for the lower level for the same reason. The furnace has an air plenum at the floor level to handle the main supply and return air intake. All return air is mixed with the air entering this plenum. The unit is self contained with the exception of the air-conditioning compressor. All of the controls are built into the main unit. The thermostat is both manually and automatically controlled.

ELECTRICAL

See the Electrical plans for the Lee Residence. As previously mentioned, electrical on-site blueprints include information on indoor lighting and power equipment from the entry switchgear (service entrance) to the light switches, receptacles, fixtures, and electrical appliances. All of the electrical layout may be identified on the architectural floor plan. Electrical schedules may or may not be found on residential plans. It is preferable to include them since they indicate any special equipment or lighting fixtures to be used in the installation. The electrical contractor may be required to determine the load calculations to ascertain the proper equipment necessary for the dwelling.

The service entrance equipment for the Lee Residence includes a panel enclosing the circuit breakers necessary for disconnecting the various branch circuits within the residence. The service entrance panel is a one-hundred twenty/two-hundred forty volt, alternating current (120/240VAC), two-hundred ampere (200A), service supplied by a 1/0 AWG USE (underground service, electrical—an NEC classification) lateral service feeder from the transformer. The circuits from the service entrance to the convenience outlets and switches are referred to as branch circuits. The power and lighting plan identifies which circuit is to be connected to what circuit breaker. This is determined from the load calculations mentioned above. The branch circuits may be directly supplied from the service entrance panel or they may be operated through a sub-panel. A sub-panel is one connected to the load side of the service entrance panel. The load side of the service entrance panel is any part of the panel supplied from the interior electrical bus (bars to which the circuit breakers [CB] are connected) *after* the main (200A) breaker. The load side of a CB is the one to which the wires are connected for the individual branch circuits.

The sub-panel may be used for convenience of location for energizing or de-energizing a circuit or, in the more modern concept, a Smart House service may be installed. A Smart House is a computerized or automatic electronic control used for controlling the circuits. A computerized system may operate complete areas of power and lighting by just touching the monitor screen identifying the area desired. An electronically controlled service can operate in the same manner by touching switches in the panel. The systems may use reduced voltages (from 120VAC to 24VAC) at the control points or switches. The reduced voltage operates electronic devices, which, in turn, close the normal 120VAC power and lighting circuits.

CHAPTER EXERCISES

Completion

1. The Lee Residence exterior walls are constructed with _____" studs.

2. The east and west exterior walls are _____ frame construction.

3. The lower-level framing may require _____ lf studs cut to fit.

4. Interior partition (non-bearing) studs are _____".

5. A minimum 6 × 6 or equivalent _____ is required over all bearing-wall openings.

6. The roof structure is a _____ system.

7. The sub-flooring to be installed at the upper level may be installed with 1" (2.5 cm) OSB or _____" CDX plywood.

8. There are _____ risers on the stairs connecting the lower level and the main level.

9. The maximum allowable span of the floor joists before blocking is necessary is _____.

10. The structural member required for closing the joist ends is referred to as a _____ joist.

11. The roof structure over the garage is identified as _____ framing.

12. The _____ contractor is responsible for all trim work.

13. Window type "Mark 4" is a _____.

14. Door "Mark _____" is a 3'–0" × 6'–8" (0.9 m × 2.0 m) door with 10 lites.

15. The lower-level hall walls are to be _____.

16. The family room ceiling is _____ A.F.F.

17. The dining room, living room, and foyer have a(n) _____ ceiling.

18. The garage requires ⅝" X GWB on the ceiling and the _____ wall.

19. The kitchen, bathrooms, and utility room are to have a(n) _____ paint applied as required.

20. The tile in the bathrooms is to be installed to _____ A.F.F.

21. The _____ selects all finish materials.

22. The den is to have paneling and _____ installed full height.

23. All interior wood trim and cabinets are to have a(n) _____ finish.

24. A _____ terra cotta or plastic pipe is often added below grade to assist in drainage.

25. A retaining wall is installed wherever there is a major change in grade _____.

26. The plastic membrane used for protection on the exterior frame walls is called _____.

27. The interior walls of the bedrooms require R–11 insulation for _____ attenuation purposes.

28. The ceilings of the bedrooms all have _____ batt or roll insulation installed for thermal protection.

29. The roof insulation is a 1½" (3.8 cm) rigid _____ insulation.

30. The dwelling masonry walls are insulated with a(n) _____ system.

31. A(n) _____ underlayment is installed over the ½" (1.3 cm) CDX plywood roof sheathing and rigid insulation for moisture protection.

32. The nails used to install the tile roofing are referred to as "_____" nails.

33. A(n) _____ system is preferred over the use of battens and nails for tile roofing.

34. The tile roofing is a(n) _____ clay tile.

35. There are _____ installed at the first course of the tile roofing to aid in the proper alignment of the tiles.

36. The tiles used for the gable ends are called _____ tiles.

37. There is a _____ installed along the ridge to allow for the passage of air from the attic spaces under the roof structure.

38. The tiles used for installation along the ridges and hips of a roof are called _____ .

39. The door schedule may include information regarding the _____ as well as the length and width of the door.

40. Window schedules usually give details on the head, _____, and sill of a window.

41. The windows identified in the window schedule are _____.

42. The specifications for the living room carpet are found on the _____ Schedule.

43. The window on the west side elevation at the _____ is a combination casement and fixed glass.

44. The entry door is a pair of 3′–0″ × 6′–8″ _____ doors.

45. The door to the patio is identified as a(n) _____ door.

46. All interior passage doors are 3′–0″ × 6′–8″, 1³/₈″, _____ doors.

47. The plot plan of the Lee Residence indicates that there are _____ trees to be planted or remain.

48. The Lee Residence plot plan indicates that there are two _____ walls, one on each side of the residence.

49. The steep slope on each side of the Lee Residence is _____ feet high.

50. The northeast property line is _____ lineal feet in length.

51. The Lee Residence has setbacks of 20′–0″ (6.1 m) and _____.

52. Mary Street has a(n) _____ surface.

53. The finish floor elevation for the lower level of the Lee Residence is _____ feet above mean sea level.

54. The lowest finish elevation above mean sea level on the Lee Residence plot plan is _____.

55. The highest finish elevation on the Lee Residence plot plan is _____ above mean sea level.

56. A _____ excavation is required to construct the lower level of the Lee Residence.

57. There is no _____ for utilities within the property lines.

58. All site improvement plumbing work is to be installed on the _____ side of the Lee Residence.

59. A _____ line is installed for the purpose of removing waste.

60. The _____ service entrance equipment is placed as conveniently near the location of the power supply as possible.

61. The plumbing plans are referred to as _____ drawings.

62. Much of the information necessary to electrical installations is found in _____ included as part of the electrical plans.

63. All utility services are located along _____.

64. The utility farthest from the Lee Residence is _____ service.

65. The metes and bounds describe the _____ of a property.

Multiple Choice

1. Structural plastics include:
   a. Skylights and vinyl plastic doors.
   b. Counter tops and decorative screen walls.
   c. Arabesques and window lites.
   d. None of the above.

2. The garage roof is classed as a:
   a. Hip roof.
   b. Mansard roof.
   c. Flat built-up roof (BUR).
   d. Gable roof.

3. The concrete footings supporting the masonry walls and structural slabs are:
   a. Lightweight concrete.
   b. Non-structural concrete.
   c. 1′–6″ × 8″ (0.46 m × 20.32 cm) monolithic footings.
   d. 2′–0″ × 1′–0″ (0.61 m × 0.31 m) with a minimum of 2–#4 rebar.

4. The top of the masonry walls:
   a. Are 8 × 8 × 16 (20.32 cm × 20.32 cm × 40.64 cm) CMU with fill insulation.
   b. Require a 2 × 8 (5.08 cm × 20.32 cm) sill plate.
   c. Are exposed when construction is completed.
   d. Require a 2 × 8 (5.08 cm × 20.32 cm) sole plate.

5. Regarding the upper level floor joists:
   a. Are 2 × 10 (5.08 cm × 25.40 cm) DF #2 or better.
   b. The bottom of the joists are 8′–2″ (2.49 m) A.F.F.
   c. Neither a nor b.
   d. Both a and b.

6. All partition (non-bearing) walls are:
   a. 8′–1″ (2.46 m) A.F.F.
   b. Constructed from DF common or HF utility stock.
   c. Require a sole plate and double plate at all walls.
   d. None of the above.

7. The exterior walls are:
   a. Framed with 2 × 6 (5.08 cm × 15.24 cm) DF construction grade lumber.
   b. Are all 8′–1″ (2.46 m) A.F.F.
   c. Require no fireblocking (firestopping).
   d. None of the above.

8. Regarding the roof trusses:
   a. There are three truss designs.
   b. There are additional gable-end trusses required.
   c. They are called scissor trusses because of their design.
   d. All of the above.

9. The garage roof is:
   a. Conventional framing.
   b. A gable roof structure.
   c. A flat roof.
   d. Made from 2 × 4 (5.08 cm × 10.16 cm) DF common stock.

10. The main entry door is:
    a. Metal-clad wood.
    b. A panel door with "half-moon" lites.
    c. Two 3'–0" × 6'–8" (0.91 m × 2.03 m) doors.
    d. All of the above.

11. The windows are:
    a. All custom made.
    b. All metal frame.
    c. Neither a nor b.
    d. Both a and b.

12. The trim used throughout the house is:
    a. Pine.
    b. Walnut.
    c. Oak.
    d. Imitation wood veneer.

13. The door and window trim:
    a. Match the baseboard.
    b. Is customized and packaged with the doors and windows.
    c. Is not a part of the door and window package.
    d. Is pre-stained.

14. The exterior trim:
    a. Matches the interior trim.
    b. Has a rough-sawn (R/S) finish.
    c. Is installed before the exterior siding.
    d. Is smooth-finished and painted.

15. Exterior trim includes:
    a. All window and door trim and fascia board.
    b. Door trim only.
    c. Window trim only.
    d. Fascia board only.

16. The wall construction category(ies) that best describe(s) the Lee Residence include(s):
    a. Post and beam, and balloon frame.
    b. Platform and balloon frame.
    c. Post and beam, and platform frame.
    d. Platform frame only.

17. The chimney stacks are:
    a. Wood frame.
    b. Masonry construction.
    c. A combination of masonry and wood frame.
    d. Installed over a 4'-0" (1.22 m) deep mat footing.

18. The exterior finish is:
    a. CMU and ship-lap wood siding.
    b. Concrete plaster and exposed CMU.

c. Brick veneer, exposed CMU and metal siding.
d. All brick veneer.

19. The sheathing for both the siding and the roof underlayments:
    a. Are ³/₈″ (0.95 cm) Masonite panels.
    b. Are either ⁵/₈″ (1.59 cm) OSB or ¹/₂″ (1.27 cm) CDX.
    c. Include ³/₈″ (0.95 cm) CDX shear panels over the sheathing.
    d. Are used with 34lb (15.45 kg) building paper.

20. The underlayment for the exterior walls is:
    a. 25lb (11.36 kg) building paper.
    b. Tyvek® plastic wrap.
    c. 7lb (3.18 kg) building paper.
    d. 20 mil Visqueen® polyethylene sheet.

21. A drain pipe used at the retaining walls for drainage:
    a. Is a solid cast-iron pipe.
    b. Is sloped from one end to the other.
    c. Is installed prior to the moisture protection.
    d. Is a perforated clay pipe sloped from center to end each way.

22. The masonry walls are:
    a. Installed immediately prior to the installation of the moisture protection.
    b. To have an asphaltic moisture protection where required.
    c. To have a cementitious moisture protection coating where required.
    d. Left without protection on the free-standing retaining walls.

23. The frame wall moisture protection in Question 3:
    a. Extends to the bottom of the roof structure.
    b. Extends only to the bottom of the gable-end truss.
    c. Is applied over the masonry walls as well.
    d. None of the above.

24. Insulation for the exterior framed walls includes:
    a. A blown material such as rockwool.
    b. 16″ (40.64 cm) wide batts or rolls.
    c. 24″ (60.96 cm) wide batts or rolls.
    d. Foam insulation.

25. The insulation for the roof is:
    a. Foil-backed batt insulation on the underside of the roof structure.
    b. 1¹/₂″ (3.81 cm) composite board rigid insulation.
    c. 1¹/₂″ (3.81 cm) coated rigid fiberglass insulation.
    d. The air space between the roofing material and the roof deck.

26. The roofing is:
    a. A one-piece S tile application.
    b. A wood shake roofing material.
    c. Asphalt composition shingles.
    d. A panelized metal roof system.

27. All roof penetrations shall include:
    a. No protection.
    b. Galvanized iron or aluminum flashings.
    c. Galvanized iron or aluminum flashings with collar.
    d. None of the above.

28. The roof slope is:
    a. 4:12 and 8:12.
    b. 8:12 and 10:12.
    c. 3:12 and 5:12.
    d. 4:12 and 6.5:12.

29. The roofing materials are installed over:
    a. ³/₄″ (1.91 cm) CCX plywood.
    b. 1″ (2.54 cm) OSB.
    c. ³/₈″ (0.95 cm) CDX plywood.
    d. ¹/₂″ (1.27 cm) CDX plywood.

30. The specifications for concrete state that:
    a. All concrete shall be smooth finish.
    b. The driveway is 6″ (15.24 cm) thick concrete.
    c. The living room slab is recessed 4″ (10.16 cm).
    d. The patio slab is 2″ (5.08 cm) thick.

31. The entry stoop:
    a. Is 21″ (53.34 cm) higher than the sidewalk approach to it.
    b. Is squared flush with the living room wall.
    c. Is level with the living room floor.
    d. Contains "flyash" for a hardener additive.

32. The exterior finish:
    a. Is all wood siding.
    b. Has exposed and painted concrete walls.
    c. Includes a wood deck and stairs finished with weather-resistant stain.
    d. All of the above.

33. The exterior doors are:
    a. To be vinyl or metal clad wood prepainted or stained.
    b. 1³/₈″ (3.49 cm) thick.
    c. All panel doors.
    d. Have no lites.

34. The service entry equipment:
    a. Is supplied with three #1/0 wires.
    b. Includes a place for the meter.
    c. Has a sub-panel on the interior side of the garage wall.
    d. All of the above.

35. The water meter is located:
    a. Inside the garage at the side entry door.
    b. In the utility room.
    c. On the face of the east retaining wall.
    d. None of the above.

36. The gas meter is placed:
    a. Outside the wall of the utility room.
    b. Is installed by the plumber.
    c. In the garage.
    d. Next to the retaining wall on the east side.

37. The material specified for the framing:
    a. Is all cedar wood.
    b. Is Douglas or Hemlock Fir, as noted.

  c. Is all fire-treated lumber.
  d. Both b and c.

38. The roofing material:
  a. Is to be manufactured by Life-Tile.
  b. Is specified as a one-piece S tile.
  c. Is specified as a concrete Monier Tile.
  d. Is a concrete shake tile.

39. All electrical convenience outlets are to contain:
  a. A split-wired receptacle.
  b. A #14AWG THNN wire from the power supply.
  c. A duplex receptacle manufactured by Hubbell, or equal.
  d. None of the above.

40. The finish grade elevation at the POB is:
  a. 675.74 m.
  b. 2212.25'.
  c. 674.3 m.
  d. 2213.0'.

41. The height of the slope at the retaining walls is:
  a. 20'–0".
  b. 7'–0".
  c. 12'–0".
  d. 4'–0".

42. Mary Street is parallel to the:
  a. north property line.
  b. The northwest property line.
  c. The southeast property line.
  d. The south property line.

43. There are two:
  a. Sewer lines shown.
  b. Street lamps indicated.
  c. Fire hydrants located on the plan.
  d. None of the above.

44. The off-site electrical service:
  a. Is a lateral service.
  b. Is parallel to the south side of Mary Street.
  c. Both a and b.
  d. Neither a nor b.

45. The landscaping indicates:
  a. The ground cover is all clover grass.
  b. There are fifteen trees on the property.
  c. There is a hedge along the front side of the dwelling.
  d. The contours are gradual throughout the property.

46. The structure set-backs are:
  a. 20'–0" (6.1 m) from the south property line and 30'–0" (9.14 m) from the southeast property line.
  b. 20'–0" (6.1 m) from the south property line and 20'–0" (6.1 m) from the southwest property line.
  c. No set-backs are indicated.
  d. Plotted from the northwest and northeast property lines.

47. The patio at the lower level is:
    a. A combination of masonry stem wall and concrete slab.
    b. A monolithic slab construction.
    c. Has a 6″ (15.24 cm) concrete slab.
    d. None of the above.

48. All concrete used for the Lee Residence is:
    a. Structural concrete.
    b. Reinforced with WWF throughout.
    c. 4″ (5.08 cm) thick throughout.
    d. A high-early concrete mix.

49. The interior footings at the main level are:
    a. Located wherever a depressed slab construction occurs.
    b. Referred to as *thickened slabs*.
    c. Both a and b above.
    d. Neither a or b above.

50. The foundation and structural walls in the Lee Residence:
    a. Are of concrete construction.
    b. Are 10″ (25.4 cm) thick.
    c. May be changed from masonry to concrete at the discretion of the owner.
    d. None of the above.

51. As shown on the plans for the Lee Residence all masonry walls are:
    a. Double wythe.
    b. Reinforced with horizontal reinforcement at 24″ (0.61 m) O/C.
    c. Grouted only in reinforced cells.
    d. 8″ (20.32 cm) CMU.

52. The thickened slab separating the foyer and the living room is:
    a. 9.4 m long × 60.9 cm wide × 20.3 cm deep.
    b. 16′–0″ long × 2′–0″ wide × 4″ deep.
    c. 4.11 m long × 0.3 m wide by 10.2 cm deep.
    d. 19′–0″ long × 1′–0″ wide × 4″ deep.

53. The total stair riser height at the entry stoop is:
    a. 68.58 cm high.
    b. 22.86 cm high.
    c. 20.32 cm high.
    d. 17.78 cm high.

54. The finish elevation of the living room slab is:
    a. 8′–2″ (2.49 m) above the lower level.
    b. 8′–0″ (2.44 m) above the lower level.
    c. 7′–10″ (2.39 m) above the lower level.
    d. None of the above.

55. The finish floor elevation above sea level for the lower level is:
    a. 2207.0′.
    b. 1380 km.
    c. 2219.5′.
    d. 1381 km.

56. Moisture protection refers to:
    a. Below-grade and on-grade protection.
    b. Sheathing and siding applications.
    c. Roofing applications.
    d. All of the above.

57. All below-grade moisture protection installations should include:
    a. Asphalt or pitch.
    b. Protection board.
    c. Cementitious materials.
    d. All of the above.

58. The Lee Residence moisture protection system is:
    a. Cementitious.
    b. Asphaltic.
    c. Both a and b.
    d. Neither a nor b.

59. An aid in removing moisture from the below-grade walls is:
    a. A perforated drain pipe.
    b. A sump pump.
    c. A copper pipe.
    d. All of the above.

60. The two retaining walls extending perpendicular to the east and west walls are:
    a. 12'–0" (3.7 m) long.
    b. To be moisture protected.
    c. As high as the masonry walls of the lower level.
    d. All of the above.

61. The order in which the water supply system is installed from the street to the structure is:
    a. Main tap, corporate cock, meter cock, main valve, and meter.
    b. Main tap, corporate cock, meter, curb cock, and main valve.
    c. Main tap, corporate cock, meter valve, and main valve.
    d. Either b or c.

62. The electrician is responsible for all off-site and site improvement work including:
    a. Inspection of the installation.
    b. Installation of the power supply at the utility service.
    c. Back-filling all trenching regardless of trade.
    d. From the power tap to and including the service entrance equipment.

63. The power tap for the service is located:
    a. On the south side of Mary Street.
    b. On a pole along the property line.
    c. With a street-lighting circuit.
    d. None of the above.

64. The service entrance equipment has a capacity of:
    a. 250A.
    b. 200A.
    c. 100A.
    d. 150A.

65. There is a necessity for cooperation between the electrical contractor and:
    a. The plumbing contractor.
    b. The roofing contractor.
    c. The HVAC contractor.
    d. None of the above.

True or False

T F   1. The Tyvek® wrap is used for a roofing underlayment.

T F   2. Batt insulation is available in 16″ and 24″ (40.64 cm and 60.96 cm) wide sheets or rolls.

T F   3. Rigid insulation may be made from vermiculite or perlite mixed with cement.

T F   4. Depending upon the type of insulation, the material may be obtained in bags to be blown into wall cavities and ceiling (attic) spaces.

T F   5. Roof systems may include only composition shingle or tile.

T F   6. Tile systems include an asphaltic or pitch felt underlayment.

T F   7. Metal roofing systems may be applied to roofs.

T F   8. The roofing for the Lee Residence is a concrete tile over a 43lb (19.54 kg) underlayment.

T F   9. The exterior walls are insulated with fiberglass batts or rolls rated at an R–19.

T F 10. The exterior walls are the only walls to receive insulation.

T F 11. The floor and ceiling are to contain R–19 insulation between the joists.

T F 12. The specifications for the Lee Residence include insulation placed between the trusses.

T F 13. The roof insulation is to be installed prior to the sheathing.

T F 14. The tile is a one-piece clay S tile.

T F 15. The moisture and thermal wrapper used on the Lee Residence is a 7# (3.18 kg) asphalt building paper applied under the siding.

T F 16. Some specifications for the Lee Residence may be included in the keynotes.

T F 17. The utility companies install all systems to the structure.

T F 18. There are no requirements established for the electrical contractor.

T F 19. Building codes are the primary source of rules and regulations to be followed by all contractors.

T F 20. Off-site work includes all construction from the street to the structure.

T F 21. Schedules are considered a part of the specifications.

T F 22. Schedules usually supply information only for the manufacturers.

T F 23. The contractor has the option to change the foundation walls from masonry to concrete.

T F 24. Where a specification is not stated for electrical construction, the electrician can refer to a Residential Construction Code book.

T F 25. On-site construction includes all work within the property lines.

T F 26. The contractor is responsible for utility taps to the Lee Residence.

T F 27. The site improvements for the Lee Residence stop within approximately 5 lineal feet of a structure.

T F 28. Gas service is not required for the Lee Residence.

T F 29. All of the potable water supply is installed in PVC pipe.

T F 30. The rear of the property includes a septic tank, a leach bed, and a well.

T F 31. There is a generator installed for emergency purposes.

T F 32. The gas service entrance includes a meter, meter shut-off valve, and high pressure control valve.

T F 33. The electrical service entrance equipment is located on the west side of the garage.

T F 34. The service entrance is rated at 120/240VAC and 200A.

T F 35. The nearest connection to the sewer line is located 175'–0" from the residence.

T F 36. The garage slab is sloped from 6" (15.24 cm) to 4" (5.08 cm) thick with W1.4 × W1.4/6 × 6 WWF.

T F 37. All depressed slabs are 8" (20.32 cm) lower than the neighboring slab.

T F 38. A concrete curb is formed along the two sides and front returns of the garage.

T F 39. The bottom of the footings in the unexcavated areas are a minimum 2'–0" (0.61 m) below the slab.

T F 40. The retaining walls on the east and west sides of the residence are 12'–0" (3.65 m) high.

T F 41. There is a concrete cap along the top of the retaining walls.

T F 42. The monolithic slab at the patio has a footing that is 8" (20.32 cm) wide and 1'–0" (30.48 cm) deep.

T F 43. Reinforcement for the footings is #5 continuous.

T F 44. There are dowel reinforcements placed in the footings at 4'–0" (1.22 m) O/C at all stem walls.

T F 45. The recess for the stairwell is 6'–0" (1.83 m) wide × 4'–0" (1.22 m) deep × 10'–0" (3.05 m) high.

T F 46. A stem wall and footing are located under the slab along the line of the north wall at the lower level.

T F 47. Footings for all stem walls are a minimum 2'–0" × 1'–0" (60.96 cm × 30.48 cm).

T F 48. An additional footing pad is shown for the entry overhang post supports.

T F 49. There are four risers shown for the entry stoop steps.

T F 50. The living room area is depressed 4" (5.08 cm) below the foyer.

Commercial Blueprint Reading

9

The Legal Documents

Residential construction contracts are negotiated between the owner and a contractor, or, in the case of the owner-builder, with individuals or subcontractors. Residential and commercial construction are similar only in adherence to all codes and ordinances required for both.

A commercial project follows the same basic construction sequence described in the residential chapters, that is, off-sites, site improvements, and on-sites. The difference between residential and commercial construction is in the documentation requirements and the manner in which the project is supervised. The owner of a commercial development normally hires a consultant such as an architect or engineer, a construction management company, a general contractor, or any combination of them, to supervise the project. The owner gives authority to the architect or engineer to act as its representative.

See appendix IV, Legal Documents. There must be a logical sequence of events and documentation stating requirements, dividing the responsibilities, and offering some legal protection for all parties involved in a project. Whether it is the contractor, the estimator, or some field member using the blueprint, all personnel must be able to read the pertinent information influencing the work of the trade(s) and must be totally informed regarding the procedural requirements of a project. A knowledge of the legal documents assists in this endeavor. This does not mean that the field personnel must know everything described in the legal documents, but they must be informed of the requirements and penalties if the intent of the documents is not followed.

Included in the Legal Documents are the **Invitation** or **Advertisement to Bid,** the **Instructions to Bidders,** and the **Contract Documents.** The information included in these documents contain the legal requirements to be adhered to from the owner to the subcontractors selected to perform work on the project.

The Invitation to Bid

The Invitation to Bid is a letter sent to a selected list of general contractors known and qualified by an owner, developer, architect, or engineer requesting them to tender a bid on the proposed project. Only those parties who receive such a letter may bid the project. The invitation may include such information as the following:

1. Owner of project
2. Location of project
3. Bid time and date
4. Some minimal information regarding insurance

The Advertisement to Bid

The Advertisement to Bid is the same as the letter of invitation except that it is placed in a newspaper or periodical widely read in construction circles, requesting qualified general contractors to bid a project. Such an advertisement is required for government bidding. This method may also be applied when there are insufficient qualified contractors on a known list, or if the project is in an area where the owner has no knowledge of qualified general contractors.

Instructions to Bidders

The Instructions to Bidders describe what is expected of those bidding on the project. The information in the Invitation to Bid, or the Advertisement to Bid, is repeated and expanded into more detail along with other instructions, such as:

1. The cost for the plans and specifications (if required)
2. The requirements for a bid security (bond)
3. Material substitutions allowed (if any)
4. The manner in which the bid is to be handled (open or sealed bid)

CONTRACT DOCUMENTS

The contract documents are also a part of the legal documents but are separated from the others because they are only issued to the winning bidder. Sample documents may be included with the Instructions to Bidders. The contract documents may be standard or customized for certain projects. There is a variety of such documents, including those provided by the military, public works, Army Corps of Engineers, and private projects. Many private construction projects and some of the public works projects use documentation provided by the American Institute of Architects (AIA), Form A401 (revised), or the Engineering Joint Contractor Documents Committee (EJCDC) form. The contract documents include information on bid requirements, bid forms, bonding, and so on. The documents may be of the standard varieties mentioned above or customized to fit the needs of the owner, architect, engineer, and/or contractor. The following paragraphs explain the major portions of the contract documents.

General and Special Conditions

The General Conditions are the standard format governing a project. They include all of the administrative and procedural controls governing a project. Such information as the clause regarding release from injury or harm (the "hold harmless" clause), rights of rejection of bid, recision of contract, specific insurance requirements, litigation rights, payment procedures, and accounting are thoroughly explained. Instructions regarding addenda prior to acceptance of contract or work authorizations and change orders after acceptance of contract are also provided.

Special Conditions are established and incorporated into the contract documents by agreement between owner, architect/engineer, and general contractor. The changes made in the Special Conditions may modify the General Conditions, delete one or more portions of the General Conditions, or supply additional instructions inherent to the specific project.

Additional Documents

There may also be a special bid form included with the contract documents. The form may require such information as the type of company bidding (sole ownership, partnership, corporation) and the signature of the party legally appointed to sign such documents. The general contractor may be required to submit the list of subcontractors whose bids were chosen to perform. There may also be a requirement for certification of qualification by demanding bonding of the subcontractors.

There may also be a requirement for certification of qualification, known as the *bid bond, payment and/or performance bond*. Bonds are submitted only if required. Most institutional and government projects insist upon them.

CSI FORMAT

See figure 9–1. The construction sequences followed in a commercial project are established by the Construction Specifications Institute (CSI). This nationwide organization—a group composed of architects, engineers, contractors, manufacturers' technical writers, contractors, and other interested parties—has established this uniform system for identification. Every trade is identified in these specifications, from the clearing and grubbing (demolition and removal of vegetation and debris) on a site prior to any construction to the

Division 1- General Requirements
  01010 Summary of Work
  01020 Allowances
  01025 Measurement & Payments
  01030 Alternates/Alternatives
  01040 Coordination
  01060 Workmen's Comp. & Ins.
  01200 Project Meetings
  01300 Submittals/Substitutions
  01400 Quality Control
  01500 Construction Facilities
  01600 Materials & Equipment
  01700 contract Close-out

Division 2 - Sitework

  02000 Scope of Work
  02010 Subsurface Investigation
  02100 Site Preparation
  02200 Earthwork
  02500 Paving & Surfacing
  02900 Landscaping

Division 3 - Concrete

  03000 Scope of Work
  03100 Cosite Formwork
  03200 Reinforcement
  03300 Cast-In-Place Concrete
  03400 Precast Concrete

Division 4 - Masonry

  04000 Scope of Work
  04100 Mortar and Grout
  04200 Brick
  04300 Concrete Masonry Units
Division 5- Metals

  05000 Scope of Work
  05100 Structural Metal Framing
  05200 Structural Light Gauge Metal Framing

Division 6 - Wood and Plastics

  06000 Scope of Work
  06100 Rough Carpentry
  06200 Finish Carpentry

Division 7 - Thermal and Moisture Protection

  07000 Scope of Work
  07100 Waterproofing
  07200 Insulation
  07300 Roofing Tile
  07600 Sheet Metal
  07900 Sealants & Caulking

Division 8 - Doors and Windows

  08000 Scope of Work
  08100 Metal Doors & Frames
  08200 Wood & Plastic Doors
  08250 Door Opening Assemblies
  08500 Metal Windows

Division 9 - Finishes
  09000 Scope of Work
  09200 Lath & Plaster
  09250 Gypsum Board (GWB)
  09300 Tile
  09500 Acoustical Treatment
  09650 Resilient Flooring
  09630 Caspet
  09900 Painting
  09950 Wallcovering

Division 10 - Specialties

  10000 Scope of Work
  10500 Lockers
  10800 Toilet & Bath Accessories

Division 11 - Equipment

  11000 Scope of Work
  11700 Medical Equipment

Division 12 - Furnishings

  12000 Scope of Work
  12100 Office Furniture
  12200 Draperies
  12300 Rugs
  12400 Art Work

Division 13 - Special Construction

  13000 Scope of Work
  13100 Boiler
  13200 Incinerator

Division 14 - Conveying Systems
  14000 Scope of Work
  14100 Elevators
  14200 Hoisting Equipment
  14300 Conveyors

Division 15 - Mechanical

  15000 Scope of Work
  15050 Basic Mechanical Materials & Methods
  15100 Heating, Ventilation & Air Conditioning
  15400 Basic Plumbing Materials & Methods
  15450 Plumbing

Division 16 - Electrical

  16000 Scope of Work
  16050 Basic Electrical Materials & Methods
  16400 Service & Distribution
  16500 Lighting
  16600 Special Systems
  16700 Communications

FIGURE 9–1
CSI Format

finished project (certificate of occupancy). An example of a portion of the CSI format is described in the figure. It is this format that is used for the specifications for the Frontier Manufacturing Company (see chapter 10).

CHAPTER EXERCISES

Matching

Match the legal documents with the descriptions.

_____ 1. General Conditions

_____ 2. Specifications

_____ 3. Project manual

_____ 4. Special Conditions

_____ 5. Payment bond

_____ 6. Contract documents

_____ 7. Bid bond

_____ 8. Invitation to Bid

_____ 9. Bid form

_____ 10. Section 10100

_____ 11. Construction Specifications Institute

_____ 12. American Institute of Architects

_____ 13. Performance bond

_____ 14. Instructions to Bidders

_____ 15. Addendum

a. Section of Division 10
b. Specification writing organization
c. Request for bid by letter or advertisement
d. Part of legal documents describing legal responsibilities
e. A correction to the bid request
f. The manual of Specifications
g. Legal document expanding information on the Invitation
h. Supplement to General Conditions
i. The agreement
j. Form used to present bid to owner
k. A guarantee of payment
l. An assurance of contractor's ability to produce a quality project
m. A guarantee to complete a project
n. The explicit instructions regarding responsibilities of all parties
o. The trade information and directions for materials, labor, and equipment

Multiple Choice

_____ 1. The term *specification in construction* means:
   a. The legal documents.
   b. The project manual.
   c. Directions written for a trade.
   d. None of the above.

_____ 2. The Legal Documents include:
   a. The General and Special Conditions.
   b. The Specifications.
   c. The list of trade organizations.
   d. All of the above.

_____ 3. The General and Supplemental Conditions include:
   a. Responsibilities of the owner.
   b. Responsibilities of the Architect/Engineer.
   c. Responsibilities of the Contractor.
   d. All of the above.

_____ 4. A bid bond is:
   a. Supplied by the owner.
   b. Normally required for all government project bids.
   c. The same as the payment and performance bonds.
   d. Costs the bidder 100% of the bid total.

_____ 5. The Specifications:
   a. Are unnecessary for commercial and government work.
   b. Are part of the Project Manual.
   c. Include twenty division breakdowns.
   d. Are always written by the AIA.

_____ 6. There are three types of CSI Specification formats. They are:
   a. Narrowscope, widerscope, and widestscope.
   b. Broadscope, narrowscope, and informal.
   c. Informal small, informal medium, and informal large.
   d. Broadscope, mediumscope, and narrowscope.

_____ 7. The Invitation to Bid is:
   a. A request to contractors to bid on a project.
   b. A request to partake in an invitation for a party.
   c. A demand for a payment and performance bond.
   d. None of the above.

_____ 8. The bid bond:
   a. Is a requirement for most major commercial projects.
   b. Costs approximately 15% of total contract value.
   c. Both a and b.
   d. Neither a nor b.

True or False

T F   1. A payment and performance bond each require coverage for 100% of the project value.

T F   2. The Instructions to Bidders are directions on the proper estimating procedures of a project.

T F   3. The American Institute of Architects has written the basic requirements for Division 1 of the Specifications.

T F   4. A Bid Bond is always necessary with a private commercial project.

T F   5. A Specification may include a broadscope, mediumscope, and narrowscope explanation of directions for material, labor, and equipment requirements.

T F   6. An addendum is a change in Specifications made prior to the bid date.

T F   7. The Specifications include a division defining requirements for steel construction.

T F   8. General Conditions and General Requirements are interchangeable.

T F   9. The cost of bonding varies from 1.2% to 5% of project value.

T F 10. The legal documents include the contract.

Completion

1. A contract may be broken if the contractor cannot _____.

2. The Instructions to Bidders is provided along with the plans and _____.

3. The bid bond is included for the purpose of determining the _____ of a contractor.

4. Government requests for bids are normally found in _____.

5. The bid submission on government contracts and some private contracts demand a list of the _____.

6. A contract document includes the General Conditions and, possibly, a section referred to as the _____ _____.

7. The value of a bond is determined by the _____ total.

8. The _____ documents are supplied to a contractor for instructions to the bidders, bid proposals, and contract back-up.

9. A contractor that is the successful bidder may _____ on the contract only if all notification, in writing, was not provided to the contractor.

10. There are _____ trade divisions in the CSI format.

10

Commercial Plans and the Project Manual

COMMERCIAL PLAN GROUPS

Plans drawn for commercial projects are more uniform in context than residential plans. Where residential plans may have architectural and structural drawings intermingled, a commercial set of plans is organized. Likewise, a set of commercial plans can be quite large, with as many as fifty or more drawings. When a set of plans is developed for a project, the architect and engineer must also determine the materials and installation procedures to be included. The set of plans is organized in six groups and in a specific pattern. *See figure 10–1* for a typical commercial plan breakdown.

```
1. Civil (C) plans:
   a. Site plan*
   b. Plot plan
   c. Utilities plans (water, sewer, gas, and/or electrical)**
   d. Paving plan**
   e. Street improvements plans**

*The site plan may be under separate contract and not included here.

**Utilities, paving, and improvement plans may be included in the plot plan
```

FIGURE 10–1
Commercial Plan Group

```
        f. Landscape plans***
        g. Sections and details of each plan as required
     ***Landscape plans may be a separate set of plans and placed under separate contract.


     2. Architectural (A) plans:
        a. Floor plan
        b. Exterior elevation plan(s)
        c. Interior elevations (details)
        d. Reflected ceiling plan
        e. Roof plan
        f. Sections:
           (1) Longitudinal, transverse, and partial wall sections
        g. Door, window, and hardware schedules*
        h. Interior finish schedule
        j. Miscellaneous architectural details

     *These may be found in the plans, the specifications, or both


     3. Structural (S) plans:
        a. Structural General Notes*
        b. Foundation plan
        c. Structural floor plan (not at foundation level; above grade)
        d. Structural wall framing plan
        e. Masonry reinforcement plan (if masonry is used in lieu of framing)
        f. Roof framing plan
        g. Structural sections:
              (1)   Longitudinal, transverse, and partial wall sections
        h. Structural schedules:*
              (1)   Footing, reinforcement, column, pier, beam, lintel,
        joist, and so on.*

     *These schedules and the Structural General Notes may be combined on one or more sheets,
     on separate sheets as indicated, and/or in the specifications.


     4. Plumbing (P) plans:
        a. Piping isometric plan (potable water)
        b. Piping pictorial (if used)
        c. Plumbing isometric plan (waste disposal)
        d. Plumbing pictorial (if used)
        e. Piping and plumbing details
        f. Fixture schedule*
        g. Miscellaneous plumbing details

     *These may be found on the plans, in the specifications or both.
```

FIGURE 10–1
(continued)

5. Mechanical (M) plans:
   a. Floor layout (underfloor or wall supply and return, if necessary)
   b. Reflected ceiling plan (if required)
   c. Roof layout (if required)
   d. Equipment schedule(s)
   e. Equipment layout (pictorial—risers, etc.)
   f. Control diagrams
   g. Miscellaneous mechanical details

6. Electrical (E) plans:
   a. Plot plan (exterior power and lighting)
   b. Power plan (interior receptacle layout)
   c. Reflected ceiling plan (interior lighting layout)
   d. Power, lighting, fixture, and equipment schedules
   e. Equipment pictorials (one-line and riser details)
   f. Feeder and control diagrams
   g. Miscellaneous electrical details

FIGURE 10–1
(continued)

THE PROJECT MANUAL

The specifications and drawings are designed to coordinate with one another. The specifications are assembled in a book form referred to as the *project manual*. Included in the project manual are specifications for all trades involved. Specifications can be quite detailed, depending upon the size of the project. A project manual includes the following:

1. General Project Information. All parties responsible for the development of the project are included on the cover page of the project manual as well as on the set of plans. The cover page identifies the names and addresses of the Owner(s), Architect(s), Civil Engineer(s), Structural Engineer(s), Mechanical Engineer(s), and Electrical Engineer(s).

2. Index to the Specifications. These are laid out in the CSI format, divisions 1 through 16, identifying the administrative and trade responsibilities.

3. Specifying Organizations. This is a list of several organizations that have their own specifications which are incorporated into the project specifications either in writing or by inference.

4. Specifications per the CSI format. The General and Special Requirements (similar to the General and Special Conditions) and the specifications are detailed.

A typical example of a project manual is found in figure 10–2.

PROJECT MANUAL

for FRONTIER MANUFACTURING, INC.

CALIENTE, NEVADA

Owner: Frontier Manufacturing, Inc.
100 First Avenue
Caliente, Nevada 89--

Architect: Christle Associates
550 Broad Street
Las Vegas, Nevada 89109

Civil & Structural Engineers: Janus Corporation
1 Main Street
Caliente, Nevada 89--

Mechanical Engineer: Aquarius Mechanical & Plumbing, Inc.
375 Water Street
Las Vegas, Nevada 89--

Electrical Engineer: Brophy Electric, Inc.
935 Ampere Avenue
Las Vegas, Nevada 89--

FIGURE 10-2
Project Manual for Frontier Manufacturing, Inc.

GENERAL CONDITIONS

Definitions

For purposes of this contract, Frontier Manufacturing, Inc., of 100 First Avenue, Caliente, Nevada, 89—-, is referred to as "the Owner."

The term "project" described in this Specification is an office/warehouse for the Owner located at Broad Street and First Avenue, Caliente, Nevada, 89—-.

The term "contractor" means the person, firm, or corporation, identified as such in the agreement, responsible for the execution of the work contracted with the owner.

The term "subcontractor" means, without limitation, any person, firm, or corporation working directly or indirectly for the contractor, whether or not pursuant to a formal contract, that furnishes or performs a portion of the work, labor, or material, according to the drawings and/or specifications.

The term "agreement" means the construction agreement between the owner and the contractor.

The term "contract" means the agreement signed by the owner and the contractor, these Specifications, and all other documents listed as contract documents of this agreement.

The term "contract amount" means the dollar-value of the agreement as revised by approved contract change orders.

The term "work" includes all labor, material, and equipment necessary to produce the construction required by contract.

The term "change order" is a written order to the contractor, signed by the owner, issued AFTER the execution of the contract, authorizing a change in work or an adjustment in the original contract amount as agreed upon by the owner and the contractor.

The term "contract time" is the period of time allotted in the agreement for the completion of the work as revised by approved contract change orders.

Intent of the Documents

The agreement and each of the contract documents are complementary and they shall be interpreted so that what is called for by one shall be binding upon all. Should there be any conflicts in the documents, the contractor is to bring the discrepancies to the attention of the owner at once. It shall be the owner who shall make the responsible decision as to which document is correct and all other documents shall be immediately amended by addendum.

Duplication is not intended through any of the documents and no duplication for additional cost may be claimed.

Delays and Extensions of Time

Should there be excessive delays due to the owner, an employee of the owner, or a contractor of the owner, or by changes ordered in the work, or by acts of God, or by any other cause deemed by the owner as justifying the delay,

FIGURE 10–2
(continued)

the contract shall be extended by change order. The length of the extension shall be determined by the owner.

All requests for extension of contract shall be made to owner no more than ten (10) working days after such delay occurs or they shall be otherwise waived. A continuing delay need not be put into writing unless it exceeds another ten (10) working-day period. Any delays caused by other than the above shall be at the expense of the contractor at a cost of one-thousand and 00/100 dollars ($1,000) per day.

Assignments

This contract, or any rights hereunder, shall not be assigned by the contractor without the express consent of the owner.

Payment and Performance Bonds

Prior to any work, the contractor, at the discretion of the owner, shall supply the owner with a payment and performance bond in the amount of one-hundred percent (100%) of the contract. The cost of such bond shall be at the expense of the contractor.

Compliance with the Law

Contractor shall be responsible for complete compliance with all laws, including OSHA, ordinances, codes, or other regulations as may exist in the jurisdiction of authority in the locale of this contract.

Indemnification

The contractor shall indemnify and hold harmless the owner and all of the owner's heirs and assigns against any and all claims, damages, losses, and expenses, including attorney's fees, due to the performance of the work, provided that such claims, damages, losses or expenses, causing bodily harm, illness, or death due to negligence or omission of the contractor, subcontractor, or anyone directly or indirectly employed by the contractor or subcontractor, or anyone for whose acts any of them may be liable, regardless of whether or not it is caused in part by a party indemnified hereunder, and shall further indemnify and hold harmless the owner, all of the owner's heirs and assigns from the expense of such defense against all claims for damages, losses, and expenses claimed by any person, firm, or corporation.

FIGURE 10–2
(continued)

INDEX TO SPECIFICATIONS

Division 1-General Requirements
    01010 Summary of Work
    01020 Allowances
    01025 Measurement and Payment
    01030 Alternates/Alternatives
    01040 Coordination
    01060 Workmen's Compensation and Insurance
    01200 Project Meetings
    01300 Submittals/Substitutions
    01400 Quality Control
    01500 Construction Facilities and Temporary Controls
    01600 Materials and Equipment
    01700 Contract Close-out

Division 2-Sitework
    02000 Scope of Work
    02010 Subsurface Investigation
    02020 Demolition
    02100 Site Preparation
    02220 Earthwork
    02270 Slope Paving
    02510 Asphalt Concrete Paving
    02525 Prefabricated Curbs
    02580 Pavement Marking
    02720 Storm Sewerage
    02800 Site Improvements
    02900 Landscaping

Division 3-Concrete
    03000 Scope of Work
    03100 Concrete Formwork
    03210 Reinforcement Steel
    03220 Welded Wire Fabric
    03300 Cast-in-Place Concrete
    03480 Precast Concrete Specialties

Division 4-Masonry
    04000 Scope of Work
    04100 Mortar and Masonry Grout
    04150 Masonry Accessories
    04220 Concrete Unit Masonry

Division 5-Metals
    05000 Scope of Work
    05050 Metal Fastening
    05120 Structural Metal Framing
    05530 Gratings

FIGURE 10–2
(continued)

```
Division 6-Wood and Plastics
     06000 Scope of Work
     06100 Rough Carpentry
     06150 Wood and Metal Systems
     06180 Glue-Laminated Beams
     06190 Trusses
     06200 Finish Carpentry
Division 7-Thermal and Moisture Protection
     07000 Scope of Work
     07110 Sheet Membrane Below-Grade Moisture Protection
     07200 Insulation
     07300 Roofing Tile
     07460 Manufactured Siding
     07500 Membrane Roofing
     07600 Flashing and Sheet Metal
     07900 Sealants and Caulking
Division 8-Doors and Windows
     08000 Scope of Work
     08100 Metal Doors and Frames
     08200 Wood and Plastic Doors
     08250 Door Opening Assemblies
     08500 Metal Windows
Division 9-Finishes
     09000 Scope of Work
     09100 Metal Support Systems
     09200 Lath and Plaster
     09250 Gypsum Board (GWB)
     09300 Tile
     09500 Acoustical Treatment
     09650 Resilient Flooring
     09680 Carpet
     09900 Painting
Division 10-Specialties
     10000 Scope of Work
     10400 Identifying Devices
     10500 Lockers
     10800 Toilet and Bath Accessories
Division 11-Equipment
     11000 Scope of Work
     11160 Loading Dock Equipment
     11500 Industrial and Process Equipment
Division 12-Furnishings
     N.I.C.—to be Furnished by Owner
Division 13-Special Construction
     13000 Scope of Work
     13400 Industrial and Process Control Systems
     13900 Fire Suppression and Supervisory System
```

FIGURE 10–2
(continued)

```
            Division 14-Conveying Systems
                 14000 Scope of Work
                 14500 Material Handling Systems
                 14600 Hoists and Cranes
            Division 15-Mechanical
                 15000 Scope of Work
                 15050 Basic Mechanical Materials and Methods
                 15400 Plumbing
                 15500 Heating, Ventilation, and Air Conditioning
            Division 16-Electrical
                 16000 Scope of Work
                 16050 Basic Electrical Materials and Methods
                 16400 Service and Distribution
                 16500 Lighting (General Lighting and Power)
                 16600 Special Systems
                 16700 Communications



                          STANDARDS


            AIA-American Institute of Architects
            ACI-American Concrete Institute
            APA-American Plywood Association
            ASHRAE-American Society of Heating, Refrigeration, and Air-
                 conditioning Engineers, Inc.
            ASTM-American Society for Testing Materials
            AWS-American Welding Society
            CRSI-Concrete Reinforcing Steel Institute
            DHI-Door and Hardware Institute
            MIA-Masonry Institute of America
            TCA-Tile Council of America, Inc.
            UL-Underwriters Laboratories, Inc.
            WWPA-Western Wood Products Association
```

FIGURE 10–2
(continued)

SPECIFICATIONS

DIVISION 1 General Requirements

01010 Summary of Work

1.1. The contractor warrants and represents that it has carefully examined all the plans and Specifications, and all of the real property upon which the work is to be conducted, and has satisfied itself as to the conditions existing and the difficulties that may be encountered in the execution of the work which should have reasonably been discovered upon such examination, will not constitute a cause for the reformation or recision of this contract, or a modification of the amount of this contract, or its termination.

1.2. The contractor shall obtain and pay for all permits, licenses, certifications, tap charges, construction easements, inspections, and other approvals required, both temporary and permanent, to commence and complete the work at no additional cost to the owner.

1.3. The contractor shall be responsible for all the work on the site and the adjacent property regarding loss or damage resulting from its operations at no additional cost to the owner.

1.4. Contractor shall receive a full certificate of occupancy before the contractor can receive final payment for the work.

1.5. The contractor may have portions of the work performed by others by use of subcontract agreements. These agreements must be approved by the owner and shall in no way increase the cost of the project.

1.5.a. All subcontract agreements shall automatically include the General Conditions and Requirements between the owner and the contractor.

1.5.b. No contract between the contractor and the subcontractor shall be construed to be a contract between the owner and the subcontractor. No subcontractor has a right against the owner unless the contract has defaulted. Should this happen, the owner shall be liable only for the costs incurred in accordance with the subcontract agreement.

1.6. The contractor shall be fully responsible for any omissions, commissions, or errors committed by the subcontractor, or any person, firm, or corporation, or any of their respective employees, in contract with the contractor.

01020 Allowances

1.1. An allowance shall be permitted by the owner for all lighting fixtures. The fixtures included are for the plant/warehouse overhead fixtures, the office fluorescent ceiling fixtures for the offices and the display room, and the track lighting as may be required by owner. The lighting fixture allowance shall be in the amount of ten thousand three-hundred fifty and 00/100 dollars ($10,350).

FIGURE 10–2
(continued)

01025 Measurement and Payment

1.1. Each subcontractor shall submit a request for payment to the contractor as prescribed in the contract agreement. Each submission shall be made no later than the 10th day or the 25th day of each month. Requests for payment received on the 10th day shall be reimbursed on the 30th day of the same month. Requests for payment received on the 25th day of the month shall be reimbursed on the 15th day of the month following. There shall be only one payment allowed per month.

1.2. No payment shall be approved by the contractor or owner without verification of the measurement submitted with the payment request.

01030 Alternates/Alternatives

1.1. Should any of the materials, procedures, or systems be unavailable for any reason an alternative material, procedure, or system may be submitted. Should there be an alternative submitted, the contractor and/or material supplier shall submit such information and change per Section 01300.

1.2. Alternates shall only be submitted at the request of the owner or the owner's representative.

01035 Modification Procedures

1.1. Upon contract and start of construction, no work shall be done other than that established by contract. Any changes to be made due to construction problems or the owner's request shall be done by one of two (2) methods, work order or field directive.

1.1.a. Only authorized personnel shall request any contractor or subcontractor to make such changes. Changes requested shall be by written authorization only in the manner directed above. Authorized personnel include the architect, engineer, appointed superintendent, project engineer, or project manager. All other requests shall be denied.

01040 Coordination

1.1. It is the responsibility of the contractor to supply a Critical Path Chart to the owner, all selected subcontractors, and manufacturers or suppliers so that the work can be accomplished in a timely manner without confusion or delay.

01060 Workmen's Compensation and Insurance

1.1. The contractor, at its own expense, shall be responsible for maintenance of workmen's compensation in accordance with the laws of the state in which the project is being constructed.

FIGURE 10–2
(continued)

1.2. The contractor shall also supply the owner with liability insurance in the amount of one million and 00/100 dollars ($1,000,000) for injury or death and three million and 00/100 dollars ($3,000,000) for property damage. The owner shall be named as co-insurer.

01200 Project Meetings

1.1. It shall be the responsibility of the contractor and all subcontractors, manufacturer's representatives, and/or suppliers to be available for regular project meetings to be held on-site weekly for the purposes of discussing continuity, labor, material, or equipment problems, and safety. The day and time of the meeting is at the discretion of the contractor. The owner may or may not be present at these meetings.

01300 Submittals/Substitutions

1.1. The contractor shall submit to the owner, or owner's representative, for approval, all materials, equipment, and procedures to be a part of the completed project. Submittals shall be in writing and certified to be as per manufacturer's recommendations.

1.1.a. All "or equal" and alternative products or procedures are to be submitted in writing to the owner, or owner's representative, for approval. The reason for the "or equal" or alternative materials or procedures must be explained in the submittal. Such submittals must be available to the owner or owner's representative no less than ten (10) working days prior to the start of work on the project.

1.2. The owner has the right to reject any and all such submittals except in the event the material is no longer available or there is a delay in time in obtaining the material or the procedure must be changed due to the change in material.

01400 Quality Control

1.1. The contractor warrants that all materials and equipment supplied to the owner for the project are new unless otherwise specified. All work shall be free from any defects in material and workmanship.

1.1.a. All warranties or guarantees supplied by the manufacturers to the contractor or subcontractors shall be deemed as supplied to the owner as well. Prior to final payment by the owner, all copies of the warranties, guarantees shall be submitted to the owner and the said warranties/guarantees assigned directly to the owner.

FIGURE 10–2
(continued)

01500 Construction Facilities and Temporary Controls

   1.1. The contractor, at its own cost, shall be responsible that all
temporary facilities such as telephones, electrical supply, personal care
equipment, first aid equipment, potable water, and fire prevention facilities
are made available on the project.
   1.2. Fire prevention facilities and services and first aid and medical
assistance must be prominently displayed so that all persons, firms, or
corporations employed on the project may have access to them.

01600 Material and Equipment

   1.1. At the discretion of the owner, if there is sufficient room, an
area may be set aside for storage of equipment and materials. If possible, a
fence will be so provided for enclosure of the materials and equipment. It is
the responsibility of each person, firm, or corporation to make certain that
the area is secure at the end of each workday.

01700 Contract Close-out

   1.1. The contractor shall be responsible for maintenance of all records.
A copy of such records shall be provided to the owner at the time of
completion of project including manufacturers' warranties, guarantees,
certifications of workmanship and material prior to final payment and/or
retention. Where no manufacturer's warranty or guaranty exists, and,
regardless of such warranties or guarantees, all trades shall submit, in
writing, a minimum two (2) year guarantee defects in workmanship and material
which are a permanent part of the project.
   1.2. The contractor, at its own expense, shall be responsible for a
clean worksite. All rubbish caused by the contractor's employees, the
subcontractor or its employees and the suppliers or their employees shall be
removed and properly stored in containers for removal to a suitable site for
dumping.

DIVISION 2 Sitework

02000 Scope of Work

   1.1. Division 1 and the General Conditions are to be considered a part
of this division including all materials, labor, and equipment necessary to
complete the work of this division.

FIGURE 10–2
(continued)

02010 Subsurface Investigation

1.1. The owner shall provide for subsurface exploration to be conducted by a qualified soils engineering firm. The soils testing and results shall be made available, in writing, to the owner or owner's representative and the contractor and shall be become a part of these Specifications.

1.2. The report shall include the type of surface soil, the type, or types, of soil for a minimum of ten (10) feet (3.05 m) below grade, obtained by test borings or core drillings, and shall make recommendations, if any, for correcting substandard soils conditions. During excavation and grading, soils testing shall be performed to ensure the soils meet a minimum of 3,000 psf (1,360.79 kg/30.48 cm^2) design strength.

02020 Demolition

1.1. If, during the soils testing, any hazardous materials, pipes, conduits, or other possible hazards, are located, the owner shall be notified and corrections made at the expense of the owner. All materials shall be properly and safely removed from the site. All pipes shall be tested and capped at a safe distance from the site work.

1.2. No work shall be initiated until after "Call Before You Dig," or equivalent organization, is contacted and permission to proceed is given by all utilities and/or local authorities. Any structural demolition which may be located on the property shall be done by a licensed, qualified demolition and/or salvage company.

02100 Site Preparation

1.1. The contractor shall be responsible that certain vegetation is marked to remain intact or to be removed, saved, and transplanted. This shall be accomplished in cooperation with the owner, contractor, and clearing and grubbing contractor. When all vegetation to be saved is so marked, all remaining vegetation, debris, and refuse is to be cleared and removed.

02220 Earthwork

1.1. Excavate as required to achieve proper grade levels and for the mass excavation of the loading dock ramp and for working room required for laying of retaining walls on both ends of the loading dock area. Excavation for all footings to be on undisturbed earth or minimum 95% compacted soil with the minimum allowable depth, as shown on drawings, or otherwise governed by local codes.

1.2. Should the contractor contact calcite or large rock conditions which would require blasting, the owner will reimburse the contractor for the cost of such work.

1.3. Backfill at exterior walls shall be Type II soil, well compacted, to the grades specified on the plot plan. Backfill shall be performed in 8" (20.32 cm) lifts. Backfill over utilities shall conform with the utility

FIGURE 10–2
(continued)

company requirements of sand and/or Type II soil. The remainder of the site shall be graded to assure proper drainage away from the building. Remove all excess soils from the site. Grades not otherwise indicated on the plans shall be of uniform levels or slopes between points where elevations are given.

1.4. Contractor is to notify owner immediately if any excavation reveals fill or ground water.

02270 Slope Paving

1.1. The finish grading shall be completed to conform with the paving swale elevations as indicated on the plans. Rough grading must be such that the base course, aggregate (cementitious) base, and finish surface shall not exceed elevations indicated on plans.

02510 Asphaltic Concrete Paving

1.1. All paving is to be prepared from a combination of cementitious and asphaltic materials as per manufacturer's recommendations, the Asphalt Institute, and local codes and ordinances. All paving shall be installed in areas indicated on plans. Pavement design shall meet ten (10) year minimum design criteria for local areas as established by the Asphalt Institute. The following guide should be used as a *minimum* thickness required:

Soil Class	Minimum Pavement
Poor-CBR = 3.5-type, plastic when wet such as clay, fine silt, sandy loam	6″ (15.24 cm) coarse asphalt base binder (1½″ [3.81 cm] asphalt aggregate) and 1½″ (3.81 cm) asphalt topping (maximum ½″ [1.27 cm] aggregate)
Medium-CBR = 7.0-type, hard, silty sands or sand gravels containing clay or fine silt	4″ (10.16 cm) coarse asphalt base binder (1½″ [3.81 cm] asphalt aggregate) and 1½″ (3.81 cm) asphalt topping (maximum ½″ [1.27 cm] aggregate)
Good-CBR = 12-type, clean sand and sand gravel free of asphalt topping clay, silt or loam	3″ (7.62 cm) coarse asphalt base material (1½″ [3.81 cm] asphalt aggregate) and 1½″ (3.81 cm) asphalt topping (maximum)

1.2. Finish paving shall be applied with a 4″ (10.16 cm) asphalt mix at all areas over a 6″ (15.24 cm) cementitious base over 10″ (25.40 cm) approved compacted base, aggregate or sand, at all paved areas. The aggregate or sand base shall be compacted to maintain an 80% compaction rate. Base shall be tested for compaction prior to application of asphalt finish. All paving surfaces shall be properly sealed from weather deterioration as per local codes and accepted workmanship of the trade.

FIGURE 10–2
(continued)

02520 Portland Cement Concrete Paving

1.1. Curb and gutter shall be installed along the perimeter of the driveway and parking areas. Curbs shall be 18″ (45.72 cm) deep by 4″ (5.05 cm) wide (15.24 cm) concrete with 6″ (15.24 cm) exposed above finish asphalt surfacing and/or gutter. 2-#4 rebar shall be installed in curb, one 3″ (7.62 cm) from the top of the curb and the other 3″ (7.62 cm) from the bottom of the curb. The gutter shall be 12″ (30.48 cm) wide by 4″ (5.08 cm) deep with 2-#4 rebar spaced 6″ (15.24 cm) apart. All horizontal reinforcement shall be placed on chairs for proper support and binding of the concrete upon placement. The gutter base shall meet the same specifications as in Section 2510 above or shall meet the minimum DOT specifications of the local building and engineering departments.

1.2. Formwork for the approach shall be installed and shall conform to the best standards of the American Concrete Institute. All lines shall be straight and true. Concrete shall be 3500 psi (1,587.59 kg/6.54 cm^2) at 28 days per ASTM C94 using materials from one manufacturer and supplier. Reinforcement shall be installed and inspected prior to concrete placement. The concrete and reinforcement shall meet all ASTM and DOT requirements for approach installations. Should the concrete not meet proper standards it shall be repaired, or removed and replaced, as necessary, at the expense of the contractor.

1.2.a. See Division 3, Concrete, for complete requirements for concrete installations. If there are any discrepancies noted, the information in Division 3 shall prevail.

02525 Prefabricated Curbs

1.1. Precast concrete parking blocks, 6′-0″ (1.83 m) long and 5″ (12.70 cm) high, shall be installed one for each two (2) parking places, spanning one-half (½) per parking space, except at handicapped parking where the concrete block shall be placed one (1) per parking space.

02580 Pavement Marking

1.1. The paving contractor shall paint parking stalls and directional markings, including entry and exit arrows, center-line striping, and warning signage.

1.2. The parking spaces shall include two (2) handicap spaces for customer parking in front of office. Two (2) handicap spaces shall be marked at employee parking area along side of structure facing First Avenue. Handicap spaces shall be properly protected from other parking spaces with "Van Accessible" striping and otherwise identified with the necessary ADA signage requirements. All other parking spaces along the front parking area (both sides) and the side parking area shall be standard size (9′-0″ [2.74 m] wide by 19′-0″ [5.79 m] long). There are no parking spaces inside the chain-link fence and gate (North area of property).

FIGURE 10–2
(continued)

02720 Storm Sewerage

1.1. A cast iron (CI) drain shall be installed which shall receive drainage from the trench drain and swales and shall be connected to an open storm drain located to the north of the property on First Avenue. The top of the storm drain shall be even with the lowest part of the surrounding area but a minimum of 4″ (10.32 cm) lower than the trench drain at the loading dock. See plans for locations and elevations.

02800 Site Improvements

1.1. An 8′-0″ (2.44 m) high chain-link fence and traffic-control, motor-operated, roll-away gate is to be installed across the parking area/driveway on the First Avenue side of the structure as indicated on the plot plan. The fence shall be installed with one section 10′-0″ (3.05 m) long abutting the structure and the other section 18′-0″ (5.49 m) long with a 12′-0″ (3.66 m) long gate.

A second 8′-0″ (2.44 m) high chain-link fence with a 4′-0″ (1.22 m) wide personnel gate are to be installed on the opposite side of the structure extending 28′-0″ (8.53 m) O/A to the south property line wall across the easement area as per plans. Permission must be obtained from the utility company(ies) for this installation.

02900 Landscaping

1.1. Provide all labor, material, and equipment necessary to complete the seeding, sodding, landscape planting, earthwork, and edging as shown on plot and/or landscape plans. Landscape bidder shall submit a proposal and drawings for approval by the owner. Proposal shall include size, type, and number of plantings, and exact area to be sodded.

1.2. Landscape contractor shall be responsible for the installation of the topsoil to finish grade at all the rough grading. All planting areas shall be free of all debris and well drained prior to any planting. An automatic sprinkler system shall be installed in accordance with local codes and ordinances. Total proposal shall include all taxes where applicable.

END OF DIVISION

FIGURE 10–2
(continued)

DIVISION 3 Concrete

03000 Scope of Work

   1.1. Division 1 and the General Conditions are considered a part of this division. All labor, material, and equipment necessary to complete all concrete work including formwork, reinforcing, and cement finish shall be furnished by the concrete contractor.

03100 Concrete Formwork

   1.1. Formwork shall be installed for footings and sidewalks where required. Footing forms shall be installed along property line retaining wall footings, at the loading dock retaining walls and all other structure footing support. All labor materials and equipment necessary for the installation of footings shall include steel stakes, 3'-0" (0.91 m) long and 2× treated lumber or 1" (min) (2.54 cm) treated plywood for forms and any other accessories necessary for proper construction of the footings. Where sidewalks are installed standard flat forms shall be used.

   1.2. All work shall conform with ASTM standards, standards of the trade, and all local codes and ordinances. Where the soil conditions permit forms may be excluded. Refer to the engineering Soils Report made a part of these Conditions and Specifications for requirements and/or recommendations.

03210 Reinforcement Steel

   1.1. Reinforcement bar (rebar) shall be grade 60 (60 kps). Rebar shall be 2-#4 (U.N.O.) laid horizontally and continuous in footings with 48 bar diameters at all laps. Rebar shall be installed on concrete prefabricated chairs 3" (7.62 cm) from bottom of footing. Corners shall have 2-#4 rebar, 4'-0" (1.22 m) long, bent 90° at the center, and shall extend 2'-0" (60.96 cm) each way from the corner. 1-#5 rebar dowel shall be installed vertically in foundation walls or at slab perimeter at 4'-0" O/C (1.22 m) horizontally to match masonry reinforcement (see plans) with the 6" (15.24 cm) hook tied to footing rebar. Dowel rebar length shall extend 2'-0" (60.96 cm) vertically. No rebar shall be heat bent. All rebar shall be installed and inspected prior to placement of concrete.

03220 Welded Wire Fabric

   1.1. The manufacturing/warehouse concrete slab shall have W2.9×W2.9-6×6 welded wire fabric installed a minimum 1½" (3.81 cm) below the surface of the slab. The fabric shall be lapped 6" (1.27 cm) on all sides and ends. The perimeter fabric shall extend 6" (1.27 cm) beyond the edges of the slab and shall be turned down parallel at the stem wall and/or footing.

FIGURE 10–2
(continued)

03300 Cast-In-Place Concrete

1.1. Concrete footings and slabs are to be 3,500 psi (1,587.59 kg/6.54 cm²) ready-mix concrete per ASTM C94. Type III cement shall be used. Concrete shall be tested at the expense of the owner at 3 days, 7 days, and 28 days in accordance with ASTM C31 and ASTM C150. If any of the tests fail, the contractor shall, at his/her own expense, make all necessary repairs and/or replacements.

1.2. The manufacturing/warehouse concrete slab, including the loading dock, shall be 6" (1.27 cm) thick and the office slab shall be 4" (0.83 cm) thick. The exterior sidewalks shall be 5" (12.70 cm) thick and the approach apron shall be 6" (15.24 cm) thick. The manufacturing/warehouse slab shall be placed in alternate sections so that expansion joints can be inserted between placements. Flat forms shall be installed with cold key joints. The office slab may be placed as a single unit.

1.3. Concrete components shall be Portland cement, one brand; aggregate—fine sand and maximum ³/₄" (1.91 cm) DIA coarse gravel free from other deleterious substances; potable water.

1.3.a. Admixtures permitted shall be:

(1) air-entrained agent per ASTM C260

(2) hardener and dustproofer—"Lapodith," or equal, *f*

(3) non-slip additive—"Durafax" or equal,

(4) non-shrink additive—"Sika Set," or equal

1.4. The concrete contractor shall be responsible for all column support pads (footings) and expansion and contraction joints as shown on plans and/or as required by codes and ordinances.

1.5. The concrete contractor shall build into the concrete all materials furnished by others and shall secure same: including plumbing, electrical conduit, concrete inserts, anchors, hangers, hold-downs, sleeving for piping, and so on, when and where required by the other trades.

03480 Precast Concrete Specialties

1.1. A 6" (15.24 cm) wide by 8" (20.32 cm) deep precast trench drain shall be installed at the bottom of the loading ramp and abutting the loading dock. An open storm drain shall be located at the northeast corner of the drive area (see plans for location) which shall receive drainage from the trench drain and swales and shall be connected to the storm drain located to the north of the property on First Avenue. The drain shall be 3'-0" (91.44 cm) long by 2'-0" (60.96 cm) wide by 18" (45.72 cm) deep. The top of the drain shall be even with the lowest part of the surrounding area and a minimum 4" (10.16 cm) lower than the trench drain at the loading dock.

END OF DIVISION

FIGURE 10–2
(continued)

DIVISION 4 Masonry

04000 Scope of Work

    1.1. Division 1 and the General Conditions shall be considered a part of this division. Provide all labor, material, and equipment necessary to complete the structural and miscellaneous steel work indicated on the drawings. All materials to meet ASTM requirements. Install all embeds, anchors, and accessories as shown on plans or as required for a complete installation.

04100 Mortar and Masonry Grout

    1.1. Mortar shall be pre-mixed Type S or Type N as required by code and local ordinances. The pre-mix shall be supplied by one manufacturer and shall be 1800 psi (816.47 kg/6.45 cm^2), consistent with all ASTM requirements as well as local codes and ordinances. All masonry units are to be installed in a $^3/_8$″ (0.96 cm) mortar bed and head.
    1.1.a. Mortar may be used for a period of one (1) hour after mixing. Where required, a fluidifier may be used. Care must be taken to ensure that the consistency is not changed by addition of too much water.
    1.2. Grout shall be a 2000 psi (907.19 kg/6.45 cm^2) ready-mix concrete with $^3/_8$″ (0.96 cm) pea gravel. All masonry cells shall be grout filled. Where weather conditions permit, a plasticizer may be used to aid in the grout placement.

04150 Masonry Accessories

    1.1. All vertical masonry reinforcement shall be 1-#5 rebar spaced at 4′-0″ (1.22 m) O/C, horizontally, to match the dowel rebar placed in the slab or footing. 2-#5 rebar shall be additionally installed on each side of all openings and shall extend three (3) courses above the openings. 1-#5 rebar shall be added on each side of all control joints. 2-#5 rebar shall extend continuously along the east wall in the double bond beam installed over the overhead door openings.
    1.1.a. 2-#4 continuous rebar shall be installed horizontally at 4′-0″ (1.22 m) O/C, vertically, U.N.O. 2-#4 rebar shall also be installed at the roof line and 1-#4 rebar at the top of parapet. Rebar extending through control joints shall be taped with cambric a minimum 8″ (20.32 cm) each side of the joint.
    1.3. Where required, masonry Rapid Control Joints® by Duro-Wall® are to be installed the complete height of the wall. No wall shall exceed 40′-0″ clear without installation of a control joint.
    1.4. All other masonry and non-masonry accessories, although not specified, are understood to be a part of these Specifications to ensure a complete installation.

FIGURE 10–2
(continued)

04220 Concrete Unit Masonry

1.1. All masonry units shall conform to ASTM C-90. All units shall be supplied from one source. The units shall be structural concrete masonry, 8×8×16 precision, for unexposed retaining walls and exposed manufacturing/warehouse walls, f'm 1565 psi (709.88 kg/6.45 cm^2) and shall meet a total 3125 psi (1,417.49 kg/6.45 cm^2) when cured and grouted. Exposed slumpstone masonry units, 8×6×16 shall be f'm 1506.

1.1.a. All units shall be installed in a common bond. All precision masonry in the manufacturing/warehouse area shall be struck joints on the exterior and hand-tooled joints on the interior side of the units. Retaining walls shall be struck joints unless exposed. All exposed precision units shall be hand-tooled. All slumpstone units shall be hand-tooled both sides. No damaged units shall be installed.

1.1.b. All units shall be stored in a place or in a manner whereby they may be protected. All incomplete work at the end of each workday shall be braced and covered with polyethylene sheets to protect the units from moisture and dust.

END OF DIVISION

DIVISION 5 Metals

05000 Scope of Work

1.1. Division 1 and the General Conditions shall be considered a part of this division. Provide all labor, material, and equipment necessary to complete the structural and miscellaneous steel work indicated on the drawings. All materials to meet ASTM requirements. Install all embeds, anchors, and accessories as shown on plans or as required for a complete installation.

05050 Metal Fastening

1.1.a. The steel manufacturer shall provide all reinforcement bar as specified in Division 3, Concrete, and Division 4, Masonry. All rebar shall meet the ASTM requirements.

05120 Structural Metal Framing

1.1. The column supports for the glue-laminated beams shall be fabricated by a steel fabricator with all accessory parts included (base plate, 6" (15.24 cm) DIA column, top plate, and beam hinges) as per plans. The column bottom plate shall be fastened to the concrete pad with $^5/_8$" (1.59 cm)

FIGURE 10–2
(continued)

anchor or expansion bolts. Bolting for the glue-laminated beam shall be ⅝" (1.59 cm) through bolts, extending sufficiently long enough to expose a minimum ⅜" (0.95 cm) beyond the flat and lock washers and tightened nuts. The tightened nuts shall be tack welded to prevent loosening.

1.2. Hinge connectors shall be constructed of ¼" steel plate in the design shown on the plans and details. The hinge connectors may be manufactured or custom-made if a manufactured size is not available. Simpson Strong Tie Company, or equal, may be approved for the hinges.

1.3. Steel materials and accessories shall meet all ASTM, FM and local codes requirements.

05530 Gratings

1.1. A grating shall be fabricated to fit the top of the trench drain at the loading dock. The grating shall be a total of 55'-8" (15.97 m) long by 7" (17.78 cm) wide cast in two (2) sections 5'-4" (1.62 m) long and two sections 5'-0" (1.52 m) long. The casting shall have two (2) supports extending 8" (20.32 cm) to the bottom of the trench on each side of the trench as per plans.

1.1.a. A grate shall be manufactured and fitted over the 3'-0" (91.44 cm) by 2'-0" (60.96 cm) storm drain. The grate shall be of sufficient strength to withstand heavy traffic. The grate shall completely cover the precast drain with a ¼" (0.64 cm) thick by 1½" (3.81 cm) deep steel plate welded to the underside of the grate placed so as to fit into the precast drain for rigidity and support. All welding shall be continuous ¼" (0.64 cm) fillet welds on both sides of the extensions for all gratings. Flat plate joints shall be welded with continuous V groove welding both sides of plate. All flat surfaces shall be scarfed and ground smooth.

END OF DIVISION

DIVISION 6 Wood and Plastics

06000 Scope of Work

1.1. Division 1 and the General Conditions are to be considered a part of this division. Furnish all labor, materials, tools, and equipment necessary to complete all work under this division and as indicated on drawings. All lumber shall meet the Western Wood Products Association (WWPA) standards for materials. All plate stock shall be DF common or HF utility stock. All studs shall bear identification verifying stud grade. All other vertical structural members shall be DF #2 or better. All horizontal structural members shall be DF #1 or better, U.N.O.

FIGURE 10–2
(continued)

1.2. Provide and maintain temporary enclosures, fences, and barricades as required by local codes and ordinances and OSHA. If required, provide temporary door and window enclosures.

06100 Rough Carpentry

1.1. A rough-sawn 6×12 (15.24 cm × 30.48 cm), DF #1 or better, beam shall be centered in the demising wall. The top of the beam shall be 12'-0" (3.66 m) A.F.F. and shall be supported by two (2) rough-sawn 6×6 (15.24 cm × 15.24 cm), DF #2 or better, posts. The beam shall be mounted on the posts in such a way that the connections are not visible.

1.2. A 3×10 (7.62 cm × 25.40 cm), DF #2 or better, ledger shall be installed on the north and south walls of the manufacturing/warehouse for support for joists. The ledger shall be fastened with $\frac{5}{8}$" DIA × 7" (1.59 cm DIA × 17.78 cm) anchor bolts embedded in the masonry walls at 48" (1.22 m) O/C, with all necessary accessories. The top of the ledger shall be 12'-0" (3.66 m) A.F.F.

1.3. The exterior walls of the plant office, wash/restroom and break room, shall have $\frac{1}{2}$" exterior grade CDX or OSB™ sheathing. The ceiling over the plant office, wash/restroom, and break room shall be two (2) layers of $\frac{1}{2}$" exterior grade CDX or OSB™.

06150 Wood and Metal Systems

1.1. Open web joists, manufactured by Trus-Joist/MacMillan, for the manufacturing/warehouse area. Trusses shall be series TJL, 14" (35.56 cm) deep by 27'-6 $\frac{1}{8}$" (8.39 m) long, top chord, connected to the glue-laminated beam with hangers and to the ledger on the masonry walls with beam with hangers. Accessories shall be provided by the manufacturer as required for support and rigidity of the trusses. Trusses shall be spaced at 2'-0" (0.61 m) O/C.

06180 Glue-Laminated Beams

1.1. Structural glue-laminated beams shall be installed as part of the structural roof support system. All beams shall be cambered a minimum 1" (2.54 cm). The center beam shall be $6\frac{3}{4}$" × 27" × 24'-0" (17.14 cm × 0.69 m × 7.32 m), the two (2) end beams shall each be $6\frac{3}{4}$" × 18" × 31'-0" (17.14 cm × 0.46 m × 6.47 m). The one end of the two equal beams shall rest on the masonry pilasters for support. The larger beam shall be connected with a hinge connector as designed and required in Division 5, Metals. The interior end of the smaller beams shall rest on the 6" DIA (15.24 cm DIA) pipe column supports provided for the purpose.

FIGURE 10–2
(continued)

06190 Wood Trusses

    1.1. Prefabricated wood trusses, 3:12 slope, manufactured by Trus-Joist/MacMillan, for the office area. Trusses shall be constructed with a 2×6 (5.08 cm × 15.24 cm) top chord and 2×4 (5.08 cm × 10.16 cm) bottom chord. The trusses shall be constructed so as to provide the shed roof configuration as indicated on the structural framing plan. Trusses are to be mounted on the exterior of the plant west wall on a 2×10 (5.08 cm × 25.40 cm) top ledger and the bottom of the 2×8 (5.08 cm × 20.32 cm) bottom ledger at 12'-0" (2.66 m) A.F.F. All trusses, blocking, and accessories shall be supplied by the manufacturer. The truss shall include a rafter tail to extend 2'-0" (0.61 m) beyond the plate line at the eave.

06200 Finish Carpentry

    1.1. An oak wood surround shall be installed at all windows on the interior side of the exterior walls. In addition a $1/2$" (1.27 cm) to $3/4$" (1.91 cm) thick return of the same thickness shall be applied to both sides and head of each window immediately adjacent to the interior side of the window. An apron and stool of matching oak finish shall be applied to the interior side of the exterior windows. All nailing shall be with 6d finish nails, maximum $1 1/2$" (3.81 cm) long. The nails shall be slightly punched for application of a finish putty over each nail head. All joints shall be smooth and even.

    1.2. A matching 3" (7.62 cm) baseboard shall be applied at all areas where carpeting exists and in the showroom area.

    1.3. The exterior walls of the plant office shall have a $1/2$" (1.27 cm) insulating sheathing board installed with panelized $7/16$" (1.11 cm) T-1-11 siding over.

END OF DIVISION

DIVISION 7 Thermal and Moisture Protection

07000 Scope of Work

    1.1. Division 1 and the General Conditions are to be considered a part of this division. Furnish all labor, materials, and equipment necessary to complete all work under this division and as indicated on drawings.

    1.2. Work shall include a 20 mil polyethylene sheet horizontally under the slabs and footings; installation of tile and built-up roofing; insulation between office walls and ceilings adjacent to the plant, interior offices and display room.

FIGURE 10–2
(continued)

07110 Sheet Membrane Below-Grade Moisture Protection

1.1. All retaining walls shall be moisture-protected with a single-ply self-adhering bituminous membrane with $1/2''$ (1.27 cm) rigid fibrous protection board over.

1.2. Acceptable manufacturers are as follows:

Koppers   GAF   Owens Corning   Johns-Manville

1.3. The membrane shall be applied as per manufacturer's specifications and shall be approved by manufacturer with a certificate of approval and a minimum five (5) year warranty.

07200 Insulation

1.1. Install an R-11 combination thermal and batt insulation by Owens Corning in all interior office, hall, perimeter wall framing in the office areas, and the plant office, break room, and wash/restroom. Install an R-30 batt insulation in the ceiling of the offices.

1.2. A 2×4 (5.08 cm × 10.16 cm) chemically treated fire-retardant furring strip shall be installed over the interior face of the masonry on the east, west and south walls. The furring shall be applied horizontally, 2'-0'' (0.61 m) O/C, vertically, The strips shall be fastened with concrete nails or anchor bolts or screws.

1.3. A rigid roof insulation system shall be installed over the plywood deck. The system shall be a tapered insulating system by Western Insulation Company, Los Angeles, California. The manufacturer shall estimate the materials required and cut the insulation to properly fit as per the roof plan. All tapered insulation shall be directed to the roof drainage system.

1.3.a. Western Insulation shall properly protect its product from damage and weather. Any materials that must be replaced shall be at the expense of the manufacturer or contractor, whichever is deemed responsible for the damage.

1.3.b. A guarantee shall be provided for the product and its approved installation that covers a period of five (5) years.

07300 Roofing Tiles

1.1. Roofing shall be clay slate tile, variegated colors, as manufactured by EuroTile Systems, or equal. Underlayment shall be a 43 lb (19.55 kg), 36'' (91.44 cm) wide, 5-square felt laid horizontally on the roof sheathing starting from the bottom (eave line). The felts shall have a minimum 4'' (10.16 cm) lap.

1.1.a. The tile shall be laid with a maximum 5'' (12.70 cm) exposure. All tiles shall be laid in a straight and true horizontal line. No broken tiles shall be used. All broken tiles shall be replaced prior to final inspection of the roof.

FIGURE 10–2
(continued)

1.1.b. A prefabricated plastic or metal ridge vent shall be installed under the ridge along the top of the masonry wall. (See Section 07600, Flashing and Sheet Metal.)

1.2. Manufacturer shall supply a ten (10) year warranty covering workmanship and material. A certificate of acceptance by the manufacturer shall be submitted to the owner prior to release of retention payment.

07460 Manufactured Siding

1.1 The face of the end trusses above the masonry walls on each side of the office segment of the structure shall be covered with aluminum shiplap siding over $^1/_2''$ (1.27 cm) insulating sheathing with a minimum $7^1/_2$ lb (3.41 kg) moisture barrier. Materials shall meet all ASTM criteria and local codes and ordinances. Siding shall be applied with proper flashing and fasteners as recommended by the manufacturer. Siding selection shall be at the option of the owner.

07500 Membrane Roofing

1.1. The plywood roof deck shall be covered with a $2^1/_2''$ (6.35 cm), 2' × 4' (0.61 m x 1.22 m) rigid fiberglass insulation board manufactured by Owens Corning. The insulation shall be in two layers. The first layer shall be $1^1/_2''$ (6.35 cm) thick and the second layer 1" (2.54 cm) thick. The first layer shall be adhered to the roof deck with a "spot" mopping and typical insulation nails a minimum $2^1/_2''$ (6.35 cm) long. The joints shall be staggered and tape sealed. The second layer shall be mopped in place with a minimum 15 lb (6.82 kg) coating of hot asphalt. The joints shall be staggered and opposite the joints of the first layer and tape sealed.

1.2. The built-up roofing system shall be a four-ply BUR system, specification I04G by GAF with decorative white gravel topping, is hereby specified. Asphalt shall be supplied in a pre-heated tank truck. All felt materials shall be supplied by the same manufacturer. All asphalt shall be supplied by the same manufacturer. The asphalt shall be approved for use with the BUR system. The system shall be applied as follows:

Type II asphalt ply coat	@ 25 lb (11.34 kg)
Gafglas Ply 4 sheet	@ 10 lb (4.54 kg)
Type II asphalt ply coat	@ 25 lb (11.34 kg)
Gafglas Ply 4 sheet	@ 10 lb (4.54 kg)
Type II asphalt ply coat	@ 25 lb (11.34 kg)
Gafglas Ply 4 sheet	@ 10 lb (4.54 kg)
Type II asphalt ply coat	@ 25 lb (11.34 kg)
Gafglas Ply 4 sheet	@ 10 lb (4.54 kg)
Asphalt flood coat	@ 60 lb (27.22 kg)
White decorative pea gravel	@450 lb (204.12 kg)
Total weight	650 lb (294.86 kg)

FIGURE 10–2
(continued)

07600 Flashing and Sheet Metal

1.1. All sheet metal flashings and accessories for the roof shall be supplied by the sheet metal contractor. All sheet metal shall be a minimum 26 gauge galvanized steel or aluminum material with the exception of the pipe jacks, which shall be manufactured in $1/16$" (0.16 cm) thick lead and formed in the same manner as the galvanized flashings. 26 gauge galvanized steel shall be used for the coping on the manufacturing/warehouse parapets.

1.2. A prefabricated ridge vent shall be used along the ridges.

07900 Sealants and Caulking

1.1. The contractor shall provide for installation of joint sealants and caulking at all control joints. Caulking shall also be provided around all exterior doors and windows.

END OF DIVISION

DIVISION 8 Doors and Windows

08000 Scope of Work

1.1. Division 1 and the General Conditions are to be considered a part of this division. Furnish all labor, materials, and equipment necessary to complete all work under this division and as indicated on drawings. Refer to door and window schedules on the plans.

08100 Metal Doors and Frames

1.1. Exterior doors to be hollow-metal (HM) with hollow-metal frames. The door separating the offices from the manufacturing area shall also be hollow metal w/hollow-metal frame and shall be installed as a fire door to be connected to the emergency alarm system.

08200 Wood and Plastic Doors

1.1. Interior doors to have hollow-metal knock-down (KDHM) frames. See door schedule for door styles and types. All interior doors to have sound insulation fill (STC 60) in the door cores to match the sound attenuation requirements for the walls.

FIGURE 10–2
(continued)

08250 Door Opening Assemblies

1.1. All door hardware is to be supplied by one manufacturer. The hardware shall be Schlage, or equal. The following is the hardware schedule for all doors:

Front Entry—Schlage entry latch w/thumb latch handle and deadbolt, w/matching key, brass. Schlage handle to match latch. $1^{1}/_{2}$ sets butts, brass, each leaf.

Side Exterior Doors—Schlage emergency kit hardware only (no special knowledge). $1^{1}/_{2}$ sets butts, brass.

Offices and restroom—Schlage privacy latch, brass, $1^{1}/_{2}$ sets butts, brass.

1.1.a. All emergency door closers, shall be the "No Special Knowledge" type of release bar.

08500 Metal Windows

1.1. Windows shall be aluminum framed and manufactured to fit into frame or masonry wall openings. All glazing for the exterior windows shall be integrally tinted, gray, dual pane insulated glass, $^{1}/_{8}$" (0.32 cm) thick, w/$^{1}/_{2}$" (1.27 cm) air space between panes. Windows are to be installed as per plans and details. The window schedule is a part of this specification.

END OF DIVISION

DIVISION 9 Finishes

09000 Scope of Work

1.1. Division 1 and the General Conditions are to be considered a part of this division. Furnish all labor, materials, and equipment necessary to complete all work under this division and as indicated on drawings. Work is to include installation of cement plaster on exterior masonry walls, an acoustical suspension system, drywall, floor coverings, wall tile, and painting.

09100 Metal Support Systems

1.1. A metal stud framing system shall be installed for all interior office framing. Interior nonbearing walls shall be 4"–20 ga (10.16 cm–20 ga) galvanized studs and track at 24" (0.61 m) O/C. The plumbing wall between the kitchen and restroom shall be 6"–20 ga (15.24 cm–20 ga) studs and track at

FIGURE 10–2
(continued)

24″ (0.61 m) O/C. Hall walls shall be 6″–20 ga (15.24 cm–20 ga) galvanized studs and track at 24″ (0.61 m) O/C. All walls shall extend to a height of 9′-0″ A.F.F. (UNO). The demising wall between the offices and display room shall be 6″–20 ga (15.24 cm–20 ga) stud and track at 16″ (0.41 m) O/C. extending to the underside of the roof structure. All necessary accessories required shall be in accordance with the manufacturer's recommendations, codes, and local ordinances. All materials shall be supplied by American Studco Company, Phoenix, Arizona.

1.2. See Reflected Ceiling Plan for locations of ACT system. All ACT ceilings are to be 8′-0″ (2.44 m) A.F.F. Install 1″ (2.54 cm) wall angle along perimeter of all supporting walls. Install 1″ (2.54 cm) main "T" runners spaced 2′-0″ (0.61 m) O/C., with secondary cross runners spaced at 4′-0″ (1.22 m) O/C. Center the main runners in each area for aesthetic appearance. In areas where the walls are 4′-0″ (1.22 m) apart only the wall angle and main "T" runners shall be used. All joints shall be fastened with corner clips at the walls and at the cross joints.

1.2.a. The ceiling shall be suspended with 9 gauge tie wire fastened to the wood joists by a screw eye and to the runners with a clip fastener at the corners of the mains and cross secondary members. Tie wires shall be installed so as to offer support every 9 square feet of ceiling area or as necessary for proper support. Additional tie wire shall be added at each corner of the T bar ceiling structure where an electrical fluorescent fixture is to be installed. Add seismic support as may be required by local code and ordinance.

09200 Lath and Plaster

1.1. The exterior face of the exposed precision masonry walls shall have an Exterior Insulation and Finish System (EIFS) cement plaster finish with integral coloring. Coloring shall be selected by owner from standard pigmentation. All materials shall be from one manufacturer. Acceptable manufacturer(s) include:

Senergy   Dryvit   Sto Corp.

1.2. The system shall be installed as per manufacturer's specifications. The contractor shall be responsible for timely work and quality control. The contractor shall supply a written manufacturer's warranty to cover a period of ten (10) years after the manufacturer's inspection and acceptance of the work.

09250 Gypsum Board (GWB)

1.1. The office partition and plant office interior walls shall be covered with one (1) layer of ⁵⁄₈″ (1.59 cm) X (Firecode) by USG, or equal, both sides. The demising wall between the offices and showroom shall be covered with two (2) layers of ⁵⁄₈″ (1.59 cm) X (Firecode) by USG, or equal, on

FIGURE 10–2
(continued)

both sides. The perimeter walls adjacent to the exterior masonry shall have one (1) layer of ⅝″ (1.59 cm) X (Firecode) by USG, or equal, on the interior side of the framing. The office/showroom area shall also have one layer of ⅝″ (1.59 cm) X (Firecode) GWB installed on the underside of the roof trusses.

1.1.a. Drywall shall be laid horizontally with the long side perpendicular to the framing on both walls and ceilings. The sheets shall be placed so that all vertical joints on walls and the ends on the ceilings are staggered. Staggered joints shall be centered on the adjacent sheets.

1.1.b. GWB shall be fastened with a minimum 1⅛″ (2.86 cm) drywall screws spaced at 6″ O/C (15.24 cm) along the perimeter of each sheet and 9″ O/C (22.86 cm) in the field. The screws shall be applied with sufficient force to slightly indent the GWB.

1.1.c. All exposed joints on walls and ceilings shall be sealed with either paper tape or self-adhering tape and multipurpose compound. The first application shall be left to set and, when dry, sanded smooth. A second application is applied to the taped joint, allowed to set, and sanded smooth to match the GWB surface for application of paint or wallcovering. All exposed screw heads shall also be embedded in multipurpose compound, sanded and smoothed to match the GWB surface. See Finish Schedule for textures. All drywall ceilings are 8′-0″ A.F.F. (2.44 m), U.N.O.

1.1.d. All areas above the ceilings shall be fire-taped only.

09300 Tile

1.1. See Finish Schedule for location and other information regarding ceramic wall tile to be installed. Tile shall be "Dal-Tile," or equal, 4×4 (10.16 cm × 10.16 cm), color to be selected by owner from standard ranges. Bullnose tile shall be applied at all exposed ends of tile.

1.2. Tile shall be applied using a thinset cement wall application and grouted with a color matching the tiles as per manufacturer's recommendations.

09510 Acoustical Treatment

1.1. An acoustical ceiling tile (ACT) shall be installed using Armstrong Acoustical Tile, 2′ × 4′ (0.61 m × 1.22 m), 1½″ (1.91 cm) thick, treated wood fiber, fissured, 1-hour rated fire-retardant boards. See Section 09100 for the support system for this installation.

09650 Resilient Flooring

1.1. Vinyl composition tile (VCT) flooring shall be installed with an adhesive directly to the subfloor. Tile shall be placed so that it is properly centered on the floor in each area where it is used.

FIGURE 10–2
(continued)

1.2. The tile flooring shall have a 4" (5.08 cm) base, or coving of the same height. See Finish Schedule. The coving shall be backed by a 1½" (3.81 cm) concave quarter-round wood member, color selected by owner to match flooring.

1.3. The contractor shall allow for left-over material, sufficient for repairs, to be left on the project.

09680 Carpet

1.1 See Finish Schedule for location of carpet installation. Carpeting shall be DuPont, commercial grade, heavy traffic, with a rubber pad. Installation shall be by a reputable carpet contractor. Seams shall be kept to a minimum. Seams shall be installed so that the webbing or joint does not show after installation. A guarantee shall be supplied to the contractor and owner by manufacturer as to workmanship and material. A copy of the manufacturer's accreditation shall be in the hands of the owner prior to final payment and retention.

09900 Painting

1.1. See Finish Schedule for location of all interior painting and exterior elevations for exterior paint. Colors to be selected by owner from standard color ranges.

1.2. Acceptable paint manufacturers for standard paints are:

  Sinclair Paints Sherwin-Williams Paints
  Dunn-Edwards   Frazee Paints

1.3. The painting shall be applied as follows:

  Exterior Walls (to match cement plaster color) and Trim:
  Exterior Wood Trim—Oil based stain
  Standard colors selected by owner
  Underside of Overhang—one coat primer and two coats latex paint
  Interior Walls—one coat sealer, one coat primer, and one coat
    semi-gloss epoxy

END OF DIVISION

FIGURE 10–2
(continued)

DIVISION 10 Specialties

10000 Scope of Work

    1.1. Division 1 and the General Conditions are to be considered a part of this division. Furnish all labor, materials, and equipment necessary to complete all work under this division and as indicated on drawings.
    1.2. The work shall include installation of all identifying devices and personnel lockers.

10400 Identifying Devices

    1.1. Exterior signage and other identifying devices, such as exit signs and restroom identification, shall be a part of this contract and shall be installed as per all codes and ordinances. The exterior sign shall be painted on a wood background with frame and lighting to be mounted over front entry. The design shall be given to contractor by owner for production.

10500 Lockers

    1.1. Individual personnel storage lockers shall be installed for each employee and are to be located in the plant restroom for the plant/warehouse employees and in the office restroom for the office employees. The number of employees to be determined by owner (maximum of fifty).

10800 Toilet and Bath Accessories

    1.1. The contractor shall be responsible for the purchase and installation of all Restroom and Kitchen accessories including, but not limited to, mirrors, dispensers, waste depositories, and grab bars per ADA requirements.

END OF DIVISION

DIVISION 11 Equipment

11000 Scope of Work

    1.1. Division 1 and the General Conditions are to be considered a part of this division. Furnish all materials, labor, and equipment necessary to complete the installation of all of the equipment as indicated on drawings and in these Specifications.

FIGURE 10–2
(continued)

1.2. It is the responsibility of the manufacturers' erector crews to install all necessary equipment for a loading dock with all accessories and the processing system for the manufacturing area.

11160 Loading Dock Equipment

1.1. The contractor shall be responsible for proper installation of the equipment. Where required, coordination shall be applied by the various subcontractors responsible for specialty installations, such as plumbing and/or electrical.

11500 Industrial and Process Equipment

1.1. The owner shall supply the paint booth and mixing equipment used for the manufacture and finishing of residential and commercial plumbing fixtures. The contractor shall be responsible for placement and installation of the equipment as directed by the owner or manufacturer. All codes and ordinances shall be adhered to. See manufacturers' instructions, plans, and shop drawings for proper location and installation procedures.

END OF DIVISION

DIVISION 12 Furnishings—N.I.C. Supplied and installed by owner.

DIVISION 13 Special Construction

13000 Scope of Work

1.1. Division 1 and the General Conditions are to be considered a part of this division. Furnish all materials, labor, and equipment necessary to complete the installation of all of the equipment as indicated on drawings and in these Specifications. Installation of the control systems for the mixing, kiln and finishing system, and the conveying equipment are a part of this division. A systems supervisory for the fire suppression system shall also be included as a part of this division.

13400 Industrial and Process Control Systems

1.1. All trades involved with the installation of the process equipment shall also be responsible for the correct application and installation of all operating and safety controls. The drying booth, the mixing vats, kilns, and dryers are all to be installed in accordance with manufacturer requirements and/or recommendations. The contractor shall make certain that all work shall comply with OSHA, ADA, and ANSI regulations and orders.

FIGURE 10–2
(continued)

13900 Fire Suppression and Supervisory Systems

1.1. The mechanical engineer shall supply a complete fire sprinkler system for the office and manufacturing/warehouse areas. A special suppression system shall be installed in conjunction with the kiln and processing units. Shop drawings shall be submitted to the engineer and architect for approval prior to any construction.

END OF DIVISION

DIVISION 14 Conveying Systems

14000 Scope of Work

1.1. Division 1 and the General Conditions are to be considered a part of this division. Furnish all materials, labor, and equipment necessary to complete the installation of any equipment required for material handling as indicated on drawings and in these Specifications. The equipment shall include a floor-operated A-frame crane with proper electrical controls and safety features.

14500 Material Handling Systems

1.1. A conveying system shall be installed in the manufacturing/ warehouse portion of the structure for handling of parts and complete units to and from the processing areas and the warehouse storage areas.

1.2. All work shall be in accordance with manufacturer's requirements and/or recommendations as well as with local codes and ordinances. Shop drawings shall be submitted for approval. Warning devices and alarm systems shall be a part of the installation and shall meet OSHA and ANSI requirements.

1.3. Where motorized equipment is used in lieu of a conveying system, the motorized equipment shall be required to include all safety and warning devices as required by ANSI and OSHA.

14600 Hoists and Cranes

1.1. The floor-operated crane shall be installed in the manufacturing/ warehouse area by the manufacturer's installation crew. All work shall be coordinated with the contractor to ensure cooperation with all other trades. Shop drawings shall be submitted for approval prior to installation. The equipment shall meet the requirements of both ANSI and OSHA.

END OF DIVISION

FIGURE 10–2
(continued)

DIVISION 15 Mechanical

15000 Scope of Work

1.1. Division 1 and the General Conditions are to be considered a part of this division. Furnish all labor, material, and equipment necessary to complete all work under this division and as indicated on drawings.

15050 Basic Mechanical Materials and Methods

1.1. In addition to the requirements stated in Section 15000, the mechanical contractor shall be governed by the regulations established by professional engineers who have designed the installation and material requirements.

1.2. The mechanical contractor shall also be governed by the regulations of ASHRAE, OSHA, and by national, regional, and/or local mechanical and plumbing codes, where applicable. The materials used shall be as specified in the following sections.

15400 Plumbing

1.1. The plumbing contractor shall be responsible for all fee and permit costs in reference to the plumbing and piping applying to this project.

1.2. Plumbing shall include, but is not limited to, installation of all sanitary sewer, storm drainage, gas, and potable water connections from the off-sites to, and including, the appliance or fixture shut-off valves and the appliances or fixtures themselves. Fittings not specifically mentioned shall be construed to be included to make a complete installation.

1.3. Provide and install all soil, waste, vent pipes, and clean-outs for all sewer lines in accordance with local code. Provide proper drainage where necessary and ensure that all stub-outs are properly capped. Pipe and fitting sizes shall be as per plans. Where discrepancies may occur with local codes and installation recommendations, such codes and recommendations shall prevail.

1.4. Provide and install type K copper pipe for all underground potable water service and connections. Use Type K or L copper pipe for all potable water above grade pipe.

1.5. Where gas is used for heating and/or hot water heat, gas piping shall be schedule 40, black steel pipe. All below-grade gas pipe and gas pipe exposed to the atmosphere shall be wrapped with a polyethylene wrapper coating.

1.6. Insulate all cold and hot water piping as required by local codes and ordinances. Hold installation to inside of building insulation to prevent freezing.

FIGURE 10–2
(continued)

1.7. The plumbing fixture schedule is as follows:

Handicap Water closet: American "Cadet" #2108.408-18" (45.72 cm) high
                          Church #295 Or equal
Lavatories: Custom designed cultured marble one-piece lavatory
                          tops w/basins integral (color and style to be
                          selected by owner)
Mop Basin: Stainless Steel by Elkay, or equal
Scrub Basin: By American Standard or equal

15500 Heating, Ventilation, and Air Conditioning

1.1. Mechanical contractor shall supply shop drawings for the installation of the HVAC system as required.

1.2. All fees and permits for the HVAC installation are at the expense of the mechanical contractor. The HVAC equipment shall be manufactured by Lennox Corporation, or equal. The mechanical contractor shall propose two separate self-contained HVAC units.

1.3. The system for the manufacturing/warehouse area shall include one 5-ton self-contained unit with all necessary accessories. The HVAC contractor shall ascertain that the structure is sufficiently constructed to properly support the unit, controls, and accessories.

1.4. A heat exchanger with all accessories shall be installed in the office ceiling. The unit shall be a split system with the A/C compressor located outside the office on a concrete pad. The equipment shall include, but is not limited to, ductwork, grilles, registers, and other fittings as necessary for a complete installation.

1.5. Separate thermostat controls shall operate both units manually and automatically. See HVAC Plan. Coordinate all work with the plumbing and electrical contractors where required.

END OF DIVISION

DIVISION 16 Electrical

16000 Scope of Work

1.1. Division 1 and the General Conditions are to be considered a part of this division. Furnish all labor, material, and equipment necessary to complete all work under this division and as indicated on drawings.

FIGURE 10–2
(continued)

16050 Basic Electrical Materials and Methods

   1.1. In addition to the requirements stated in Section 16000, the electrical contractor shall be governed by the regulations established by professional engineers who have designed the installation and material requirements. The electrical contractor shall also conform to the latest edition of the NEC, OSHA, regional and/or local electrical codes, where applicable. The materials used shall be as specified in the following sections.

16400 Service and Distribution

   1.1. Provide for an adequate service and grounding system as shown on drawings and as described in the specifications. Conduit shall be used as a continuous ground path from appliance to distribution center. A complete equipment ground conductor shall also be supplied from each appliance to the distribution center.
   1.2. All materials shall be new and supplied by one manufacturer with shipping crates intact. The contractor shall be provided with proof of manufacturer's shipping record. All materials selected shall be as indicated in the specifications and/or electrical schedules. All equipment shall have a label and/or stamp from an approved testing laboratory such as Underwriters Laboratories (UL), and all motorized and switchgear equipment shall have nameplates which shall be supplied with the equipment. All disconnects shall be rated NEMA 1 enclosures.
   1.3. The electrical contractor shall coordinate all installation with the local utility company and shall provide connections for service when all service is inspected and approved. The electrical contractor shall further coordinate all hook-ups with contractors of other trades where cooperation is necessary for speedy execution of the contract.
   Acceptable manufacturers of the switchgear equipment are:

        Square D   General Electric   White/Westinghouse   ITT

   1.5.   There shall be two (2) distribution panels as a part of the entry switchgear, one (1) for power and one (1) for lighting.

16500 Lighting (General Lighting and Power)

   1.1. All standard lighting switches shall be Hubbell 1221-1, or equal. All duplex receptacles shall be Hubbell 5262-1, or equal. All three-wire receptacles shall be by Hubbell, or equal (minimum 25A, 240VAC). All GFCI receptacles shall be GE-TGTR115F, or equal.
   1.2. Exterior lighting installations shall be underground using schedule 80 electrical PVC conduit.

FIGURE 10–2
(continued)

    1.3. The electrical contractor has the liberty to make the best
application with the least cost and still have the installation acceptable to
all codes and regulations. Sizes of conduit shall be determined by the
electrical contractor with all connections, accessories, and wiring to be in
accordance with code. The minimum allowable size and insulation type for
conductors shall be #12AWG, THNN, for power and exterior lighting circuits,
and #14AWG, THNN, for interior lighting circuits.
    1.4. The electrical contractor shall install an empty conduit for
thermostat wiring.

16700 Communications

    1.1. A special conduit and a special circuit shall be installed for an
isolated computer system with additional junctions supplied in each office
for networking.
    1.2. The electrical contractor shall install an empty conduit for
telephone communications and for intercom and fire alarm systems. The systems
are to be installed by communications specialists who shall supply drawings
and specifications to the owner for approval.

                        END OF DIVISION

FIGURE 10–2
(continued)

    All information found in the project manual is part of the legal docu-
ments. Any discrepancies noted between the specifications and the set of
plans must be rectified prior to bidding or construction. Such problems are directed through the proper channels from subcontractor to general contractor,
and the general contractor to the architect, engineer, or both, for clarification.
In most cases the clarification request must be in writing.
    If the discrepancy is noted with sufficient time (four to ten days min-
imum) prior to a bid, an addendum may be prepared and all bidders notified.
If the discrepancy is noted following contract, the party making the discovery
must again notify the proper individual(s). If any change is to be made, the
owner, architect, engineer, or other authorized person, issues a work authorization and/or change order in writing before any work is done.

CHAPTER EXERCISES

Multiple Choice

_____   1. The project manual indicates that the owner of the Frontier Manufacturing is:
   a. Janus Corporation.
   b. Brophy Electric Company.
   c. Christle Associates.
   d. None of the above.

_____   2. The initials ASHRAE found in the list of support organizations represent:
   a. The ASHRAE Corporation.
   b. The American Society of Roofing Architects and Engineers.
   c. The Association of Standard Housing Regulations, Administration and Effort.
   d. The American Society of Heating, Refrigeration and Air–conditioning Engineers.

_____   3. Division 6 includes:
   a. Beams and supports.
   b. R/S beam, posts, sheathing, siding, joists, trusses, and roof decking.
   c. All interior framing.
   d. All of the above.

_____   4. The exterior finish specified for the Frontier Manufacturing building is:
   a. Slumpstone CMU and a one–coat stucco finish.
   b. Slumpstone and precision CMU.
   c. Precision CMU.
   d. EIFS and slumpstone.

_____   5. The HVAC includes:
   a. Radiant heating and a heat pump for the office areas.
   b. Swamp cooling for the whole building.
   c. Air–conditioning throughout.
   d. None of the above.

_____   6. Division 1:
   a. Is to be included as part of Division 12 only.
   b. Is inferred as a part of all the division.
   c. States the requirements for concrete work.
   d. All of the above.

_____   7. Division 12:
   a. Covers information regarding equipment.
   b. Is known as the Mechanical division.
   c. Is not included in the contract.
   d. All of the above.

_____   8. The format used for the project manual and specifications is called:
   a. The Legal format.
   b. The CSI format.
   c. The Contract format.
   d. The AIA format.

_____ 9. All of the divisions except Division 1 are referred to as:
   a. The trade divisions.
   b. The Special Requirements.
   c. The Instruction to Bidders.
   d. None of the above.

_____ 10. The AIA:
   a. Has a form, AIA Form 401A Rev, used in the specifications.
   b. Is an organization made up of certified architects.
   c. Is formally known as the American Institute of Architects.
   d. All of the above.

_____ 11. Division 2, Earthwork, includes:
   a. Landscaping and paving.
   b. Excavating and grading.
   c. Shoring and mass excavations.
   d. All of the above.

_____ 12. The division considered the most diversified is:
   a. Division 9, Finishes.
   b. Division 6, Wood and Plastics.
   c. Division 7, Thermal and Moisture Protection.
   d. Division 16, Electrical.

_____ 13. Included in Division 4 are:
   a. Concrete slab construction and pilings.
   b. Mortar, grout, reinforcement, and masonry units.
   c. Caulking and sealants.
   d. Clay roofing tiles.

_____ 14. The division that will normally be responsible for supplying steel reinforcement in commercial construction projects is:
   a. Division 3, Concrete.
   b. Division 4, Masonry.
   c. Division 5, Metals.
   d. Division 6, Wood and Plastics.

_____ 15. The divisions most commonly considered in carpentry construction include:
   a. Divisions 1, 4, and 14.
   b. Divisions 6, 9, and 12.
   c. Divisions 6, 8, and 9.
   d. Divisions 6, 14, and 15.

True or False

T F 1. The American Institute of Architects has written the basic requirements for Division 1 of the Specifications.

T F 2. A Specification may include a broadscope, mediumscope, and narrowscope expansion of directions for material, labor, and equipment requirements.

T F 3. The Specifications include a division defining requirements for steel construction.

T F 4. General Conditions and General Requirements are interchangeable.

T F   5. There are six major areas covered in a blueprint.

T F   6. A blueprint is a set of plans or drawings.

T F   7. Most commercial blueprints include schedules describing information not found directly on a plan.

T F   8. The Specifications include information for sixteen (16) divisions.

T F   9. A change in plans issued after contract is referred to as an addendum.

T F 10. Division 11, Equipment, of the Specifications supplies information regarding swimming pool construction.

T F 11. Divisions 10 through 14 of the Specifications are often referred to as the "Specialty Divisions."

T F 12. The work described in Division 9, Finishes, includes finish carpentry.

T F 13. The Project Manual includes information regarding the owner, architect, and engineering companies that took part in the development of the plans for a project.

T F 14. The Project Manual is a complete separate document not affiliated with the legal documents.

T F 15. Thermal and Moisture Protection are included in Division 8.

Completion

1. Commercial _____ are broken down into six major groups.

2. Specifications supply information on _____ divisions.

3. Structural plans may include _____ for reinforcement, columns, and beams.

4. A(n) _____ is written to advise of changes in bidding procedures or plans.

5. A section of Division 2, identified as _____, requires that all hazardous materials must be removed from a job–site prior to any other work.

6. Information on dumbwaiters is found in Division _____.

7. No corrections in the workplace after contract should be done without a written change order or work _____.

8. Sheet metal work is included in Division _____.

9. The _____ determines the strength requirement for concrete.

10. _____ is the section of Division 16, Electrical, stating the requirements for intercom systems.

11. A(n) _____ drawing is normally used to show the plumbing connections.

12. The power requirements for the Frontier Manufacturing are found in the specifications or _____.

13. The site facilities are supplied by the _____.

14. _____ and _____ are the materials to be installed for roofing on the Frontier Manufacturing building.

15. The exposed portions of the perimeter walls are constructed of _____ CMU.

16. The steel columns used for the glu–lam beams are _____" DIA.

17. _____ wood and steel joists are by Trus–Joist/MacMillan.

18. The size of the center glu–lam beam is _____ × _____ × _____.

19. The plant office is finished with _____ siding.

20. There a total of _____ windows in the main office area.

11

Off-Sites and Site Improvements

Each project has the possibility of off-site construction work. In the case of the Frontier Manufacturing Company, there is work involving the entry approach onto the property and retaining walls. These items are further discussed in the succeeding sections of this chapter.

See C-1, Site Plan, and C-2, Plot Plan, Frontier Manufacturing, Inc. The site plan and legal description on the plan indicate the benchmark is located at Broadway and Main Street at elevation 500.0′ (152.4 m). The datum point is identified at the intersection of Broad Street and First Avenue next to the project at elevation 504.0′ (153.62 m). The point of beginning (POB) for the project is the northwest corner, nearest the datum point, starting at elevation 507.0′ (154.53 m). The length of the property is 260.0′ (79.25 m) along the north property line, 125.0′ (38.1 m) along the east property line, 240.0′ (74.37 m) along the south property line, and 126.59′ (38.58 m) along the west property line.

The specifications for the site improvements include excavating and grading, surfacing (asphalt or concrete), landscaping, and, if necessary, concrete and masonry construction. Following the CSI format, information for these trades is located in Division 2, Earthwork; Division 3, Concrete; Division 4, Masonry; and Division 5, Metals."

EARTHWORK

The Entry Approach (Apron)

See figure 11–1 and refer to C-2 Plot Plan. The approach is 26′–0″ (10.97 m) long and 15′–0″ (4.57 m) wide from street curb to interior (top) end of approach at

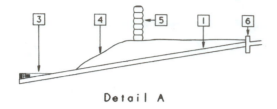

Detail A

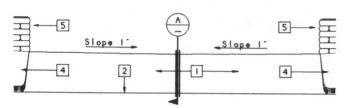

KEYNOTES

1. 5" thick concrete approach (see specs)

2. First Avenue street level-elevation 504.0'

3. Sidewalk beyond (N.I.C.)

4. Berm or landscaping

5. Masonry perimeter wall

6. Curb and gutter

FIGURE 11–1
Entry Approach

parking lot. The finish-grade elevations are indicated with a point (+) and the elevation on the plot plan. The plan indicates that the finish grade at the entrance is at elevation 507.5' (154.69 m) and the street elevation is 504.0' (153.62 m). Therefore, the apron must slope 3'–6" (1.07 m) from the parking area to the street (approximately $4^{1}/4$" per foot [10.8 cm per 30.48 cm]). It is constructed in concrete and ties into the asphalt parking area and the street.

Curb and Gutter

See figure 11–2. The curb and gutter detail and the Specifications for Division 2 indicate that the curb is 4" (10.16 cm) wide by 18" (45.72 cm) deep with a 6" (15.24 cm) exposure above the finish asphalt surface. The elevation of the curb and gutter will vary with the elevation of the finish surface throughout the project

FIGURE 11–2
Curb and Gutter

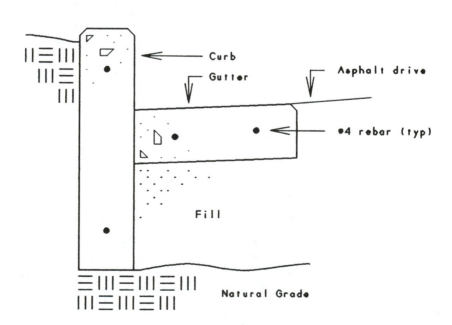

parking and driveway areas (U.N.O.). The exposed height will always remain the same. This detail is similar to the U.S. Department of Transportation (DOT) detail for curbs and gutters and is followed in most areas of the country.

The roof drains are extended into the interior curbs at the office portion or onto splash blocks around the plant/warehouse to direct water from the structure into the swales (see section below) constructed in the parking areas.

Asphalt Surfacing

Refer to C-2, Plot Plan and Specifications. The finish surface elevations of the parking areas and driveways are noted on the plot plan with the highest elevations nearest the curb and gutter and the lowest elevations along the center line of these areas. The whole of the east end slopes to the loading dock. The asphalt surfacing is specified indicating a 10″ (25.4 cm) sand or gravel base with a 4″ (10.16 cm) cementitious base and a 6″ (15.24 cm) asphalt surface and seal coating overall. The specifications also note that the finish surface shall be striped for parking and for traffic direction.

Swales and Drains

Refer to C-2, Plot Plan. Another construction note regarding the surfacing is the requirement for swales and a basin installed in the asphalt. A swale is, by definition, a natural depression, or man-made, in the earth that allows water to flow from one point to another, or may be constructed in any finished surfacing such as the asphalt surfacing on the plan. They are constructed to divert surface water away from the structure and into a drainage basin or into the street where drainage already exists. The swale in the west parking area directs the flow to the entry approach as does the one on the north side of the structure from the security fence and gate. The swale at the southeast corner of the drive area directs water away from the loading ramp.

See figure 11–3. Water is drained from the loading ramp area through the installation of a 6″ (15.24 cm) wide by 8″ (20.32 cm) deep trench drain, with a steel grate, at the base of the loading dock. The drawing indicates that the drain is constructed with 4″ (10.16 cm) thick concrete on the sides and bottom. A bulkhead (diverter wall) is installed at the north end of the drain to accommodate a 6″ (15.24 cm) DIA (ID) cast-iron steel pipe.

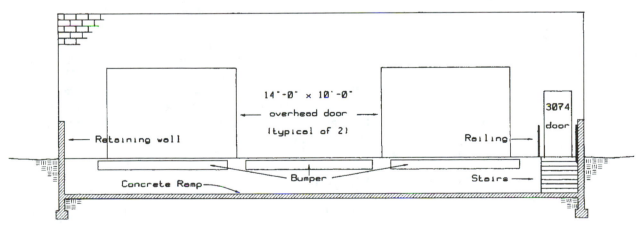

FIGURE 11–3
Loading Dock, Full View

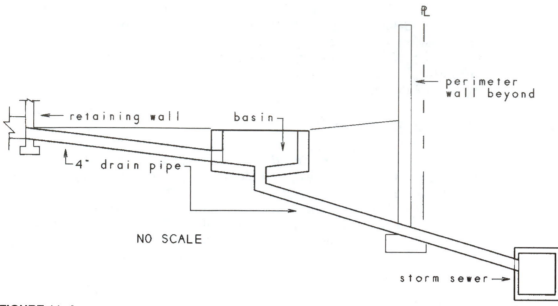

FIGURE 11–4
Drainage System

See figure 11–4 and refer to C-2, Plot Plan. The pipe is installed to an open storm basin, 3'–0" (91.44 cm) long by 2'–0" (60.96 cm) wide by 18" (45.72 cm) deep, located in the northeast area of the drive, as shown on the plot plan. The connection point of the pipe at the trench drain and the basin is called an *invert*. An invert is the point at which a change in depth of a drain, basin, or sewer connection occurs. Another pipe is connected between the basin and the storm sewer along First Avenue. The purpose of the basin is to provide additional drainage to reduce the possibility of an overflow of the trench at the loading dock.

CONCRETE

Concrete Loading Dock and Service Area

Refer to figure 11–3; also see A-2, Architectural Plans, East Elevation. The loading dock deck and the sloped dock entry area, extending the full length of the east end of the warehouse, are both 6" (15.24 cm) thick. A concrete pedestrian stair is built into the dock on the north end. The concrete dock driveway is 4'–0" (1.22 m) below the finish floor and dock elevation and is installed over a 10" (24.5 cm) compacted base extending 20'–0" (6.1 m) to the east from the loading dock. The area is sloped from the finish elevation of the driveway asphalt surfacing to the base of the loading dock, or 2'–8" (81.38 cm) in 20'–0" (6.1 m) (approximately $1^{1}/2$" per foot [3.81 cm per 30.48 cm]).

Concrete Sidewalks

Refer to C-2, Plot Plan. In addition, there are concrete sidewalks surrounding three sides of the office area and along the south side of the structure to the manufacturing area exterior side door. The sidewalks are 3'–0" (91.44 cm) wide and 5"

(12.7 cm) thick over 4" (10.16 cm) compacted fill. The entry sidewalk (from the main sidewalks to the office entry) is 6'–0" (1.83 m) with the same specifications.

MASONRY

Masonry Retaining Walls

Refer to figure 11–3 and A-2, Architectural Plans, East Elevation. The masonry retaining walls on the north and south sides of the loading dock extend 20'–0" (6.1 m) from the east end of the structure to the end of the loading ramp. The retaining walls are installed over a 1'–6" × 1'–0" (45.72 cm × 30.48 cm) footing. A solid 8 × 2 × 16 (20.32 cm x 5.08 cm × 40.64 cm) concrete cap block is installed over the top of each wall, therefore, the walls are 8'–2" (2.49 m) deep at the structure, 4'–2" (1.27 m) of which is exposed above the finish floor elevation of the dock. A maximum depth of 5'–6" (1.68 m) is exposed from the dock to the east end of each wall.

An additional depth of 2'–0" (60.96 cm) is added to the depth of the retaining wall below the finish ramp elevation to the top of the footings. When concrete or masonry walls are constructed along a slope, or a change in depth of a structure occurs, the footings are usually installed in steps. Steps occur as often as required to maintain a minimum depth below grade, usually 1'–4" (0.41 m) to 2'–0" (0.61 m) in length. The steps in the retaining wall for the loading dock are installed to accommodate the masonry units along the slope; that is, the equivalent of one or two lengths of block (16" [40.64 cm] to 32" [81.28 cm]) and one or two courses of block (8" [20.32 cm] to 16" [40.64 cm]) high. The masonry for these walls is a smooth-faced precision 8×8×16 (20.32 cm × 20.32 cm × 40.64 cm) CMU. In geographic locations where the frost line is deeper, the footings are not stepped but are all maintained below the frost line.

Masonry Perimeter Walls

See figure 11–5 and refer to C-2, Plot Plan. Also refer to figure 1–9. There are slumpstone fence walls surrounding the property. The slumpstone block is 8×6×16 (20.32 cm × 15.24 cm × 40.64 cm). The plot plan indicates that the east and south walls are 8'–0" (2.44 m) above finish grade. The north wall extending westward from the east property line to the chain–link fence is also 8'–0" (2.44 m)

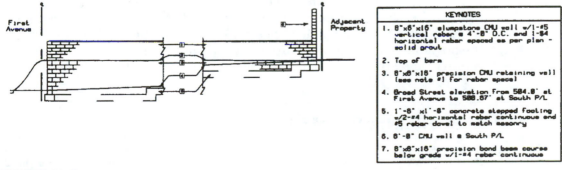

FIGURE 11–5
Slumpstone Fence Walls

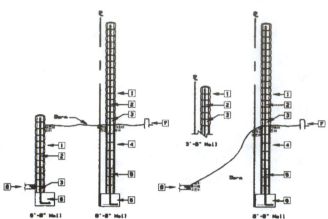

FIGURE 11–6
Slumpstone Retaining Walls

above finish grade. The remaining north wall extending westward to the west property line from the chain-link fence and the west wall are 3'–0" (0.91 m) above finish grade.

The elevation at the corner of Broad Street and First Avenue is identified as elevation 504.0' (153.62 m). The elevation of the landscaping and berm between the walls and parking curbs is 508.68' (155.04 m). The depth for these retaining walls on this project is, therefore, 5'–4" (1.62 m). The 3'–0" (0.91 m) high perimeter wall along Broad Street requires a tapered masonry retaining wall similar to the walls at the loading dock. The retaining wall tapers from 5'–4" (1.62 m) at the northwest corner of the property (the corner of Broad Street and First Avenue) to a minimum 8" (2.44 cm) at the southwest corner (on the Broad Street side).

The south and east walls require no retaining wall since the adjoining properties are at approximately the same elevation as the finish grade of the property. All masonry below finish grade are 8×8×16 (20.32 cm × 20.32 cm × 40.64 cm) smooth-faced precision units.

The specifications note that all of the masonry walls are solid grouted with a grout cap. A grout cap is made from an additional amount of grout, approximately 1" (2.54 cm) to 2" (5.08 cm) high, installed on top of the wall and rounded to a smooth finish. The grout cap is often used in lieu of a standard masonry slab cap, especially when used with slumpstone or natural stone.

See figure 11–6. A retaining wall is required for the north and west perimeter walls from street level to the finish grade level to aid in the prevention of erosion of the soil between the property and the sidewalks. An additional 6'–0" (1.83 m) slumpstone wall is noted that parallels the perimeter walls adjacent to the sidewalk *(Figure 12–5).* This is frequently done to prevent the possibility of earth erosion from the retaining wall. This information, too, is provided by the engineer and included in the specifications.

STEEL REINFORCEMENT

Refer to figures 11–2 through 11–6, also see S-1 and S-2, Structural Plans. The plans and the specifications indicate that the concrete loading dock and driveway area, extending the full length of the east wall, include 6 × 6/W2.9 × W2.9 WWF

(10.24 cm × 10.24 cm/W2.9 × W2.9) embedded in the concrete. The specifications further note that the footings require 2–#4 horizontal rebar and the walls and slabs have 1–#5 horizontal and vertical rebar as specified in the details in Figures 12–2 and 12–3. The perimeter fence walls are to have 2–#4 rebar (U.N.O.) and 1–#5 vertical dowel rebar in the footings. 1–#5 rebar is inserted vertically in the walls at 4'–0" (1.22 m) O/C, horizontally, to match the footing dowels. The fence walls also include 1–#4 horizontal rebar spaced at 4'–0" O/C, vertically, in the 8'–0" (2.44 m) walls and in the top course of the 3'–0" (0.91 m) walls.

BELOW-GRADE MOISTURE PROTECTION

See C-2, Plot Plan and refer to figures 11–2 through 11–6. All retaining walls are to be protected with moisture protection according to the specifications. The protection system is a self-adhering bituminous membrane "installed as per manufacturer's specifications." This statement is not an unusual one because most systems—moisture protection, insulating, surfacing, and so on—must be installed per the manufacturer's specifications to be able to gain approval and certification for the installation. Many manufacturers will allow only those companies with trained personnel who have passed a manufacturer's certification on their products and procedures to install the system.

FENCES AND GATES

Refer to C-2, Plot Plan. Additional site improvements include two 8'-0" (2.44 m) high chain-link fences and gates on the north and south sides of the structure. The fence on the north side is divided into two equal fixed sections with a 14'–0" (4.27 m) long rolling gate, electrically operated, centered in the fence. The fence on the south side is 28'–0" (8.53 m) long including a 4'–0" (1.22 m) wide swing gate for personnel use. The fence and gate is located on the sidewalk along the south side of the structure at the juncture of the office and manufacturing/warehouse.

UTILITIES

Refer to C-2, Plot Plan. The water, gas, and electrical service utilities are located in a 15'–0" (4.57 m) wide easement along the south side of the property. The electric power enters from the adjoining property to the east. The water and gas utilities enter from Broad Street on the west. These utilities enter the structure at the west end of the manufacturing/warehouse structure. All metering is established on the exterior of the building within the fence. The architect/engineer has been granted permission to construct the masonry and chain-link fences across the easement as per utility company and local codes and ordinances. The utilities extend approximately 130'–0" (39.62 m) from the street to the point of entry into the structure.

The sanitary and storm sewer lines are located on the north side of the property. The storm drainage system has been previously discussed. The sanitary sewer is located at the northwest corner of the manufacturing/warehouse structure and extends to the First Avenue sewer main.

LANDSCAPING

There are no specifics for the landscaping other than that noted on the plot plan and in the specifications. All landscaping is to be under separate contract between the owner and the landscape architect. The information included in the specifications is to be a part of the landscape contract.

SITE ELECTRICAL

There are two lamps built into the 3'–0" (91.44 cm) perimeter wall at the entry approach and floodlights mounted on the top of the parapet as indicated on the plot plan.

CHAPTER EXERCISES

True or False

T F   1. The benchmark is located at Broad Street and First Avenue.

T F   2. The property is on the corner of Main Street and Broadway.

T F   3. The legal description states that the property is separate from any other industrial or commercial properties.

T F   4. The north and south boundaries are the same length.

T F   5. The construction included in this chapter is referred to as the on-site construction.

T F   6. The POB is farthest from the datum point located at Broad Street and First Avenue.

T F   7. Most of the work included in this chapter is covered in Divisions 6 through 16.

T F   8. There are no utility easements within the boundaries of the Frontier Manufacturing Company property.

T F   9. The entrance to the property is made from Broad Street.

T F 10. The property is enclosed with a chain-link fence.

Matching

_____ 1. Approach   a. Point above sea level

_____ 2. Swale   b. Department of Transportation

_____ 3. Cementitious   c. Plan with natural contours

_____ 4. DOT   d. Location of property

_____ 5. Plot plan   e. Starting point of survey

_____ 6. Elevation   f. Sloped earth or surface to direct water flow

_____ 7. Legal description   g. Starting point of property layout

_____ 8. Datum point   h. Finish grades noted in this plan

_____ 9. Point of beginning   i. Entry to the property

_____ 10. Site plan   j. Cement-like materials

Completion

1. All work except the structure is included under site _____ or off-site construction.

2. The _____ ramp and approach apron (ramp) are both installed with 3,500 psi (1587.6 kg/6.45 cm²) concrete.

3. The north property line of the Frontier Manufacturing Company is _____ feet.

4. The depth of the curb surrounding the parking/driveway is _____ cm.

5. The 2.78 m and 0.91 m high perimeter walls have exposed masonry units called _____.

6. The size of all below-grade masonry units at the retaining walls are _____ .

7. All asphalt surfacing shall be laid over a _____" (_____ cm) compacted base material.

8. The lowest area of the parking/driveways leading away from the structure is a(n) _____.

9. The lowest area of the loading dock ramp includes a 6" (15.24 cm) wide _____ drain.

10. All water runoff is directed to the _____ drain on First Avenue.

11. A _____ pipe connects the trench drain to a storm drain on the northeast corner of the property.

12. All curb and gutter installations are to meet the requirements of the federal _____.

13. The asphalt surfacing is _____ cm thick.

14. The sidewalks are _____" deep over 4" (10.16 cm) compacted base.

15. The loading dock ramp is 6" (15.24 cm) deep, 3500 psi (1587.59 kg/6.45cm²) concrete with _____ WWF 1¹/₂" (3.81 cm) below the concrete surface.

16. The retaining walls on both sides of the loading dock have a 20.32 cm × _____ cm × 40.64 cm concrete cap on top.

17. The perimeter retaining walls are _____' (1.62 m) deep.

18. All masonry walls are placed on _____ (45.72 cm × 30.48 cm) footings.

19. The exposed walls on the west property line are _____' high.

20. To prevent the berm from eroding away from the perimeter walls, exposing the retaining walls, another _____, 6'–0" (1.83 m) wall may be installed.

21. There are _____ fences installed between the perimeter walls and the structure.

22. A(n) _____ operated rolling gate is installed on the north side of the structure.

23. The _____ plans are under separate contract to the owner, therefore, the plans are not included with the Frontier Manufacturing Company blueprint.

24. There is a(n) _____ on the south side of the property for use by the utility company(ies).

25. The plot plan indicates the installation of a $1\frac{1}{2}$" (3.81 cm) DIA water service copper pipe and a 1" (2.54 cm) DIA insulated black gas service pipe by _____' (39.62 m) from the street to the structure.

Multiple Choice

_____ 1. The datum point used for the survey of the Frontier Manufacturing Company property is located:
   a. At Broad and Main Streets.
   b. At elevation 504.0' (153.62 m) above sea level.
   c. On the Plot Plan only.
   d. Is not shown.

_____ 2. The Legal Description of the property indicates:
   a. The range location.
   b. The township location.
   c. Where the records are located.
   d. All of the above.

_____ 3. Site improvements and off–sites are:
   a. Both included as one area.
   b. All construction on a property excluding the structure.
   c. Both A and B.
   d. Neither A nor B.

_____ 4. The property point of entry (apron or approach) on the Plot Plan:
   a. Is located on First Avenue just off Broad Street.
   b. Is 30' (9.14 m) wide.
   c. Is asphalt surfaced.
   d. None of the above.

_____ 5. The curb and gutter to be installed along the perimeter of the paved areas is:
   a. Installed per DOT Specifications.
   b. Machine-formed.
   c. Asphalt formed.
   d. 4" (10.16 cm) by 18" (45.72 cm) with a 12" (30.48 cm) wide gutter.

_____ 6. The property measures:
   a. 260.0′ × 125.0′ × 240.0′ × 126.02′.
   b. 38.41 m × 74.37 m × 79.25 m × 36.1 m.
   c. Neither A nor B.
   d. Both A and B.

_____ 7. The asphalt surfacing for the driveway/parking areas is specified as follows:
   a. 6″ (15.24 cm) asphalt surface over 4″ (10.16 cm) cementitious base over 12″ (30.46 cm) compacted base.
   b. 6″ (15.24 cm) asphalt surface over 4″ (10.16 cm) cementitious base over 10″ (25.40 cm) compacted base.
   c. 4″ (10.16 cm) asphalt surface over 6″ (15.24 cm) cementitious base over 10″ (25.40 cm) compacted base.
   d. 10″ (25.40 cm) asphalt surface over 12″ (30.48 cm) cementitious base over 6″ (15.24 cm) compacted base.

_____ 8. Swales are sloped in the asphalt for:
   a. Aesthetic design purposes.
   b. Keep vehicles from crashing into structure.
   c. Direct the water flow away from the property.
   d. Direct the water flow onto the landscaping.

_____ 9. The trench drain and the open storm drain on the property:
   a. Are installed to remove water from the loading dock area and the western portion of the property.
   b. Are installed with a connecting CI pipe.
   c. Are for aesthetic design only.
   d. None of the above.

_____ 10. The approach apron and loading ramp both:
   a. Include W2.9 × W2.9–6 × 6 WWF.
   b. Are 3,500 psi (1,587.59 kg/6.45 cm²).
   c. Are 6″ (15.24 cm) thick.
   d. All of the above.

_____ 11. All retaining walls are:
   a. 8′–0″ (2.44 m) high.
   b. Constructed using smooth-faced precision 8″ × 8″ × 16″ (20.32 cm × 20.32 cm × 40.64 cm) CMU.
   c. Constructed from 8″ × 6″ × 16″ (20.32 cm × 15.24 cm × 40.64 cm) slumpstone CMU.
   d. Exposed to view.

_____ 12. The change in elevation of the site walls occurs:
   a. At the junction of the chain-link fence on the north side of the structure and at the southwest corner of the property.
   b. At the junction of the chain-link fence on both sides of the structure.
   c. At the junction of the southwest corner and the east end of the entry approach.
   d. At the northwest and northeast corners of the property.

_____ 13. The entry approach is 26′ (7.92 m) long by 15′ (4.57 m) wide by:
   a. 24.5 cm deep.
   b. 10.16 cm deep.

      c. 15.24 cm deep.
      d. 5.08 cm deep.

_____ 14. The trench drain and open storm drain:
      a. Remove water from the whole east section of the property.
      b. Connect with the storm sewer on First Avenue.
      c. Are both precast concrete units.
      d. All of the above.

_____ 15. The landscape areas:
      a. Are included in the contract.
      b. Are to have no trees or shrubbery.
      c. Are to be automatically sprinkled.
      d. None of the above.

_____ 16. If used, the additional perimeter retaining wall shall be:
      a. Constructed from slumpstone CMU of the same size as the perimeter walls.
      b. 6'–0" (1.83 m) high O/A.
      c. Installed parallel, and adjacent, to the public sidewalk or street.
      d. All of the above.

_____ 17. All perimeter walls shall be installed with:
      a. A 2" (5.08 cm) high concrete cap.
      b. A grout cap.
      c. No reinforcement.
      d. None of the above.

_____ 18. Steel reinforcement is:
      a. Supplied by the steel fabricator.
      b. Deformed #4 and #5 rebar.
      c. Installed as per plans and specifications.
      d. All of the above.

_____ 19. The chain-link fence:
      a. Is 12'–0" (3.66 m) high.
      b. To include one electrically operated rolling gate.
      c. Extends east and west from the structure.
      d. None of the above.

_____ 20. All site improvements/off-sites include:
      a. All construction inside and outside the property excluding the structure.
      b. All construction, including the structure.
      c. All construction within the property boundaries only.
      d. All construction having to do with grading and excavating only.

12

On-Sites—The Office

The Frontier Manufacturing Company structure has two separate and totally different construction requirements. The office construction includes many items similar to a residence, such as the concrete slab, the framing, and the roof structure requirements, whereas, the manufacturing/warehouse facility requires many methods and materials that are not found in residential construction. The construction of the slab, a loading dock, the equipment installation requirements, the structural roof system and the roofing, and even the personal care (wash/restroom and break room) facilities, are much different. The understanding of the blueprints and the construction techniques are, therefore, separate. This chapter shall discuss the office construction.

MAIN OFFICE AREAS

See S-1, Foundation Plan, Frontier Manufacturing Company and figure 12–1, foundation detail. The foundation plan indicates an 8×8×16 (20.32 cm × 20.32 cm × 40.64 cm) masonry foundation (stem) wall over a 2'–0" × 1'–0" (0.61 m × 0.30 m) concrete footing. The stem walls are 2'–0" (0.61 m) deep along the north, south, and west sides of the office area. This footing depth will vary in accordance with geographic location, the soils report, and weather conditions

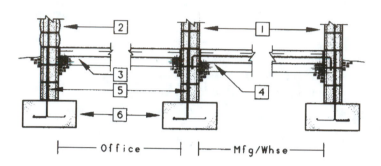

FIGURE 12–1
Foundation Details

KEYNOTES
1. 8x8x16 smooth face CMU (typ UNO) w/#5 rebar spaced 32" O.C. horizontalluy
2. 8x6x16 slumpstone CMU
3. 4" concrete slab - 3000 psi w/W1.4xW1.4/6x6 WWF
4. 6" concrete slab - 3500 psi w/W2.9xA2.9/10x10 WWF and #4 rebar hook @ 4'-0" O.C. east and west ends
5. #4 horizontal rebar spaced 32" O.C. vertically
6. 2'-0"x1'-0" concrete footing -3500 psi w/2-#4 rebar continuous and 1-#5 rebar dowel at 48" O.C. horizontally to masonry rebar

as noted in chapter 3, as well as with local codes and ordinances. The detail also indicates that the footing contains 2–#4 continuous horizontal rebar and 1–#5 rebar dowel to match the masonry wall reinforcement. The specifications state that there shall be a minimum rebar lap, horizontally and vertically, of 48 bar diameters (2'–0" [0.61 m]) for #4 rebar and 40 bar diameters (2'–1" (0.63 m), or 2'–0" (0.61 m), nominal, for #5 rebar. For this reason the dowel in the footing extends a maximum 2'–0" (0.61 m) above finish floor (A.F.F.), so that, if required, the dowel and vertical wall rebar can be tied together for rigidity and continuity.

Concrete Floor

The floor slab for the office is 48'–0" (14.6 m) by 34'–4" (10.46 m) by 4" (5.1 cm) deep and rated at 3000 psi (1360.8 kg/6.45 cm²) at 28 days. The concrete slab is placed abutting the masonry wall on all sides, requiring the installation of an isolation (moisture) control joint along the perimeter of the slab. The east wall, adjoining the warehouse, is included in the manufacturing/warehouse construction.

Exterior Wall Construction

See sheets A-2, Architectural, S-1 and S-2, Structural. The office walls above grade are 8×6×16 (20.32 cm × 15.24 cm × 40.64 cm) solid grouted slumpstone masonry to a height of 12'–0" (3.66 m) A.F.F. Reinforcement for the masonry walls is indicated in the keynotes of the foundation plan and in the structural wall sections.

The specifications further note that the exterior walls above the masonry on the north and south sides, to the underside of the roof, are to have panelized aluminum shiplap siding over ¹/₂" (1.27 cm) sheathing over the end trusses. The color is to be selected by the owner.

Structural Roof

See sheets A-3, Architectural Roof Plan, and S-3, Structural Roof Plan. The roof over the main office area is a 3:12 truss hip roof. The trusses are to have a 2×6 (5.08 cm × 15.24 cm) top chord and a 2×4 (5.08 cm × 10.16 cm) bottom chord spaced at 24" (0.61 m) O/C in all directions. The ridge of the roof structure is level with the height of the wall between the office and manufacturing/warehouse structure (20'–0" [6.10 m]) at a 3:12 slope (⅛ roof pitch). The trusses are fastened to a 2 × 10 (5.08 cm × 25.40 cm) ledger at the masonry wall, and a 2 × 8 (5.08 cm × 20.32 cm) ledger at the bottom chord, 12'–0" (3.66 m) A.F.F. A rafter-tail extending 2'–0" (0.61 m) horizontally, beyond the plate line is also included. The roof is sheathed with 4' × 8' × ½" (1.22 m × 2.44 m × 1.27 cm) CDX plywood or exterior grade Oriented Strand Board (OSB)®.

Interior Construction

See sheets A-1 and A-2, Architectural Plans, and S-2, Structural Plan. The interior office walls are non-bearing partition walls to a height of 9'–0" (2.74 m) A.F.F., at 24" (0.61 m) O/C, using 4" (10.16 cm), 20 gauge, galvanized steel studs. The hall partitions and the plumbing wall between the office bathroom and kitchen are 6" (15.24 cm), 20 gauge, galvanized steel stud. The east/west demising wall between the showroom and the offices is 12'–0" (3.66 m) A.F.F., using 6", 20 gauge, galvanized steel studs at 16" (15.24 cm) O/C, to the underside of the roof trusses. An exposed 6×12 (15.24 cm × 30.48 cm) DF #1, R/S, wood beam, located over the reception area, is installed as part of the separation wall. The beam is supported by two exposed 6×6 (15.24 cm × 15.24 cm) DF #2, R/S, wood posts (one on each end).

The interior of the perimeter slumpstone masonry has 2" (5.08 cm) a thermal insulating wall system (Styrostud®, or equal). There are 2 × 4 (5.08 cm × 10.16 cm) furring strips installed at each corner and at the top and bottom of the wall system to aid in the installation of drywall. The strips are screwed or nailed directly to the masonry. All interior walls are to have a combination of R–11 thermal and sound batt insulation in the stud walls.

The Finish Schedule

See figure 12–2. The finish schedule supplies information through the use of number and/or letter identification with corresponding notes inserted with the numbers and/or letters in the same way as is done with keynotes. The schedule is broken down into six areas:

1. Location (room, room number, building, and so on)

2. Floor applications

3. Base applications (baseboard, coving, vinyl base, and so on)

4. Wall applications (north, south, east, and west of each location)

5. Ceiling finish applications (drywall, ACT, exposed, and so on)

6. Remarks (special information regarding heights of ceilings, and so on)

Finish Schedule							
LOCATION	FLOOR	BASE	WALLS N	WALLS S	WALLS E	WALLS W	CEILING	REMARKS
Office #1	2	1	1	1	1	1	1	
Office #2	2	1	1	1	1	1	1	
Office #3	2	1	1	1	1	1	1	
Office #4	2	1	1	1	1	1	1	
Office #5	2	1	1	1	1	1	1	
Office #6	2	1	1	1	1	1	1	
Reception	3	1	1	1	1	1	1	
Showroom	3	1	1	1	1	1	1	
Plant Office	1	3	1	1	1	1	2	
Kitchen	3	2	1,2,3	1,2,3	1,2,3	1,2,3	1	
Restroom	3	2	1,2,3	1,2,3	1,2,3	1,2,3	1	
Wash Room/ Restroom	1	3	1,2,3	1,2,3	1,2,3	1,2,3	2	
Break Room	3	3	1,2,3	1,2,3	1,2,3	1,2,3	2	

FLOORS:
1. Exposed concrete
2. Carpet
3. Vinyl composition tile

BASE:
1. Wood trim – 3"
2. Coving
3. 4" vinyl base – self-adhering

WALLS:
. Paint
. Ceramic tile

CEILINGS:
1. Acoustical tile
2. 5/8" "X" GWB

NOTES:
1. All finish materials to be selected by owner from standard styles and colors.
2. See specifications for other information.
3. Exterior walls of plant office, break room and restroom areas are to be covered with T-1-11 siding

FIGURE 12–2
Finish Schedule, Frontier Manufacturing, Inc.

Drywall

Per the finish schedule, all interior partition walls are specified with one layer of 5/8" (1.59 cm) X GWB extending the full height of the walls (9'–0" [2.74 m]). The interior office partitions shall have GWB on both sides. The demising wall has two layers of 5/8" (1.59 cm) X GWB both sides full height to the underside of the roof structure, 12'–0" [3.66 m]). The specifications also state that the underside of the trusses shall have one layer of 5/8" (1.59 cm) X GWB. All drywall above ceiling height is to be fire-taped.

Ceramic Tile

The finish schedule shows that 4" (10.16 cm) square wall tiles are installed on the kitchen walls between the backsplash over the counters and the wall cabinets, and to a 6'–0" (1.83 m) height on all walls in the balance of the kitchen and the office restroom. The tiles are embedded in a thinset mortar and grouted. The colors are to be selected by the owner.

Acoustical Ceiling

Refer to the finish schedule and see A-4, Reflected Ceiling Plan and Figure 12–3. A ceiling system, known as *an acoustical ceiling tile (ACT) system*, is installed

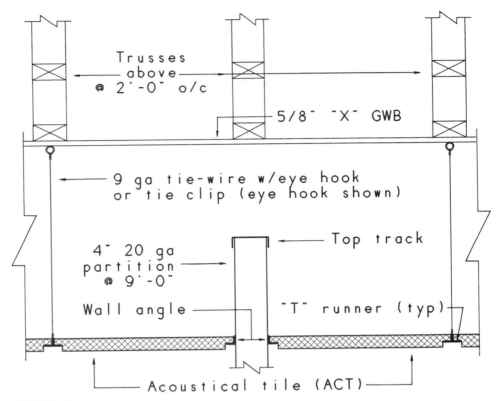

FIGURE 12–3
Acoustical Ceiling Tile (ACT) System

using a compressed fiber board cut into sizes of 2×2 (0.61 m $\times$ 0.61 m) or 2×4 (0.61 m $\times$ 1.22 m). The tiles range in thickness from $1/2''$ (1.27 cm) to $1^1/2''$ (3.81 cm), with smooth or fissured surfaces. The smooth surfaces are usually under $3/4''$ (1.91 cm), offering less acoustical control and normally have no fire rating. The thicker tiles with fissured surfaces are rated from $3/4$ to 1 hour fire resistance. The fissures in the tiles not only offer acoustical attenuation, but an aesthetic appearance as well. The tiles are supported by horizontal wall angles and T runners and tie wires attached to the runners and roof structure.

Interior Wood Finishes, Doors, and Windows

Refer to the Finish Schedule; figures 12–4 and 12–5, Door and Window Schedules. These schedules are like the finish schedule in that they identify each door or window. A door or window is identified by a number or letter called a *mark*. When the doors are marked with numbers, the windows are marked with letters, and vice versa. A door or window schedule includes:

1. Mark (the identifying number or letter)
2. Door or window size (manufacturer's identification or custom size)
3. Door or window description*
4. Remarks (special information pertinent to the door or window such as manufacturer's requirements and the like)

---

*The description includes door or window size, materials for the framework, glazing requirements, exterior or interior use, and so on.

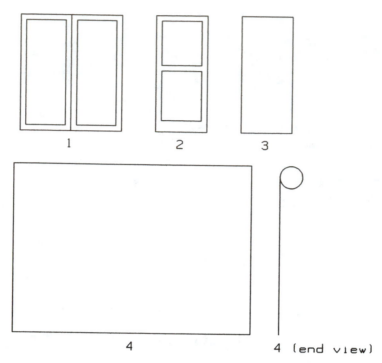

DOOR SCHEDULE				
MARK	SIZE	DESCRIPTION	QTY	REMARKS
1	pr 3'-0"x7'-0"	aluminum storefront	1	anodized finish
2	3'-0"x7'-0"	hollow metal w/HM frame	3	pre-painted by mfr.
3	3'-0"x7'-0"	birch. s/c. 13/8". flush	9	stain grade
4	14'-0"x10'-0"	steel overhead roll-up	2	motorized

FIGURE 12–4
Door Schedule

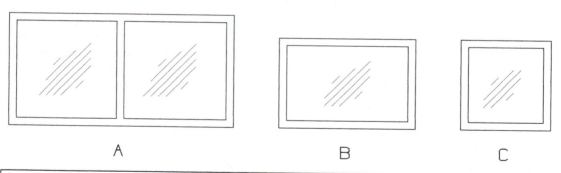

WINDOW SCHEDULE				
MARK	SIZE	DESCRIPTION	QTY	REMARKS
A	10'-0" x 5'-0"	Fixed	2	Fit masonry opening
B	6'-0" x 4'-0"	DO	3	DO'
C	4'-0" x 4'-0"	DO	5	DO
'NOTE: Plant office window made for frame construction.				

FIGURE 12–5
Window Schedule

The specifications and/or the window schedule state all interior window trim is to be stained oak wood surrounding the windows to match the baseboard located in the carpeted and showroom areas (noted in the finish schedule). The window trim includes surround trim at the windows with a stool and apron.

All windows are aluminum-framed with fixed, fire-retardant, vandal-proof, tinted, double-insulating plastic glass. All exterior doors are hollow-metal (HM) doors and frames. Where there are window lights (lites) in the doors, they are also both fire retardant and vandal proof. All interior doors are solid core, birch, flush with stain finish to match the oak trim and are to include knock-down hollow-metal (KDHM) frames.

Carpeting and Flooring

The floors of the restrooms, kitchen, break room, reception area, and show-room are to have vinyl composition tiles on the floors. The tiles may range in size from 8″ (20.32 cm) to 12″ (30.48 cm) squares. The specifications and finish schedule note that the owner is to select the size, style, and color. The carpeting is specified as commercial grade with pad and edge tacking. Again, the color and style are selected by the owner. The carpeting is installed in all of the main office areas except as noted.

Painting and Wall Coverings

Refer to figure 12–2, Finish Schedule. The specifications state that all exposed interior walls that are not covered with tile are to be painted. The R/S exposed beam and support posts are to be stained with a dark walnut stain. Unless otherwise directed by the owner, there are no walls that are to have any other wall covering (wallpaper, paneling, vinyl, etc.).

Roofing

The specifications indicate that the 3:12 sloped roof over the office area is a *clay S* tile over a 43 lb underlayment, a bituminous sheet material. Each tile is exposed as per manufacturer's directions and nailed directly to the sheathing with a tile-tie system or batten boards. Tile-ties are commonly used with the Spanish clay barrel or S tile. Batten boards are 1×4 (2.54 cm × 5.08 cm) boards installed horizontally (parallel to the eave and spaced according to the allowable exposure of the tiles. These boards may be installed for the installation of a variety of tiles, such as the Spanish clay barrel, clay or concrete S tiles, clay or concrete "flat" tiles, and panelized wood, metal, or plastic roofing systems. The specifications also call for a ridge vent. The vent may be pre-manufactured of galvanized metal or structural plastic. A ridge trim should also extend along the ridge and hips for additional weather protection. The tile used does not require a rake trim since the roof has no rakes (barges). A rake trim is a specially formed tile unit that fits over the rake of a gable roof.

CHAPTER EXERCISES

Completion

1. The size of the office area is 48'–0" × _____.

2. The exterior office walls are constructed with _____ CMU.

3. There is 2 × 4 (5.08 cm × 10.16 cm) _____ on the interior side of the perimeter walls.

4. The concrete slab is _____ psi (_____ kg/6.45 cm²).

5. A _____' demising wall is built between the offices and the showroom.

6. All interior _____ are constructed 9'–0" A.F.F.

7. The batt insulation in the ceiling is rated at _____.

8. The windows and doors are both _____ and vandal proof.

9. The drywall required for all interior walls is _____.

10. The roof system is a(n) _____ truss roof system.

11. The roofing is applied over a(n) _____ deck.

12. The interior doors are all 3'–0" × 7'–0" flush _____.

13. All offices and halls are to be _____.

14. The perimeter of the concrete slab abutting the masonry walls has a(n) _____ joint installed.

15. The top of the footings are _____' deep below grade.

True or False

T F   1. There is rigid insulation used in the office area.

T F   2. The framing is all wood stud using construction grade 92$\frac{1}{2}$" × 2 × 6 DF studs.

T F   3. The restroom is not equipped for use by persons with disabilities.

T F   4. The kitchen includes a sink and refrigerator.

T F   5. All the offices are the same size.

T F   6. The entry doors to the offices are called hollow-metal doors.

T F   7. There are three entrances into the office area.

T F   8. All office doors shown on the floor plan are marked with a circled #2.

T F   9. The measurements from the exterior outside corner to the windows is to the center of the windows.

T F 10. There is a pony wall and countertop shown at the reception area.

T F 11. All floors are to be covered with VAT except the showroom.

T F 12. All frame walls contain an insulation that controls both heat and sound transmission.

T F 13. The door exiting to the plant area is a hollow-metal door and frame.

T F 14. All windows on each side of the office structure are the same size.

T F 15. The foundation wall is constructed with 20.32 cm × 20.32 cm × 40.64 cm precision CMU.

T F 16. The trusses have a top chord of 2 × 6 and a bottom chord of 2 × 4.

T F 17. The underside of the trusses is to have ¹/2″ X GWB installed.

T F 18. A R/S 6 × 12 beam and 6 × 6 posts are installed in the demising wall at the reception area.

T F 19. The roofing called for is a Spanish S tile over a 43 lb underlayment.

T F 20. The roof is sloped 3″ per lineal foot.

Multiple Choice

_____ 1. The concrete for the footings is rated at:
   a. 2500 psi (1136.36 kg/6.45 cm²)
   b. 4000 psi (1818.18 kg/6.45 cm²)
   c. 3500 psi (1590.91 kg/6.45 cm²)
   d. 3000 psi (1363.64 kg/6.45 cm²)

_____ 2. The perimeter of the concrete slab has a(n):
   a. Construction joint installed.
   b. Expansion joint installed.
   c. Isolation joint installed.
   d. All of the above.

_____ 3. The exposed exterior office walls are:
   a. Steel framed walls at 24″ (60.96 cm) O/C.
   b. 8×8×16 (20.32 cm × 20.32 cm × 40.64 cm) slumpstone masonry.
   c. Wood framed walls with 2 × 6 (5.08 cm × 15.24 cm) studs at 16″ (0.41 cm) O/C.
   d. Exposed 8×6×16 (20.32 cm × 15.24 cm × 40.64 cm) slumpstone masonry.

_____ 4. The roof system consists of:
   a. Sloped trusses with 2 × 6 (5.08 cm × 15.24 cm) top chord and ¹/2″ (1.27 cm) plywood.
   b. A tile roofing material and 43 lb (19.55 kg) underlayment.
   c. Both A and B.
   d. Neither A nor B.

_____ 5. The structural interior wall framing consists of:
   a. 2 × 6 × 92¹/2″ (5.08 cm × 15.24 cm × 2.35 m) studs with sill plate and double top plate.
   b. 4″ × 9′–0″ (5.08 cm × 2.74 m) 20 ga galvanized steel studs and track.
   c. 6″ × 9′–0″, (15.24 cm × 2.74 m) 20 ga galvanized steel studs and track.
   d. 2 × 4 × 10′–0″ (5.08 cm × 10.16 cm × 25.4 m) wood framing with sill plate and double top plate.

_____ 6. The concrete slab is:
   a. 3000 psi (1363.64 kg/6.45 cm²) and 4″ (5.08 cm) thick.
   b. 2500 psi (1136.36 kg/6.45 cm²) and 6″ (15.24 cm) thick.
   c. 4000 psi (1818.18 kg/6.45 cm²) and 2″ (5.08 cm) thick.
   d. None of the above.

_____ 7. The stem wall is:
   a. 1′–6″ (0.46 m) deep.
   b. 2′–0″ (0.61 m) deep.
   c. 1′–8″ (0.51 m) deep.
   d. Slumpstone masonry.

_____ 8. The truss system requires that the trusses:
   a. Have a sill plate under the trusses.
   b. Have ¹/₂″ (1.27 cm) GWB fastened to the top chord.
   c. Are exposed.
   d. Have ⁵/₈″ (1.59 cm) X GWB fastened to the underside.

_____ 9. The interior office partitions comprise:
   a. ⁵/₈″ (1.59 cm) X GWB on both sides of a 6″ × 9′–0″ (15.24 cm × 2.74 m) 20 ga stud and track.
   b. ⁵/₈″ (1.59 cm) X GWB on both sides of a 4″ × 9′–0″ (5.04 cm × 2.74 m) 20 ga stud and track.
   c. ¹/₂″ (1.27 cm) X GWB on both sides of a 6″ × 9′–0″ (15.24 cm × 2.74 m) 20 ga stud and track.
   d. ¹/₂″ (1.27 cm) X GWB on both sides of a 4″ × 9′–0″ (5.08 cm × 2.74 m) 20 ga stud and track.

_____ 10. The interior walls contain:
   a. R–19 thermal batt insulation.
   b. R–11 combination thermal and sound insulation.
   c. R–11 thermal insulation.
   d. R–19 combination thermal and sound insulation.

_____ 11. The wall dividing the showroom from the office areas:
   a. Is insulated the same as the other walls.
   b. Is 12′–0″ (3.66 m) tall to the underside of the roof structure.
   c. Has a wood beam and posts installed within the wall.
   d. Includes all of the above.

_____ 12. The windows are manufactured with:
   a. Steel frames and plate glass.
   b. Aluminum frames with fire-protection and vandal-proofing glazing.
   c. Single-hung windows.
   d. Sliding glass windows.

_____ 13. The entry doors are referred to as:
   a. A storefront entry.
   b. Is composed of a pair of 3′–0″ × 7′–0″ (0.91 m × 2.13 m) doors.
   c. Are fully glazed.
   d. All of the above.

_____ 14. The kitchen is finished with:
a. Base and wall cabinets along north and east walls.
b. Is 9'–0" × 6'–0" (2.74 m × 1.83 m).
c. Has a drywall ceiling.
d. Painting full height of all walls.

_____ 15. The restroom is finished with:
a. Standard fixtures and all ceramic walls.
b. Handicap facilities with ceramic tile to 6'–0" (1.83 m) A.F.F.
c. Has a 7'–0" (2.13 m) ceiling.
d. None of the above.

13

On-Sites— Manufacturing/Warehouse

See *Architectural and Structural Plans.* As previously mentioned, the construction for the manufacturing/warehouse area, referred to hereafter as *the plant area,* includes special materials and procedures not found in residential construction. These requirements are found in the specifications in the Project Manual and the various schedules included with them. The work necessary is under more careful scrutiny, including more stringent government and owner inspections of materials, installations, care in storage, and so on. Most of the details are explained in the plans through the use of keynotes.

CONCRETE

Concrete Footings

In accordance with the specifications, the concrete footings are 2'–0" × 1'–0" (0.61 m × 0.30 m) at 3,500 psi (1,587.6 kg/6.45 cm²). The concrete requirement for the slab, as per the specifications, is also 3,500 psi (1,587.6 kg/6.54 cm²) at 6" (15.24 cm) thick. The footings continue completely around the structure and along the face of the loading dock with step footings from the main slab level to the bottom of the loading wall. The retaining walls on each side of the loading dock also have step footings from the loading dock to their ends.

Refer to figure 1–8, Keynotes, and see the details on Structural Plans. The drawing in figure 1–8 is the same detail describing the column supports for the plant as the detail in the plans. The roof support system requires additional concrete where interior column supports are located. A special footing, referred to as a *mat footing*, is placed where the columns are installed. These are done at the same time as the perimeter footings are placed. This area at the mats is left undone until the columns are installed and the roof structure completed. Concrete is then placed over the mats with control (isolation) joints and finished to the level of the main slab areas.

Concrete Slab

See figure 13–1. Per the specifications, as mentioned above, the concrete requirement for the slab is 3500 psi (1,587.6 kg/6.45 cm²), 6″ (15.24 cm). The slab is placed in sections with a cut-back at the column footings. The slab sections are placed in staggered pours. Flatwork forms are installed to form the six sections shown on the foundation plan. The forms are used to separate the slab sections as well as to form a keyed joint, referred to as a *cold-key expansion joint*. Three sections may be placed at one time. For example, the northwest end, southwest end, and the middle section on the south side may be placed at the same time. This leaves the three other areas open for future installation. When the concrete in the first three areas cures, the forms are removed for the next placement. A moisture barrier is installed at the "keyed" joints (thin strip of polystyrene foam, neoprene, bituthene, and the like), and the remaining areas are placed.

See figure 13–2. A 6 × 6/W2.9×W 2.9 welded wire fabric is embedded in the slab prior to the placement. There may or may not be rebar in the concrete, depending upon the locale and structural requirements. If rebar were required, it would be placed horizontally in the perimeter of the slab with a hook (bent portion of rebar) placed vertically downward in the masonry and the longer portion extending into the slab. Such reinforcement is usually spaced at 4′–0″ (1.22 m) O/C. When a slab abuts a wall, instead of extending over the wall, an isolation control joint completely surrounding the finished slab is required. There may also be requirements for additives in the concrete for additional strengthening, for reducing slippery surfaces, or for keeping dust from adhering to the concrete. These are required only if demanded by the owner, architect, or engineer.

Loading Dock

Refer to figure 11–3. The loading dock is installed with the same compressive strength concrete (3,500 psi [1587.6 kg/6.45 cm²]) and reinforcement requirements as required for the footings.

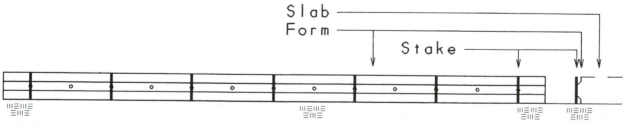

FIGURE 13–1
Flat Formwork

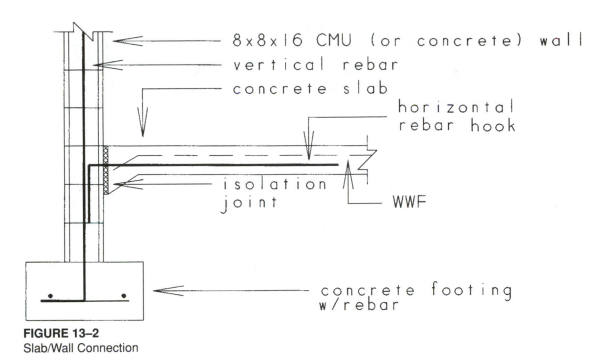

FIGURE 13–2
Slab/Wall Connection

MASONRY

The plant walls are 8×8×16 (20.32 cm × 20.32 cm × 40.64 cm) precision (smooth-faced) CMU. The plans show that the walls are 16'–0" (4.88 m) high on the north, east, and south sides, and 20'–0" (6.10 m) high on the west side adjacent to the office area. The specifications also supply information for the mortar, grout, and reinforcement. The walls are solid grouted for both strength and fire resistance. A solid-grouted masonry wall is rated as a two-hour (minimum) fire-retardant wall if standing alone, as are these walls.

See Sheet S-1, Structural Floor Plan and details. There is additional strengthening and thickening of the walls where the roof structure requires special wall support. These supports may be steel beam columns, concrete columns, or a combination of steel and concrete, or they may be reinforced masonry pilasters. Concrete, steel, or concrete and steel are used with concrete wall or steel construction. Where the main walls are constructed of masonry, the supports are reinforced masonry pilasters.

A sheet metal coping is installed over a 2 × 8 (5.08 cm × 20.32 cm) DF common, or HF utility, continuous wood cap on the top of the masonry walls. Where weather concerns are prevalent, a PTMS (mudsill) may be required. Fasteners, sufficiently long enough to penetrate into the masonry, without damaging the coping, are used for the installation. The fasteners are installed at all sheet metal laps and at 2'–0" (0.61 m) O/C between laps.

ROUGH CARPENTRY

Wall Framing

The office and personnel areas within the plant, like the main office area, are also constructed with metal stud framing to 9'–0" (2.74 m) A.F.F., using 6" (15.24 cm), 20 gauge studs, at 24" (0.61 m) O/C, in all walls, and 6" (15.24 cm),

20 gauge joists (unpunched) at 16″ (0.41 m) O/C for the ceilings. The exterior walls are covered with $^1/_2$″ (1.27 cm) exterior grade CDX or OSB® sheathing outside and $^5/_8$″ (1.59 cm) X GWB on the interiors. The walls and ceiling also have R–11 thermal and sound batt insulation identical to the office areas. The exterior (top) of the ceiling joists are covered with a double layer of $^1/_2$″ (1.27 cm) CDX plywood.

Roof Structure

Refer to sheet S-3, Structural Plans and figure 1–8. The plant roof is supported by a combination of steel pipe columns, glue-laminated beams, and open web trusses. The steel support columns are 6″ (10.16 cm) DIA with bottom plate attachment for installation on the concrete mats. Six $^5/_8$″ (1.59 cm) anchor or expansion bolts are installed in the mat, to which the column is bolted and welded into place. The top of the column has a metal, welded beam seat large enough to allow for a glu-lam beam to rest. The opposite end of the beam rests on a steel plate inserted in the top of masonry pilasters or with straps embedded in the masonry wall and pilaster. The total beam is actually constructed from three separate beams, one $6^3/_4$″ × 27″ × 24′–0″ (14.61 cm × 0.69 m × 7.32 m) center beam, and two $6^3/_4$″ × 18″ × 31′–0″ (14.61 cm × 0.46 m × 9.45 m) beams, which are connected with specially fabricated hinge connectors. The hinge connectors may be pre-manufactured or may require customizing. Whenever a metal support accessory is custom-made it must meet all standards which may be even more stringent than the manufactured accessory.

Roof Joists and Ledger

The roof joists are TJL, 14″ × 27′–$6^1/_8$″ (0.36 m × 8.36 m) at 24″ (0.61m) O/C, spanning each way from the glue-laminated beams to a ledger at the masonry walls. The ledger is a 3 × 10 (7.62 cm × 25.40 cm) fastened along the north and south walls, parallel to the glu-lam beam. The height of the top of the ledger must match the height of the top of the glu-lam beam. The joists are connected to the glu-lam and the ledger with hangers recommended by the manufacturer. The manufacturer also supplies all necessary accessories for a complete system. The roof deck is 4′ (1.22 m) × $^5/_8$″ (1.59 cm) CDX, 5-ply, in either 8′ (2.44 m) or 12″ (3.66 m) lengths of exterior glued plywood over the roof joist system.

Built-Up Roofing (BUR)

See sheet A-3, Architectural Plans. A roof is considered flat where no slope exists or the slope is up to, and including, a 3:12 slope. Many varieties of roofing felts and procedures are found in BUR. The procedures vary from a *single-ply* (one layer) application such as an EPDM (*E*thylene, *P*ropylene and *D*iene *M*onomer) or an SBS (a modified, layered bitumen sheet) to a *multi-ply* system with as many as five plies of standard roofing felts made from rag, paper, fiberglass, or other fibrous materials, which are compressed into rolls with asphalt or coal-tar pitch. BUR installations are frequently used for garage roofs in residential construction. BUR was very popular with residential roofing because of its reasonable cost, but its lack of durability in some areas of the country has minimized its use in recent years. This roofing system is still used heavily in commercial and industrial construction.

The roofing system used for the plant roof is one of the asphalt multi-ply systems. The roof deck is plywood over which an insulating system is applied. The built-up roofing (BUR) system is applied over the insulation. The specifications note several roofing material manufacturers, but the system specified is a GAF (manufacturer's name) I04G. The number and letter code is the manufacturer's way of identifying the system and the materials as well as knowing what base is used with the system. The symbols are identified as follows:

1. I = insulated deck
2. 0 = no base sheet
3. 4 = 4 plies of "Gafglas Ply 4" asphalt-impregnated rolls
4. G = gravel surfacing over the final layer and flood coat

The materials are applied in the following manner:

1. There are 4 applications (one on insulated deck and three between roof plies) of Type II asphalt ply coat each at 25 lb (11.34 kg).
2. There are four plies of the asphalt-impregnated roll material.
3. A flood coat of 60 lb (27.22 kg) is applied over all.
4. 450 lb (304.12 kg) of white gravel is embedded in the flood coat.

The weights noted in each of the items above and the specifications are the quantities required for 100 square feet (9.29 m^2), or 1 square (sq), of roof area.

DOORS AND WINDOWS

Refer to Door and Window Schedules, figures 12–4 and 12–5. There are three personnel doors and two overhead garage doors in the exterior masonry walls. The personnel doors are located on the north near the plant office and on the south next to the electrical supply equipment (transformer and switchgear). The third door is in the plant west wall where it enters the main hall in the office area. The overhead doors are located at the east end of the building at the loading dock. The personnel doors are hollow metal (HM) doors with hollow metal (HM) frames. The garage doors at the loading dock on the east end are motorized 16 gauge metal roll-up doors with hollow-metal (HM) steel frames.

There are two windows installed in the plant office only. There is one exterior window in the masonry wall and one in the office wall inside. The exterior window is identified in the same manner as the main office area windows. The plant interior window is a clear plastic laminate.

FINISHES

Exterior Wall Finish

See figure 13–3. The precision CMU plant walls are to be covered with an exterior cement plaster system. The system is both aesthetic and insulating, thus the name given the system, *Exterior Insulation and Finish System (EIFS).* The plastering

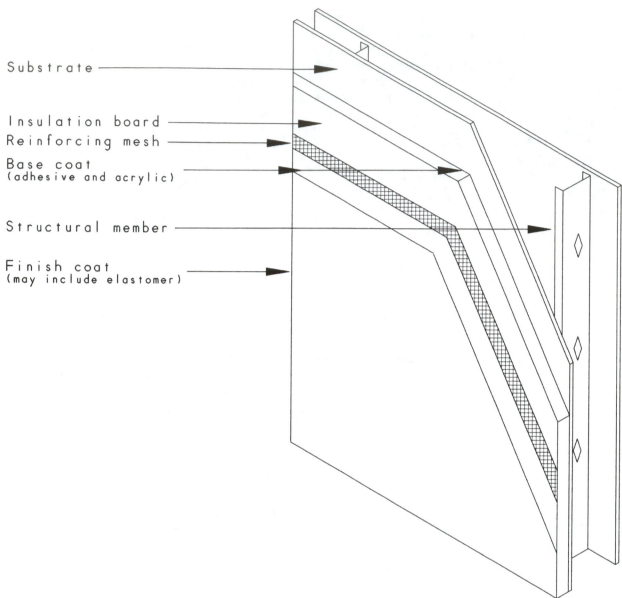

FIGURE 13–3
Exterior Insulation and Finish System

is similar to a two-coat stucco without metal lath. The material is applied over a polyisocyanurate or polystyrene foam base with a fiber reinforcing mesh (nylon, krylon, polyester, and so on) and a base coat that is both an adhesive and sealer. After the curing of the base coat, the final coat is applied with or without integral coloring and with various aesthetic finishes such as a sand finish, a Spanish lace texture, or a rough trowel finish. Each layer applied is normally not more than $1/8''$ (0.32 cm) nor less than $1/16''$ (0.16 cm) thick. The coatings may be applied like paint, that is, they may be sprayed or rolled.

Drywall

Refer to Finish Schedule, figure 12–2. All interior walls and ceiling of the plant office are specified with one layer of $5/8''$ (1.59 cm) X GWB, extending the full height (9′–0″ [2.74 m]) of the walls and the full area of the ceiling. The partitions between the office and the wash/restroom, and the wash/restroom and break room, have ⁵/₈″ (1.59 cm) X GWB on both sides. All walls and drywall ceilings not covered with tile are to be textured for painting.

Ceramic Tile

Refer to Finish Schedule, figure 12–2. 4″ (10.16 cm) square wall tiles are installed to a 6′–0″ (1.83 m) height on all walls in both the employee wash/restroom and break room. The tiles are embedded in a thinset mortar and grouted. The colors are to be selected by the owner.

Wall Coverings

Refer to figure 12–2, Finish Schedule. All exposed interior drywall that is not covered with tile is to be painted. The plant office and personnel area exterior wall face has a ⁷/₁₆″ (1.11 cm) thick T–1–11 panelized siding, available in sizes of 4 × 8 to 4 × 12 sheets, installed over the plywood sheathing. T–1–11 has the appearance of a board-and-batten siding. Board-and-batten is an original aesthetic wood siding utilizing 2 × 12 (5.05 cm × 30.48 cm), select DF or pine boards, installed vertically on the walls, with a 1 × 4 (2.54 cm × 10.16 cm) or 2 × 4 (5.08 cm × 10.16 cm) select grade member over the board seams (joints).

Painting

All exposed interior drywall that is not covered with tile is to be painted. The interior of all masonry walls are painted with a sealer, primer, and oil-based latex finish coat. The underside of the roof structure is also painted to match. The exterior of the plant office is also painted to match the plant walls.

HEATING, VENTILATION, AND AIR-CONDITIONING (HVAC)

There are five gas-fired air-handling units mounted on the roof. Two air-conditioning units (heat pumps), one mounted on the roof. One supplies air-conditioning for the plant (10-ton unit) and the second supplies air to the office areas (5-ton unit). The duct work for the office areas is mounted in the sloped trusses and ceilings of the offices. The duct work for the plant area is fastened to the roof joists with supply registers spaced equally along the north and south sides of the building. A room air-conditioner is supplied for the plant office at the owner's option.

PLUMBING

See figure 13–4. There is one water closet and one large washbasin in the restroom. This is also the locker room. The basin is a commercial/industrial type with a foot pedal operation so that several persons can wash simultaneously.

FIGURE 13–4
Washbasin. Courtesy of International Sanitary Ware Manufacturing Co.

The lockers are placed along two walls, the east wall, and the south wall next to the shower area. There are three floor drains installed, two (one in the shower area) in the restroom and one in the break room.

ELECTRICAL POWER

The transformer outside the southwest corner of the plant supplies power to switchgear located on the inside of the wall at the same location. The switchgear supplies power to all of the machinery—mixers, kilns, spray booth and conveyors—that are located throughout the plant. One A-frame floor crane is included in the plant construction. The power to the crane is supplied by the electrical contractor when the manufacturer's erector representative completes the installation of the crane.

The 800 VAC switchgear supply controls each piece of equipment, or series of equipment, with a separate power supply breaker on the main panel. All plant power outlets are 240VAC, 25A (minimum), three-wire, twist-lock receptacles. All convenience outlets are the standard 120VAC, 15A or 20A, duplex receptacles. The electrical contractor installs only the power supply disconnects for the crane and spray booth.

The electrical contractor is responsible for supplying and installing 240VAC disconnects and outlets for plug-in connections to the motors for the overhead doors. The door installers make the necessary connections to the outlet.

Interior Plant Lighting

See sheet E-1, Plant Lighting Plan. Plant lighting is installed between the roof joists. The light fixtures are 400W, 208VAC, with high-intensity halogen vapor lamps, with self-contained transformers. There are thirty-seven (37) lamps as per the lighting plan. Separate lighting is supplied to the plant office, wash/restroom, and break room.

EQUIPMENT INSTALLATIONS

Manufacturing equipment and the location(s) are determined by the owner and are not included in the contract (N.I.C.). All equipment is to be installed by the equipment erector (a representative of the manufacturer) or by the owner after completion of contract.

CHAPTER EXERCISES

Completion

1. The plant area has a concrete slab that is _____ kg/6.45 cm².

2. The _____ wall at the plant is a maximum 2'–0" deep.

3. The loading dock is _____' deep from top to bottom.

4. The retaining walls on each side of the loading dock are _____ CMU.

5. The plant office has a roof that is double _____ CDX or OSB.

6. There are two _____' wide overhead doors.

7. The electrical switchgear is located on the _____ corner of the plant.

8. The masonry wall is 16'–0" on _____ side(s) of the building.

9. There are _____ gas-fired heating units.

10. The steel columns used for the glu-lam beams are _____" DIA.

11. _____ wood and steel joists are by Trus-Joist/MacMillan.

12. The size of the center glu-lam beam is _____ × _____ × _____.

13. The plant office is finished with _____ siding.

14. There a total of _____ windows in the plant office area.

15. The smaller glu-lams are _____ × _____ × _____ each.

True or False

T F   1. The crane is installed by the electrical contractor.

T F   2. The slab is divided into two separate placements, three areas in each.

T F   3. The concrete is formed with a flying gang form system.

T F   4. The plant masonry walls are grout-capped.

T F   5. The plant is 86′–8″ × 57′–4″, excluding the loading dock.

T F   6. There are four personnel doors entering into the plant area.

T F   7. The owner supplies all equipment for the manufacturing areas.

T F   8. The light fixtures for the plant area are incandescent 200W.

T F   9. The exterior walls of the plant are coated with an Exterior Insulating Finish System.

T F   10. The restroom has a standard vanity basin for washing.

T F   11. The exterior doors are all hollow metal and hollow-metal frame.

T F   12. The masonry walls are struck flush on the interior side for painting.

T F   13. The overhead doors are motor-driven.

T F   14. The length of the building including the loading dock is 97′–4″.

T F   15. The large square in the manufacturing area is the location of paint booth.

Multiple Choice

_____   1. The electrical switchgear is located:
   a. Outside with the transformer.
   b. Nearest to the loading dock.
   c. Inside on the northwest corner of the plant area.
   d. Inside on the southwest corner of the plant area.

_____   2. The plumbing installation includes:
   a. Connections for a vanity basin and shower.
   b. Connections for four floor drains.
   c. Connections for two water closets.
   d. None of the above.

_____   3. The interior masonry plant walls are to be:
   a. Painted from floor to roof structure.
   b. Left exposed with the natural masonry gray color.
   c. Covered with drywall.
   d. Covered with T–1–11 siding.

_____   4. The roofing for the plant roof material is:
   a. GAF BUR system IO4G.
   b. Insulated with pre-formed tapered insulation.
   c. Both a and b.
   d. Neither a nor b.

_____ 5. The plant office/personnel area is:
   a. Located on the northeast corner of the plant building.
   b. Constructed of wood frame and siding.
   c. Constructed with metal stud frame and exterior siding.
   d. None of the above.

_____ 6. The break room is used for:
   a. The locker room.
   b. The lunch room.
   c. Dressing area.
   d. None of the above.

_____ 7. The plant office is:
   a. Connected to the air-conditioning system.
   b. To be supplied with a room air-conditioner.
   c. Located next to the office entry door.
   d. Windowless.

_____ 8. The manufacturing area has:
   a. An overhead crane operated from the floor.
   b. An overhead crane with overhead crane run and operator.
   c. A floor crane operated from the floor.
   d. No crane at all.

_____ 9. The mechanical contractor:
   a. Responsible for both the gas and electrical heating and cooling systems.
   b. Responsible for the installation of the plant equipment.
   c. Must supply the electric power to the equipment.
   d. All of the above.

_____ 10. The slab for the plant/warehouse:
   a. Is 6" thick.
   b. Has W2.9–W2.9/6–6 WWF.
   c. May have horizontal rebar along the slab perimeter.
   d. All of the above.

_____ 11. The exterior surface of the plant walls:
   a. Is painted to match the slumpstone color.
   b. Is finished with a two-coat stucco system and painted.
   c. Has an EIFS system installed over the masonry.
   d. Is finished with a one-coat stucco system.

_____ 12. The roof structure includes:
   a. Glue-laminated beams and TJI truss joists.
   b. $^1/_2$" (1.27 cm) CDX plywood deck with insulation and BUR over.
   c. Both a and b.
   d. Neither a nor b.

_____ 13. The original name for T–1–11 siding is:
   a. Board and batten siding.
   b. Shiplap siding.
   c. V-groove siding.
   d. Wood shingle siding.

_____ 14. The loading dock area is:
    a. 6'–0" (1.63 m) above finish grade.
    b. All concrete construction.
    c. Concrete and masonry construction.
    d. At grade level.

_____ 15. The wall height at the west end of the plant is:
    a. 20'–0" (6.10 m).
    b. 20'–4" (6.20 m).
    c. 16'–0" (4.88 m).
    d. None of the above.

Fundamental Everyday Mathematics

The purpose of this section is to offer the instructor and the student an alternate chapter in the event mathematics review is required.

ADDITION AND SUBTRACTION

See figure 1. All forms of work require some mathematics, in the field or in an office. Each day the field crews are measuring for excavations, trenching layouts, or concrete, masonry, or lumber layouts; or calculating the number of courses of material for a roof installation; and so on. This is true even of blueprint reading. When looking at a drawing, there are multiple measurements indicated. Many of these measurements must be added or subtracted from one another to attain the correct measurement being sought for a layout or installation. For example, the measurement from the corner of a building to the center of a window and the center of a door are shown in a frame wall. There is no measurement given for the wall on either side of the window or the door. This is common in architectural blueprints where frame construction is called out. For example, the window measurement (on figure 1) (symbol 4040) is 4'-0" wide by 4'-0" high and the door measurement (symbol 3068) is 3'-0" wide by 6'-8" high. The wall measurements are as follows:

Window width:	4'-0" wide
Wall measurement to center of window from the corner:	3'-6"
Door width:	3'-0" wide

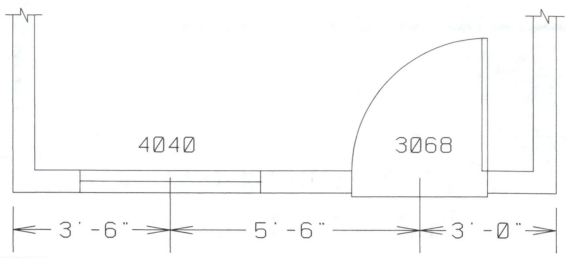

FIGURE 1
Partial Wall Plan

Wall measurement to center of door from the corner:	3′-0″
Distance from center of window to center of door:	5′-6″
Total wall length:	12′-0″

Therefore, the wall measurements between the door and corner, between the window and door, and the window and corner, are:

3′-0″–(½ × 3′-0″) = 3′-0″–1′-6″ = 1′-6″ **wall between corner and door**
3′-6″–(½ × 4′-0″) = 3′-6″–2′-0″ = 1′-6″ **wall between corner and window**
12′-0″–(1′-6″ + 4′-0″ + 1′-6″ + 3′-0″) = 2′-0″ **wall between door and window**

This is blueprint reading and is actually what the layout carpenter in the field must do on a daily basis.

FRACTIONS AND DECIMALS

See appendix III, Inch to Fraction or Decimal Part of a Foot. The chart in appendix III shows both the fractional and decimal equivalent of inches per foot. Like the chart, the numbers as used above can be written in the same two ways. The average calculator uses the decimal system. When calculating by hand (written), the fraction is often used. For example, the numbers could be written as follows:

3′-6″ = $3^1/_2$ ft (fraction) or 3.5 ft (decimal)
10′-4″ = $10^1/_3$ ft (fraction) or 10.33 ft (decimal)
5′-7″ = $5^7/_{12}$ ft (fraction) or 5.58 ft (decimal)
3′-0″ = 3 ft or 3.0 ft (decimal)

RATIO AND PROPORTION (MULTIPLICATION AND DIVISION)

Another use of fractions in construction in the field is the almost daily application of the ratio and proportion formulas (equations). The dictionary defines a ratio as "a fixed relation in degree, number, and so on, between two similar things; proportion; in mathematics, the quotient of one quantity divided by another of the same kind, and usually expressed as a fraction." When two such ratios, or fractions, are placed in a format forming an equation, they become one of the common simple algebraic expressions in any of the following ways:

$$a:b = c:d \qquad a/b = c/d \qquad a \div b = c \div d$$

See figure 2. The proportion formula can be readily used when three of the four parts of the equation are known. One of the most common uses for proportion equations is found in framing for roof structure calculations for **rise and run.** For example, the **span** in a transverse section of a $\frac{5}{12}$ gable is 40 lf (lineal feet). The run of a true gable is one half ($\frac{1}{2}$) the distance of the span. With the proportion formula (equation), the *rise* of the gable at the ridge can be determined. The rise is determined as 8'-4" as follows:

Span (exterior bearing wall to opposite exterior bearing wall) = 40'-0"

Run ($\frac{1}{2}$ of the span) = 20'-0"

The roof slope is $\frac{5}{12}$ (5 unit rise for each equal 12 units horizontally) = $\frac{5}{12}$

The denominator (bottom number of the slope fraction)—$\frac{5}{12}$—is the run (horizontal measurement) and the numerator (top number) is the rise (vertical measurement). Since the other measurements (span and run) are in feet, the unit measure for the $\frac{5}{12}$ is also converted to feet as follows:

5 lf/12 lf

As noted above, the run is the horizontal measurement from exterior bearing wall to the center (ridge) of the gable. The calculation is as follows:

$$\frac{a}{b} = \frac{c}{d}$$

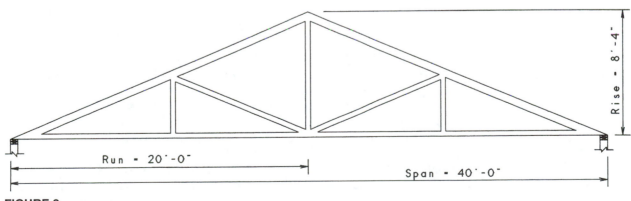

FIGURE 2
RISE and RUN

Where:

a = 5 lf
b = 12 lf
c = the unknown (x lf)
d = 20 lf

Therefore:

$$\frac{5\ lf}{12\ lf} = \frac{x\ lf}{20\ lf}$$

The numerator on one side of the equation is multiplied by the denominator (called cross-multiplication) on the opposite side as follows:

5 lf · 20 lf = x lf · 12lf

The unknown part of the equation (x) is to be left on one side by itself. This is done by dividing both sides of the equation by the 12 as follows:

100 lf ÷ 12 lf = (x lf · 12 lf) ÷ 12 lf

Since 12 lf ÷ 12 lf = 1 lf, the equation becomes as follows:

100 lf ÷ 12 lf = x lf · 1 lf
or
100 lf ÷ 12 lf = x lf

Thus:

x lf = 8.33 lf or 8⅓ feet or 8'-4" rise

It should be noted here that the angle formed at the junction of a rise and run is a right angle (90°). This is important for calculations of rafter lengths. The use of the right angle is discussed in the section making use of the Pythagorean theorem.

Proportional calculations can be used in other situations as well. For example, a plot plan in a blueprint is the only place that indicates a retaining wall along one of the property lines. The information on the plan indicates that the height of the wall is 6.0' (civil engineering style measurement) above grade. No length is indicated. How can the length be determined? There are two solutions to the problem. *The best possible solution is to get an answer from the engineer or architect.* Verify that the wall exists and, if so, ascertain if there is any other information needed.

Where time may be of the essence and the information is not available, the alternative is to use the proportion formula. This is one of the rare times when "scaling" (measuring with a rule or scale of some kind) is allowed. The architectural, engineering, and estimating professions frown on this procedure except in this type of situation. **The measurements indicated on a plan will otherwise take precedence over scaling in all instances.**

The plan is scaled at 1" = 20.0'. The wall measures 3½" on the plan as determined by use of a tape measure. The inches are broken down into any desired increments (for example, ⅛", ¼", ½") to produce a fraction. This fraction is used in the proportion calculation. In the example, the inches are converted into ⅛″ increments. The following are part of the proportion formula: that fractional value calculated in the conversion and the scale of the plan (in this case 1″ = 20.0′). The 20 lf is the horizontal measurement of the scale and is, therefore, the denominator of the fraction with an unknown value for the numerator. The 8 from the ⅛″ breakdown is the denominator of the other fraction in the proportion. The length of the wall is determined to be 70 lf:

$$3\tfrac{1}{2}'' = ([3 \cdot 2] + 1) = \tfrac{7}{2}$$

There are eight ⅛″ increments in each 1″, therefore:

$$\overset{4}{{}^{7}/_{\cancel{2}}} \cdot {}^{\cancel{8}}/_{8}'' = {}^{(7 \times 4)}/_{8}'' = {}^{28}/_{8}''$$

The formula is:

$$\frac{a}{b} = \frac{c}{d}$$

Where:

a = 28 (convert to lf)
b = 8 (convert to lf)
c = the unknown (x lf)
d = 20 lf

Therefore:

$$\frac{28\ \text{lf}}{8\ \text{lf}} = \frac{x\ \text{lf}}{20\ \text{lf}}$$

28 lf · 20 lf = x lf · 8 lf
560 lf ÷ 8 lf = (x lf · 8 lf) ÷ 8 lf
x lf = 70 lf

The answer for this proportion calculation will be identical for any of the above fractions suggested. For example, the 3½″ in ¼″ increments = ¹⁴/₄″, and in ½″ increments = ⁷/₂″, and so on.

PYTHAGOREAN THEOREM (3-4-5 SYSTEM)

See figure 3. One other commonly used formula in construction is the Pythagorean theorem. Most field personnel use this formula frequently and probably never know it. The system is called the *3-4-5 system.* This system is used to determine whether or not a true right angle exists at a foundation or slab, or the framing corner is square, horizontally and/or vertically. The layout is stated as follows: If one side measures 3 units (inches, feet, and so on) and the perpendicular side measures 4 units of the same measure, then the diagonal between the ends of them must equal 5 units of the same measure. In other words, the theorem states that "the sum of the squares of two sides of a right triangle is equal to the square of the hypotenuse (diagonal length opposite the

FIGURE 3
Pythagorean Theorem (3-4-5
SYSTEM)

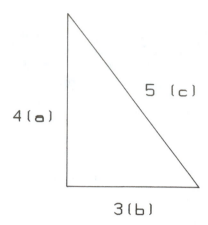

4 (a)

5 (c)

3 (b)

right angle) of the triangle." The *square* of a number is the number multiplied by itself, such as 1 · 1 or 2 · 2. It is written mathematically as follows:

$c^2 = a^2 + b^2$

Where:

c^2 = the hypotenuse (diagonal)
a^2 = the one side
b^2 = the perpendicular side

In the 3-4-5 system, the theorem is determined as follows:

c^2 = 5 (diagonal)
a^2 = 4 (perpendicular or vertical [altitude])
b^2 = 3 (base or horizontal)

Therefore, if:

$c^2 = a^2 + b^2$

Then:

$(5 \cdot 5) = (4 \cdot 4) + (3 \cdot 3)$
$25 = 16 + 9$
$25 = 25$

Thus a true right triangle (or a true right angle) is formed. As previously mentioned, this formula is also used for determining the lengths of rafters. The truss manufacturer uses this formula along with the rise and run for this purpose. Carpentry contractors also use the formula for determining the lengths of conventional rafters. As an example, with the run and rise determined in the previous calculation, the rafter length can be calculated as follows:

Rise = 8.33 lf
Run = 20 lf
Rafter length = ?

Using the Pythagorean theorem, the rafter length is calculated as follows:

Where:

$c^2 = a^2 + b^2$

$c^2 = (8.33 \text{ lf})^2 + (20 \text{ lf})^2$

$c^2 = 69.39 \text{ ft}^2 + 400 \text{ ft}^2$

$c^2 = 469.39 \text{ ft}^2$

The square root (c) = 21.67 lf

Lumber is purchased in even lineal-foot increments, therefore, the length purchased is 22 lf.

LINEAL (LINEAR) MEASURE

See figure 4. Lineal measurements for determining perimeters (length around), heights, and depths of properties, buildings, rooms, and so on, are basic to construction calculations. To obtain square measure, two lineal measurements are required; for volume, three lineal measurements are required.

For example, an architect is preparing a conceptual estimate for an owner. Part of the information to be determined includes the size of the slab and the exterior wall framing for "shell" construction (exterior walls only). The rectangular building footprint measures 100 lf by 73 lf. The slab area and volume, the quantity of plate stock, sill plate and studs can be determined quickly. All of the measurements start with the lineal feet of perimeter or the lengths of two sides as follows:

100 lf + 100 lf + 73 lf + 73 lf	= }
or	} 346 lf
(100 lf · 2) + (73 lf · 2)	= }

The concrete slab for the structure is 6" thick.

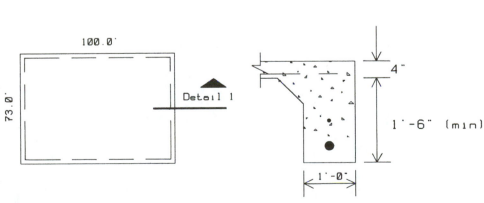

FIGURE 4
Lineal Measure

METRIC CONVERSIONS

See figure 5 and appendix III. All federal government work since 1994 requires plans to be dimensioned in metrics. It is hoped that all projects will be in metrics eventually, since most of the world uses them. To assist in calculations with the most common metric measures converted from metrics to equivalent English (American) measures, use the following conversions:

Lineal Measure	Square Measure	Volume Measure
1 in = 2.54 cm or 25.4 mm	$1\ in^2 = 6.45\ cm^2$	$1\ in^3 = 16.38\ cm^3$
1 ft = 0.3048 m	$1\ ft^2 = 0.0929\ m^2$	$1\ ft^3 = 0.0283\ m^3$

The metric equivalents of mass and liquid volume are calculated as follows:

1lb = 0.454 kg; 2.2 lb = 1 kg   3.79 gal = 1 L (liter); 1 gal = 0.264 L (liter)

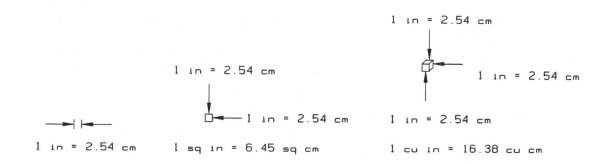

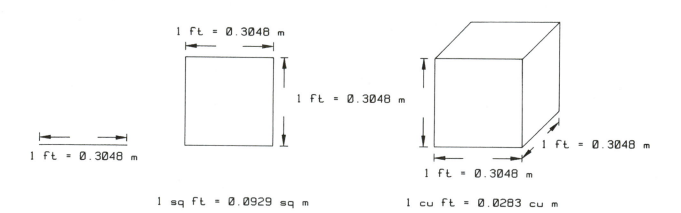

LINEAL   SQUARE   CUBIC

FIGURE 5
English/Metric Conversions

Note: in^2 = square inches (sq in); in^3 = cubic inches (cu in); ft^2 = square feet (sq ft); ft^3 = cu ft (cu ft).

See appendix III, Rebar (Standard Sizes). One other frequently noted measure is in reference to reinforcement steel bar (rebar). Rebar is sized in ⅛″ diameter (DIA) increments. For example, a #4 bar = ⅛″ or ½″ DIA.

Many specifications refer to the laps in rebar in terms to the number of diameters of the rebar. The specification for standard footing installations may state "2–#4 rebar shall be installed continuously in the footing. There shall be 48 diameter laps at all ends of the rebar and at the corners." The length of the laps are calculated as follows:

#4 = ⅛″ (½″)

    6

⅛″ · 48̶ laps = 4″ · 6 = 24″ or 2′-0″ laps

ADDITIONAL EXERCISES

Hint: When calculating combinations of addition and subtraction, *add* all of the positives (+) together, then *add* all of the negatives together (-), then *subtract* the negative (-) total from the positive (+) total.

Addition and Subtraction

The property measures as follows:

North property line	= 766.0′
East property line	= 361.5′
South property line	= 738.67′
West property line	= 370.0′

1. Determine the total lineal feet of the perimeter of the property.
2. Determine the combined east and west property line length.
3. Convert the measurements shown above into feet and inches (0′-0″).
4. The slab in figure 4 measures a total of _____ lf.
5. The depth of the slab and footing in figure 4 is _____ deep.
6. Subtract the combined east/west footage in question 2 from the total lineal feet of the plat referred to in question 1.
7. The structure that is to be built on the slab in figure 4 requires 346 lf of sill plate fastened to the slab. Deduct the quantity of sill plate required for two sides of the slab, one long side and one short side.
8. There are 692 lf of double top plate required for the perimeter walls. Determine the quantity required for the same two sides as for the sill plate in question 2.
9. A delivery of lumber is made that includes 31,368 lf of 2×4, DF #2. The load also includes some 2×6, DF #2. The total lineal feet of lumber delivered is 104,572 lf. Determine the quantity of 2×6 delivered.

Fractions and Decimals

10. Add the following fractions:
    ½" + 4¼" + 21¼" + ⁵⁄₁₆" + ⅛" =

11. Subtract the following fractions:
    52⅞" - 12½" - 10¼" - 19⅛" =

12. Determine the total of the following:
    175⅓ lf + 300 lf - 275¾ lf =

13. Calculate the answer for the following problem:
    12.66   lf + 175.5 lf - 90.99 lf + 67.66 lf - 200.17 lf =

Hint: When calculating combinations of addition and subtraction, *add* all of the positives (+) together; *add* all of the negatives (–) together; then *subtract* the negative (–) total from the positive (+) total.

Multiplication and Division

Hint: When calculating combinations of multiplication and division, *multiply* first, then *divide*.

14. 1¼" · ½" =
15. 75.35 lf · 131.8 lf ÷ 52.1 lf =
16. 21¾ " ÷ 2" · 44¼" =
17. 357.08 lf · 260.01 lf =
18. 357.08 km ÷ 260.01 km =
19. 5,286 ft · 2 = _____ mi
20. 350 cu ft (ft³) ÷ 27 cu ft (ft³) = _____ cu yd (yd³)

Metrics

1. The dimension shown on a plan is 101'-10". What is the metric equivalent?
2. A plot plan measures 245'-0" × 133'-0". Calculate the area.
3. Calculate the same area in metrics.
4. A mass excavation is 60'-0" × 40'-0" × 10'-0". Calculate the volume in cubic feet and cubic yards. (1 cu yd = 27 cu ft).
5. Calculate the same volume in cubic meters.

General

1. A specification for rebar notes that the vertical wall rebar is a #8 that must be lapped 72 bar diameters. Determine the size of the lap.
2. The rise of a sloped roof is 14'-0" and the run is 24'-0". Calculate the length of a rafter excluding any overhang.

3. The lengths of a rectangular structure are 161 lf by 65 lf. Calculate the lineal feet of perimeter.

4. Calculate the area of the flat plane of the structure in question 3.

5. Calculate the volume of concrete (in cubic yards) necessary for this area if the slab is 6″ thick. Note: 27 ft^3 = 1 yd^3.

CONSTRUCTION ABBREVIATIONS

A	area
AB	anchor bolt
AC	alternate current
A/C	air conditioning
ACT	acoustical ceiling tile
A.F.F.	above finish floor
AGGR	aggregate
AIA	American Institute of Architects
AL, ALUM	aluminum
AMP	ampere
APPROX	approximate
ASPH	asphalt
ASTM	American Society for Testing Materials
AWG	American wire gauge
BD	board
BD FT (BF)	board foot (feet)
BLDG	building
BLK	black, block
BLKG	blocking
BM	board measure
CC	center to center, cubic centimeter
CEM	cement
CER	ceramic
CFM	cubic feet per minute
CIP	cast-in-place, concrete-in-place
CJ	ceiling joist, control joint
CKT	circuit (electrical)
CLG	ceiling
CMU	concrete masonry unit
CO	cleanout (plumbing)

COL	column
CONC	concrete
CONST	construction
CONTR	contractor
CU FT(ft³)	cubic foot (feet)
CU IN(in³)	cubic inch(es)
CU YD(yd³)	cubic yard(s)
d	pennyweight (nail)
DC	direct current (elec.)
DET	detail
DIA	diameter
DIAG	diagonal
DIM	dimension
DN	down
DO	ditto (same as)
DS	downspout
DWG	drawing
E	East
EA	each
ELEC	electric, electrical
ELEV	elevation, elevator
ENCL	enclosure
EXCAV	excavate, excavation
EXT	exterior
FDN	foundation
FIN	finish
FIN FLR	finish floor
FIN GRD	finish grade
FL, FLR	floor
FLG	flooring

FLUOR	fluorescent	N	North
FOB	free-on-board, factory-on-board	NEC	National Electric Code
FOM	face of masonry	NIC	not in contract
FOS	face of stud, flush on slab	NOM	nominal
FT	foot, feet		
FTG	footing	O/A	overall (measure)
FURN	furnishing, furnace	O.C. (O/C)	on center
FX GL (FX)	fixed glass	OD	outside diameter
		OH	overhead
GA	gauge	O/H	overhang (eave line)
GAL	gallon	OPG	opening
GALV	galvanize(d)	OPP	opposite
GD	ground (earth/electric)		
GI	galvanized iron	PC	piece
GL	glass	PLAS	plastic
GL BLK	glass block	PLAST	plaster
GLB,GLU-LAM	glue-laminated beam	PLT	plate (framing)
GRD	grade, ground	PR	pair
GWB	gypsum wall board	PREFAB	prefabricate(d)(tion)
GYP	gypsum	PTN	partition
		PVC	polyvinylchloride pipe
HB	hose bibb		
HDR	header	QT	quart
HDW	hardware	QTY	quantity
HGT/HT	height		
HM	hollow metal	R	right
HORIZ	horizontal	RD	road, round, roof drain
HP	horsepower	REBAR	reinforced steel bar
HWH	hot water heater	RECEPT	receptacle
		REINF	reinforce(ment)
ID	inside diameter	REQ'D	required
IN	inch(es)	RET	retain(ing), return
INSUL	insulation	RF	roof
INT	interior	RFG	roofing (materials)
		RH	right hand
J, JST	joist		
JT	joint	S	South
		SCH/SCHED	schedule
KG	kilogram	SECT	section
KL	kiloliter	SERV	service (utility)
KM	kilometer	SEW	sewer
KWH	kilowatt-hour	SHTHG	sheathing
		SIM	similar
L	left, line	SP	soil pipe (plumbing)
LAU	laundry	SPEC	specification
LAV	lavatory	SQ FT (ft²)	square foot (feet)
LBR	labor	SQ IN (in²)	inch(es)
LDG	landing, leading	SQ YD (yd²)	square yard(s)
LDR	leader	STA	station
LEV/LVL	level	STD	standard
LIN FT (LF)	lineal foot (feet)	STIR	stirrup (rebar)
LGTH	length	STL	steel
LH	left hand	STR/ST	street
LITE/LT	light (window pane)	STRUCT	structural
		SUSP CLG	suspended ceiling
MAT'L	material	SYM	symbol, symmetric
MAX	maximum	SYS	system
MBF/MBM	thousand board feet, thousand board measure		
		T&G	tongue and groove
MECH	mechanical	THK	thick
MISC	miscellaneous	TOB	top of beam
MK	mark (identifier)	TOC	top of curb
MO	momentary (electrical contact), masonry opening	TOF	top of footing
		TOL	top of ledger
		TOP	top of parapet

TOS	top of steel		w/o	without
TR	tread, transition		WC	water closet (toilet)
TRK	track, truck		WDW	window
TYP	typical		WI	wrought iron
			WP	waterproof, weatherproof
UF	underground feeder (electrical)		WT/WGT	weight
USE	underground service entrance cable (electrical)		YD	yard
W	West		Z	zinc
w/	with			

SYMBOLS

&	and		″	ditto, inch, -es
∠	angle		′	foot, feet
@	at		%	percent
#	number, pound		ø	diameter

Reference Tables

TABLE 1–1
Inch to Fraction or Decimal Part of a Foot

Inch	Fraction	Decimal
1″	1/12 ft	0.083 or 0.08 ft
2″	1/6 ft	0.166 or 0.17 ft
3″	1/4 ft	0.25 ft
4″	1/3 ft	0.33 ft (0.34 ft)
5″	5/12 ft	0.417 or 0.42 ft
6″	1/2 ft	0.5 ft
7″	7/12 ft	0.583 or 0.58 ft
8″	2/3 ft	0.66 ft (0.67 ft)
9″	3/4 ft	0.75 ft
10″	5/6 ft	0.833 or 0.83 ft
11″	11/12 ft	0.916 or 0.92 ft

TABLE 1–2
English to Metric Equivalents

English		Metric
Lineal		
1 in	=	25.4 mm
1 ft	=	0.3048 m
1 yd	=	0.9144 m
1 mi	=	1.60934 km
Volume		
1 qt (liquid)	=	0.946353 L
1 gal	=	0.00378541 m^3
Weight		
1 oz (avdp)	=	28.3495 gm
1 lb (avdp)	=	0.453592 kg
Power		
1 HP	=	0.7457 kw

TABLE 1–3
Metric to English Equivalents

Metric		English
Lineal Measure		
1 mm	=	0.03937 in
1 cm	=	0.3937 in
1 m	=	39.37 in
1 m	=	3.28084 ft
1 m	=	1.09361 yd
1 km	=	0.621371 mi
Area		
1 cm^2	=	0.15499 in^2
1 m^2	=	1,549.9 in^2
1 m^2	=	10.7632 ft^2
1km^2	=	0.386 mi^2
Volume		
1 cc (cm^3)	=	0.6102 in^3
1 L	=	1.05669 qt (liquid)
1 m^3	=	35.314 ft^3
1 m^3	=	1.308 yd^3
1 m^3	=	264.172 gal
Weight		
1 kg	=	2.2046 lb
1 metric ton	=	2,204.6 lb
Power		
1 kw	=	1.34102 HP

TABLE 1–4
Drawing Scales

Plan Use	Ratio	Metric Length	English Equivalent (approx)
Details			
	1:1	1000 mm = 1 m	12″ = 1′-0″ (Full scale)
	1:5	200 mm = 1 m	3″ = 1′-0″
	1:10	100 mm = 1 m	1½″ = 1′-0″
	1:20	50 mm = 1 m	½″ = 1′-0″
Floor Plans:			
	1:40	25 mm = 1 m	⅜″ = 1′-0″
	1:50	20 mm = 1 m	¼″ = 1′-0″
Plot Plans:			
	1:80	13.3 mm = 1 m	3/16″ = 1′-0″
	1:100	12.5 mm = 1 m	⅛″ = 1′-0″
	1:200	5 mm = 1 m	1″ = 20′-0″
Plat Plans:			
	1:500	2 mm = 1 m	1″ = 50′-0″
City Maps (and larger):			
	1:1250	0.8 mm = 1 m	1″ = 125′-0″
	1:2500	0.4 mm = 1 m	1″ = 250′-0″

TABLE 1–5
Masonry Dimensions

	English to Metric					
	BRICK					
	Nominal English Sizes			Nominal Metric Sizes		
	W	H	L	W	H	L
Modular	4″	8″	8″	100mm	200mm	200mm
Roman	4″	6″	12″	100mm	150mm	300mm
Norman	4″	8″	12″	100mm	200mm	300mm
SCR	6″	8″	12″	150mm	200mm	300mm
	CMU					
Stretcher	8″	8″	16″	200mm	200mm	400mm

TABLE 1–6
Rebar (Standard Sizes)

BAR	DIAMETER (SIZE)
#2	$\frac{1}{4}''$
#3	$\frac{3}{8}''$
#4	$\frac{1}{2}''$
#5	$\frac{5}{8}''$
#6	$\frac{3}{4}''$
#7	$\frac{7}{8}''$
#8	$1''$
#9	$1\frac{1}{8}''$
#10	$1\frac{1}{4}''$
#11	$1\frac{3}{8}''$
#14	$1\frac{3}{4}''$
#18	$2\frac{1}{4}''$

TABLE 1–6A
Welded Wire Fabric

Roll	Sheet
6x6 - W1.4xW1.4	6x6 - W2.0xW2.0
6x6 - W2.9xW2.9	6x6 - W2.9xW2.9
6x6 - W4.0xW4.0	6x6 - W4.0xW4.0
6x6 - W5.5xW5.5	4x4 - W1.4xW1.4
4x4 - W1.4xW1.4	4x4 - W2.9xW2.9
4x4 - W2.9xW2.9	
4x4 - W4.0xW4.0	

If the letter designation D is added, the fabric is deformed similar to rebar.

WWF is made into sheets or rolls depending upon the size and quantity required.

TABLE 1–7
Framing Ratios Per Stud Spacing

Spacing	Constant	Decimal Equivalent
12″ O/C	1	1.000
16″ O/C	$\frac{3}{4}$	0.750
18″ O/C	$\frac{2}{3}$	0.667
20″ O/C	$\frac{3}{5}$	0.600
24″ O/C	$\frac{1}{2}$	0.500
32″ O/C	$\frac{3}{8}$	0.375
36″ O/C	$\frac{1}{3}$	0.333

TABLE 1–8
Nail Sizes

2d: 2 pennyweight x 1″ long
4d: 4 pennyweight x 1¼″ long
6d: 6 pennyweight x 1½″ long
8d: 8 pennyweight x 1¾″ long
10d: 10 pennyweight x 2″ long
16d: 16 pennyweight x 3″ long
20d: 20 pennyweight x 3½″ long
straw nail = 10d x 6″ long
spike = any nail 20d or larger x 6″ long

TABLE 1–8A
Surface Finishing Abbreviations, Yard and Structural Lumber

Abbreviation	Definition
S1S	Smooth surface, one side
S1S1E	Smooth surface, one side, one end
S1S2E	Smooth surface, one side, two ends
S2S	Smooth surface, two sides
S2S1E	Smooth surface, two sides, one end
S2S2E	Smooth surface, two sides, two ends
S3S	Smooth surface, three sides
S3S1E	Smooth surface, three sides, one end
S3S2E	Smooth surface, three sides, two ends
S4S	Smooth surface, four sides
S4S1E	Smooth surface, four sides, one end
S4S2E	Smooth surface, four sides, two ends
R/E	Resawn (same as S1S or S1S2E)
R/O or R/S	Rough sawn (no smooth surfaces)

TABLE 1–9
Glue-Laminated Timber Sizing

Width		Depth	
Nominal	Actual	Nominal	Actual
3″	2¼″	8″ (6¾″)	9″
4″	3⅛″	10″ (5⅛″)	10½″
6″	5⅛″	8″ (5⅛″)	9″
8″	6¾″	6″ (5⅛″)	6″
10″	8¾″	6″ (3⅛″)	7½″
12″	10¾″		
14″	12¼″		
16″	14¼″		

TABLE 1–10
Light Gauge Framing, Size and Weight per Lineal Foot

Size (Inches)	Metal Gauge	Net Weight (lb/lf)
Studs		
1½"	25	0.443
1½"	20	0.700
2½"	25	0.509
2½"	20	0.810
3"	25	0.555
3"	20	0.875
3¼"	25	0.575
3¼"	20	0.910
3½"	25	0.597
3½"	20	0.944
3⅝"	25	0.608
3⅝"	20	0.964
4"	25	0.641
4"	20	1.014
5½"	20	1.240
6"	20	1.290
Joists		
6"	20	1.486
6"	18	1.889
6"	16	2.339
6"	14	2.914
8"	18	2.215
8"	16	2.411
10"	16	3.142
10"	14	3.908

Courtesy of American Studco Corp.

TABLE 1–11
Roof Slope Table

SLOPE RATIO	PITCH RATIO	CONVERSION FACTOR	WASTE FACTOR	
3:12	⅛	1.03	.05	1.08
3.5:12	⁷⁄₂₄	1.04	.05	1.09
4:12	⅙	1.05	.05	1.10
4.5:12	⁹⁄₄₈	1.06	.05	1.11
5:12	⁵⁄₂₄	1.08	.05	1.13
5.5:12	¹¹⁄₄₈	1.10	.05	1.15
6:12	¼	1.12	.05	1.17
6.5:12	¹³⁄₄₈	1.14	.05	1.19
7:12	⁷⁄₂₄	1.16	.05	1.21
7.5:12	¹⁵⁄₄₈	1.18	.05	1.23
8:12	⅓	1.20	.05	1.25
10:12	⁵⁄₁₂	1.30	.05	1.35
12:12	½	1.45	.05	1.50
18:12	¾	2.0	.05	2.05
24:12	1	2.0	.05	2.05

TABLE 1–12
Numbers and Their Squares and Approximate Square Roots

Number	Square	Sq. Root	Number	Square	Sq. Root
1	1	1.000	51	2601	7.141
2	4	1.414	52	2704	7.211
3	9	1.732	53	2809	7.280
4	16	2.000	54	2916	7.348
5	25	2.236	55	3025	7.416
6	36	2.449	56	3136	7.483
7	49	2.646	57	3249	7.550
8	64	2.828	58	3364	7.616
9	81	3.000	59	3481	7.681
10	100	3.162	60	3600	7.746
11	121	3.317	61	3721	7.810
12	144	3.464	62	3844	7.874
13	169	3.606	63	3969	7.937
14	196	3.742	64	4096	8.000
15	225	3.873	65	4225	8.062
16	256	4.000	66	4356	8.124
17	289	4.123	67	4489	8.185
18	324	4.243	68	4624	8.246
19	361	4.359	69	4761	8.307
20	400	4.472	70	4900	8.367
21	441	4.583	71	5041	8.426
22	484	4.690	72	5184	8.485
23	529	4.796	73	5329	8.544
24	576	4.899	74	5476	8.602
25	625	5.000	75	5625	8.660
26	676	5.099	76	5776	8.718
27	729	5.196	77	5929	8.775
28	784	5.292	78	6084	8.832
29	841	5.385	79	6241	8.888
30	900	5.477	80	6400	8.944
31	961	5.568	81	6561	9.000
32	1024	5.657	82	6724	9.055
33	1089	5.745	83	6889	9.110
34	1156	5.831	84	7056	9.165
35	1225	5.916	85	7225	9.220
36	1296	6.000	86	7396	9.274
37	1369	6.083	87	7569	9.327
38	1444	6.164	88	7744	9.381
39	1521	6.245	89	7921	9.434
40	1600	6.325	90	8100	9.487
41	1681	6.403	91	8381	9.539
42	1764	6.481	92	8464	9.592
43	1849	6.557	93	8649	9.644
44	1936	6.633	94	8836	9.695
45	2025	6.708	95	9025	9.747
46	2116	6.782	96	9216	9.798
47	2209	6.852	97	9409	9.849
48	2304	6.928	98	9604	9.899
49	2401	7.000	99	9801	9.950
50	2500	7.071	100	10000	10.000

Bid Documents

INVITATION TO BID
CHRISTLE & Associates
550 Broad Street
Las Vegas, Nevada 89000
(300)555-5555

October 30, 1998

Sir(s)Madame(s):

You are invited to bid on a General Contract, including mechanical and electrical work, for a combination office/warehouse, wood frame and masonry construction, approximately 6,569 square feet. All bids must be on a lump-sum basis; aggregate bids will not be accepted.

Drawings and specifications may be obtained from the Architect along with the Instructions to Bidders at a cost of two-hundred dollars ($200.00), non-refundable. A maximum of four (4)sets may be purchased by any one company.

Plans may also be examined at the following plan room locations:

The Plan Room   The Bid Depository
35 Atlantic Avenue   156 Pacific Avenue
Las Vegas, Nevada   Las Vegas, Nevada

A bid (security) bond valued at fifteen percent (15%) of the bid must accompany each bid submitted in accordance with the Instructions to Bidders. The Architect and Owner reserve the right to reject any and all bids or waive any irregularities due to discrepancies in the bids.

(Signed) Steven Christle
Architect and Agent for
J.M. Land Co./Frontier Manufacturing
Caliente, Nevada

Advertisement to Bid

BID: November 15, 1998, office/warehouse, owned by J.M. Land Co., Caliente, NV, Project 12726, is open for bid. Christle Associates, Las Vegas, NV, (300) 555-5555, is representing the owner. Sealed bids are requested on a general contract, including mechanical and electrical work, for a wood frame and masonry structure approx. 6,569 square feet. All bids to be lump sum: no segregated bids accepted. Bids to be received until 3PM PST, Thurs, November 15, 1998, at 550 Broad Street, Las Vegas, NV. No and read publicly. Plans and specifications may be examined at:

The Plan Room	The Bid Depository
35 Atlantic Ave.	156 Pacific Ave.
Las Vegas, NV	Las Vegas, NV

Copies may be obtained from the architect at a cost of $200/set, nonrefundable, maximum 4 sets. Bid bond of 15% of total bid proposal to be submitted with the bid in accordance with the Instructions to Bidders. Owner reserves right of refusal of any bid.

By order of:
Christle & Associates, Las Vegas, Nevada.

GLOSSARY

A

abbreviation shortening of a word or group of words.

ABS (acrylonitrile butadiene styrene) plastic pipe used for plumbing construction.

abut joining end-to-end.

accelerator a concrete additive used to speed the curing time of freshly poured concrete.

acoustical referring to the study of sound transmission or reduction.

acoustical tile/acoustical ceiling tile (ACT) a combination of products such as vegetable, mineral, wood, cork, or metal, formed into boards or tiles.

acrylic a thermoplastic material used with resins, paints, and other plastic materials.

additive *see* admixture.

adhesive a bonding material used to bond two materials together.

adjacent touching; next to.

admixture any material other than water, aggregate, fiber reinforcement, or cement, added to a concrete mix.

advertisement to bid *see* Invitation to bid.

aggregate fine, lightweight, coarse, or heavyweight grades of sand, vermiculite, perlite, or gravel added to cement for concrete or plaster.

air entrainment minute bubbles of air mixed into concrete or mortar to aid in the plasticity of a mix; also improves resistance to frost.

air handling unit a mechanical unit used for air conditioning or movement of air as in direct supply or exhaust of air within a structure.

allowable load maximum supportable load of any construction component(s).

allowable span maximum length permissible for any framing component without support.

anchor bolt   a J- or L-shaped steel rod threaded on one end for securing structural members to concrete or masonry.

apron   (1) a sloped concrete pad on a property used as an approach for a garage or entry to or from a street; (2) A strip of finish trim installed under the window stool to hide the drywall edge.

arabesque   a design of plant forms or geometric figures formed into a complicated pattern used for decorative purposes.

architect   a qualified, licensed person that creates and designs drawings for a construction project.

architect's scale   a rule with scales indicating feet, inches, and fractions of inches.

area   (1) the calculation of the size of a plane (flat surface) in square units (square feet, square yards, and so on); (2) a designated space.

asphalt   the general term for a black material produced as a by-product of oil (asphalt) or coal (pitch or coal tar).

awning window   a window that is hinged at the top and the bottom swings outward.

azimuth   an angle measured from true north and expressed in degrees, minutes, and seconds

B

backfill   any deleterious material (sand, gravel, and so on) used to fill an excavation.

backup   a masonry wall used to support an exterior masonry finish.

balloon framing   wall construction extending from the foundation to the roof structure without interruption; used in residential construction only.

baluster   a vertical member supporting a balustrade.

balustrade   a series of balusters supporting a horizontal railing.

barge rafter   an extension of the gable end of a roof structure used to support a decorative framing member or roofing material.

baseboard   a finished trim member applied on the finished wall at the junction with the finished floor.

batt insulation   an insulating material formed into sheets or rolls with a foil or paper backing; to be installed between framing members.

batten   a board strip used to hide the joint between two larger boards known as *board and batten finish construction.*

beam   a large horizontal structural member made of concrete, steel, stone, wood, or other structural material to support the structure above a large opening.

benchmark   an area base reference point elevation above mean sea level.

berm   a raised earth embankment; the shoulder of a paved road; the area between the curb and gutter and a sidewalk.

bibb   also known as a *hose bibb;* a faucet used to connect a hose.

bi-fold   a double-leaf door used primarily for closet doors in residential construction.

bird block   *see* frieze block.

bird mouth   a notch cut into a roof rafter so that it can rest smoothly on the top plate.

bitumen   the general term used to identify asphalt and coal tar.

blanket insulation   *see* batt insulation; available in rolls up to 24'-0" long.

blocking   specifically, a piece of wood fastened between structural members to strengthen them; generally, solid or cross-tie wood or metal cross-tie members to perform the same task.

blueprint   a term derived from the original development process; (1) a single sheet copied from a master copy (velum, and so on) with blue lines on a blue background, or with black lines on a white background, showing some part of a construction project; (2) the complete set of drawings of a construction project.

board foot   a piece of lumber 12" long by 12" wide by 1" thick.

board measure   a system of measure used for freighting lumber based on the board foot.

bond   as used with masonry, the interlocking system of brick or block to be installed as running or common bond, stack bond, English bond, Flemish bond, and so on.

brick   a masonry unit usually, of clay base, used for both structural and aesthetic appearance.

bypass door   a sliding or track-mounted door in which the leaves can be moved past one another.

C

calcium chloride   a concrete admixture used for accelerating the cure time.

California Bearing Ratio (CBR)   a system used for determining the bearing capacity of a foundation.

cement   a material that, when combined with water, hardens due to chemical reaction; the basis for a concrete mix.

cement plaster   a mixture of gypsum, cement, hydrated lime, sand, and water, used primarily for exterior wall finish.

cementitious   able to harden like cement.

chair   used to support horizontal rebar prior to the concrete placement.

chord   top or bottom member of a truss.

cold key   *see* keyway.

collar tie   horizontal framing member tying the raftering together above the plate line.

common rafter   a structural member that extends without interruption from the ridge to the plate line in a sloped roof structure.

computer-aided design and drafting (CADD)   the computer design program used for drawing a set of blueprints or any component thereof.

computer-aided drafting (CAD)   see computer-aided design and drafting (CADD).

computer-aided engineering (CAE)   the same system using software specifically for engineering requirements (structural, mechanical, civil, and electrical).

concrete masonry unit (CMU)   manufactured into primarily modular concrete units in lightweight hollow, heavyweight hollow, and solid block forms similar to brick.

contour line   solid (finish grade—plot plan) or dashed lines (natural grade—site plan) showing the elevation of the earth on a project.

contract documents   a portion of the Legal Documents.

corner bead   galvanized metal form (L-shaped) used for protecting outside corners in drywall and plaster installations.

cross brace   wood or metal diagonal bracing used to aid in structural support between joists and beams.

cubic measure   the area of a plane multiplied by the depth or height of a second plane perpendicular to the first; formula: $V = Ah$.

cutting plane line   a heavy broken line with arrows, letters, and numbers at each end indicating the section view that is being identified.

D

dampproofing   better identified as moisture protection; a surfacing used to coat and protect concrete and masonry from moisture penetration.

datum point   *see* bench mark; identification of the elevation above mean sea level.

dead load   the weight of a structure and all its fixed components.

deformed bar   steel reinforcement bar with ridges to prevent the bar from loosening during the concrete curing process.

diagonal brace   a wood or metal member placed diagonally over wood or metal framing to add rigidity at corners and at 25'-0" feet of unbroken wall space.

diazzo print   dry blueprint process developing blue lines on a light background; wet blueprint process in black on white background.

dimension line   a line on a drawing with a measurement indicating length.

drywall   finishing material for walls made of gypsum and paper; types include Gypsum wall board, Sheetrock®.

E

earthwork   excavating and grading.

easement   a portion of land on or off a property which is set aside for utility installations.

eave   the lowest edge on a gable roof.

elastomer   synthetic polymer; *see* polymer.

elevation   an exterior or interior orthographic view of a structure identifying the design and the materials to be used.

embed   any component (anchor bolt, wall-to-joist strap, and so on) that is installed within the foundation, slab, or wall of structure to assist in the installation of another component.

erection   referring to structural steel installations.

estimate   a calculation of labor, material, and equipment costs of a project.

F

face   the exposed side of a framing or masonry unit; a type of brick (also called *common*).

fascia   an exterior trim member used at the eave of a roof to hide the rafter ends.

finish   any material used to complete an installation that provides an aesthetic or finished appearance.

fire stop/draft stop/fire blocking   a framing member used to reduce the ability of a fire's spread.

firewall/fire separation wall/fire division wall   any wall that is installed for the purpose of preventing the spread of fire.

fixed window   a window that does not open.

flashing   metal or plastic strips or sheets used for moisture protection in conjunction with other construction materials.

flat   in roofing, any roof structure up to a 3:12 slope.

flexural strength   the ability to resist bending pressure without failure of the material.

fly ash   fine, powdery coal residue used with a hydraulic (water-resistant) concrete mix.

footing   the bottom-most member of a foundation; supports the full load of the structure above.

form   a temporary construction member used to hold permanent materials in place.

found   identification of the corner of a property.

foundation   the support member(s) of any structure; includes footing, foundation wall, and/or slab.

G

gable roof   *see* roof.

galvanize   a coating of zinc primarily used on sheet metal.

gauge   the thickness of metal or glass sheet material.

glaze   to install glass.

glu-lam (GLB)   glue-laminated beam made from milled 2x lumber bonded together to form a beam.

grade   an existing or finished elevation in earthwork; a sloped portion of a roadway; sizing of gravel and sand; the structural classification of lumber.

gravel   earth materials such as crushed rock ranging in size from $1/4''$ to $3''$ in diameter.

gravel stop (strip)   the edge metal used at the eaves of a built-up roof to hold the gravel on the roof.

green   uncured or set concrete or masonry; freshly cut lumber.

ground-fault-circuit-interrupter (GFCI or GFI)   an electrical receptacle installed for personnel safety at outdoor locations and near water supply fixtures.

gypsum   a mineral (hydrous calcium sulfate) powdered and compressed into wallboard (GWB) and used in plaster.

H

habitable space   in residential construction, the interior areas of a residence used for eating, sleeping, living, and cooking; excludes bathrooms, storage rooms, utility rooms, and garages.

hanger   metal fabrication made for the purpose of placing and supporting joists and rafters.

hardware   any component used to hang, support, or position another component; e.g., door and window hardware, hangers, and so on.

header   a framing member used to hide the ends of joists along the perimeter of a structure (also known as a *rim joist*); the horizontal structural framing member installed over wall openings to aid in the support of the structure above (also referred to as a *lintel*).

header course   in masonry, a horizontal row of brick laid perpendicular to the wall face; used to tie a double wythe brick wall together.

head joint   the end face of a brick or concrete masonry unit to which the mortar is applied.

heating, ventilating, and air conditioning   *see* HVAC.

hidden line   a dashed line identifying portions of construction that are a part of the drawing but cannot be seen, e.g., footings on foundation plans or wall cabinetry in floor plans.

hip roof   a structural sloped roof design with sloped perimeters from ridge to plate line.

hopper window   a window that is hinged at the bottom and with a top that swings inward.

hose bibb   a faucet used to connect a hose.

HVAC   the term given to all heating and air-conditioning systems; the mechanical portion of the CSI format, division 15.

hydraulic cement   a cement used in a concrete mix capable of curing under water.

I

I beam   *see* S beam.

index mark   a datum point in a survey used as the reference point for the survey.

insulating glass   a glazing assembly of dual glass with an air space between and sealed in a framework.

insulation   any material capable of resisting thermal, sound, or electrical transmission.

insulation resistance   the R factor in insulation calculations; a material capable of resisting electrical flow.

invitation to bid   the bid request from an owner, or a representative of the owner, to contractor.

isometric drawing   a drawing in which all horizontal lines are drawn at an angle of 30° above the horizontal, and all vertical lines are 90° (perpendicular to the true horizontal), with a 120° angle between.

J

jack rafter   a part of the roof structure raftering that does not extend the full length from the ridge beam to the top plate.

jalousie window   a movable, louvered, multiple-pane glass window; the individual louvered panes open outward in the same manner as the awning window.

jamb   the finish framing member installed in window or door openings.

J bolt   *see* anchor bolt.

joint compound   a dry (which requires mixing with water) or pre-mixed material used with a paper of fiber tape for sealing indentations and breaks in drywall construction.

joist   a structural horizontal framing member used for floor and ceiling support systems.

joist hanger   *see* hanger.

K

keyway   also known as a *cold key*; and interlocking depression formed in concrete used to add structural stability to the next lift or placement adjoining the key.

kiln   a heating unit or oven used to bake ceramics, cure and dry masonry units, and dry out lumber; *see* kiln-dried lumber.

kiln-dried lumber   lumber that is seasoned under controlled conditions, removing from 6% to 12% of the moisture in green lumber.

king post   in conventional framing, the vertical structural roof member extending from the ceiling joist to the ridge; in trusses, the vertical structural member extending from the bottom chord of the truss to the topmost point of the truss.

king stud   the full-length stud from bottom plate to the top plate supporting both sides of a wall opening.

kips (kps)   a measurement of force equal to 1,000 pounds.

knee wall   vertical framing members supporting and shortening the span of the roof rafters.

L

laminate   the process of stacking and bonding several layers of material together to form a single unit.

lateral   underground electrical service.

lath   backup support for plaster; may be of wood, metal, or gypsum board.

lavatory   bathroom; vanity basin.

lay-in ceiling   a suspended ceiling system; *see* acoustical.

leach line   a perforated pipe used as a part of a septic system to allow liquid overflow to dissipate into the soil.

leader   in drafting, the line to which an arrowhead is placed and used to identify a component.

ledger   structural framing member used to support ceiling and roof joists at the perimeter walls.

legend   a description of the symbols and abbreviations used in a set of drawings.

light (lite)   a pane of glass.

light-gauge metal framing   metal stud framing used in lieu of wood framing; consists of track and studs or joists.

linoleum   *see* resilient flooring.

lintel   *see* header.

live load   any movable equipment or personnel weight to which a structure is subjected.

M

m shape beam   *see* structural steel.

mansard roof   a combination of a flat roof and steep sloped sides similar to a hip roof.

masonry   manufactured materials of clay (brick), concrete (CMU), and stone used as components in the completion of a structure.

mean sea level   average height of the surface of the sea.

mechanical plan   the layout for heating and air conditioning.

member   structural component.

membrane roofing   built-up roofing.

mesh   common term for welded wire fabric, plaster lath.

metal stud   *see* light-gauge metal framing.

meter   in measurement, the equivalent to 39.37"; used to measure the flow of water, electricity, gas, and so on.

metrics   an international system of measurement based on the meter (length), liter (liquid measure, volume), and gram (weight).

mil   0.001".

minute   1/60th of a degree or angle.

mix design   the proportioning of cement, sand or aggregate, water, and additives (if required) to produce the desired concrete.

modular   construction design based on 4" square.

module   a prefabricated component or structure.

moisture barrier   a material used for the purpose of resisting exterior moisture penetration.

monitor roof   clearstory; a raised portion of a roof above the ridge where windows and/or ventilators are installed.

monolithic concrete   concrete placed as a single unit including turndown footings.

mortar   a concrete mix especially used for bonding masonry units.

N

natural grade   existing or original grade elevation of a property.

neoprene   a highly oil-resistant synthetic rubber.

nominal size   original cut size of a piece of lumber prior to milling (surfacing) and drying; size of masonry unit, including mortar bed and head joint.

non-bearing   not supporting any structural load.

O

on center (O/C)   the distance between the centers of two adjacent components.

open   any exposed construction component(s).

open web joist   roof joist made of wood or steel construction with a top chord and bottom chord connected by diagonal braces bolted or welded together.

orange peel finish   a textured plaster finish for drywall applications creating a slightly roughened surface.

oriented strand board (OSB)   a resin and fiber strand mixed with compressed and heated plies of wood chips and strands manufactured into a three-ply panel to be used in lieu of plywood.

orthographic projection   opening an object into flat-plane surfaces positioned at 90° to one another.

P

package air conditioner or boiler   an air conditioner or boiler in which all components are packaged into a single unit.

pad   in earthwork or concrete foundation work, the base materials used upon which to place the concrete footing and/or slab.

paint grade   a finish designation for lumber unsuited for stain and lacquer or varnish.

paper-backed lath   plaster lath with a moisture-resistant paper barrier attached.

parapet   an extension of an exterior wall above the line of the roof.

parging   a thin moisture protection coating of plaster or mortar over a masonry wall.

partition   an interior wall separating to rooms or areas of building; usually non-bearing.

plan view   a bird's-eye view of a construction layout cut at 5'-0" above finish floor level.

plaster   a mixture of cement water and sand.

platform framing   also known as *western framing*; structural construction in which all studs are only one story high with joists over.

plumbing   the general term used for both water supply and liquid waste disposal; specifically, in drawings and specifications, the waste disposal system.

plywood   thin sheets of veneer wood with the wood grain on adjoining sheets at 90° to one another, compressed and glued together in an odd number of plies (3, 5, and so on).

point of beginning (POB)   the point on a property from which all measurements and azimuths are established.

polyester   synthetic resin used for fabrics as well as an additive for concrete and mortar.

polyethylene   thin plastic sheet material used as a vapor barrier.

polymer   an organic chemical compound used in the manufacture of styrene, urethane, and methyl methacrylate; may be used as an additive for concrete.

polypropylene   synthetic fiber used for carpet backing and roofing materials.

polystyrene   the generic chemical name for Styrofoam.

polyurethane   used as a finishing material similar to varnish; also used as a foam insulation.

polyvinyl chloride (PVC)   a plastic material commonly used for pipe and plumbing fixtures.

Portland cement   one variety of cement produced from burning various materials such as clay, shale, and limestone, producing a fine gray powder; the basis of concrete and mortar.

post-and-beam construction   a type of wood frame construction using timber for the structural support.

post-tensioning   the application of stretching steel cables embedded in a concrete slab to aid in strengthening the concrete.

pressure treatment   impregnating lumber with a preservative chemical under pressure in a tank.

purlin   a horizontal framing member spanning between rafters.

Q

quarry tile   an unglazed clay or shale flooring material produced by the extrusion process.

quick set   a fast-curing cement plaster.

quoin   a masonry unit (stone, CMU, or brick) larger than the filed masonry; may be used as a header; more commonly used for aesthetics at masonry outside corners.

R

R factor   the numerical rating given any material that is able to resist heat transfer for a specific period of time.

raceway   any partially or totally enclosed container for placing electrical wires (conduit, tray, and so on).

rafter   in sloped roof construction, the framing member extending from the ridge or hip to the top plate; *see* common rafter, jack rafter.

rake   *see* barge; the angle of slope in a roof structure.

random length   a mix of lumber lengths, such as 8 lf, 14 lf, 24 lf, and so on, without specific length requirements, equaling a total length.

ready-mix concrete   a prepared concrete mix from a batch plant and freighted for use on a project.

rebar   *see* reinforcement steel bar.

red iron   *see* structural steel.

reinforcement steel bar a steel rod with or without deformed ridges used for adding strength to concrete and masonry; in increments of $1/8''$ DIA.

resilient flooring   a vinyl plastic floor finish material formed into sheets and tiles.

ribbon   in balloon framing, the support for the ledger supporting the floor joists at the second floor level.

ridge   the highest point on a sloped roof.

rise and run   the vertical length (rise) and the horizontal length (run) from plate line to the point where the rise intersects the span (see *span*).

roll roofing   a type of built-up roofing material made of a mixture of rag, paper, and asphalt.

roof pitch   the ratio of total span to total rise expressed as a fraction.

roofing   the materials used for moisture protection on a roof structure including composition shingle, wood shake and shingles, tile (clay, concrete and slate), and built-up roofing (BUR).

S

saddle   in framing, a support for intersecting beam construction or column mount; in roofing, a metal formed sheet (also known as a *cricket*) placed on the upper side of a chimney or skylight to move water away from them.

scale   a system for measuring proportionate lengths on a drawing.

schematic   a one-line drawing for electrical circuitry or isometric plumbing diagrams.

scissors truss   a truss constructed to the roof slope at the top chord with the bottom chord designed with a lower slope for interior vaulted or cathedral ceilings.

scratch coat   first coat of plaster placed over the lath in a three-coat plaster system.

scupper   an opening in a parapet wall attached to a downspout for water drainage from the roof.

scuttle   attic or roof access with cover or door.

sealant   a material used to seal off openings against moisture and air penetration.

section   a vertical drawing showing architectural or structural interior design developed at the point of a cutting-plane line on a plan view; the section may be transverse—the gable-end—or longitudinal—parallel to the ridge.

seismic design   construction designed to withstand earthquakes.

septic system   a waste system used in lieu of a sewer system that includes a line from the structure to a tank and a leach field.

shear wall   a wall construction designed to withstand shear pressure caused by wind or earthquake.

shoring   temporary support made of metal or wood used to support other components.

sidelight (sidelite)   a narrow, fixed window installed adjacent to a door.

sill plate   also referred to as a *mudsill;* the lowest framing member fastened to the concrete or masonry foundation; may be redwood or pressure-treated lumber (PTMS); used to deter termite infestation.

skew   twisted.

slab-on-grade   the foundation construction for a structure with no crawl space or basement; may be a monolithic concrete placement.

slider/sliding door or window   a door or window construction in which one of two halves moves horizontally on a track with the other half a fixed leaf.

slump   the consistency of concrete at the time of placement.

snap-tie/form-tie   a bolt-like rod used as a spacer for concrete formwork (plyform) that can be broken off at each end to remove the forms upon curing of the concrete.

soffit   a framed drop ceiling; enclosure of a roof overhang.

solar panel   also called a *solar collector;* a panel used to collect the sun's rays for heating or electrical power supply.

span   the horizontal distance between exterior bearing walls in a transverse section.

specifications   the written instructions detailing the requirements of construction for a project.

square   in geometric design, a figure that has all four sides equal and all angles at 90°; in measurement, a number multiplied by itself; in roofing, 100 square feet.

structural steel   heavy steel members larger than 12 gauge identified by their shapes, which include the W beam (wide-flanged), the S beam (junior), and M steel (miscellaneous) such as plate and tubular steel and angle iron.

stucco   cement plaster applied in one-, two-, or three-coat applications.

stud   wood or metal vertical wall framing members.

subfloor   the rough plywood flooring placed over floor joists upon which the finish floor material is placed.

symbol   a pictorial representation of a material or component on a plan.

T

tail/rafter tail   that portion of a roof rafter extending beyond the plate line.

tensile strength   the maximum stretching of a piece of metal (rebar and so on) before breaking; calculated in kps.

tensioning   pulling or stretching of steel tendons to aid in reinforcement of concrete.

terrazzo   a mixture of concrete, crushed stone, calcium shells, and/or glass, polished to form a tile-like finish; used for entries, patios, plazas, and so on.

title block   a portion of a drawing sheet that includes some general information about the project.

top chord   the topmost member of a truss.

top plate   the horizontal framing member fastened to the top of the wall studs; usually doubled.

transition piece   in sheet metal ductwork, a reducer.

truss   a prefabricated sloped roof system incorporating a top chord, bottom chord, and bracing.

typical   meaning the same throughout the drawing(s) unless noted otherwise (U.N.O.).

U

underlayment   the material applied over the subfloor upon which finish materials are placed.

urethane   a plastic foam material; *see* polyurethane.

V

valley   the reverse of a hip.

valley rafter   a structural roof member extending from the ridge to the plate or an intersecting roof structure.

vapor barrier   construction material used to resist moisture penetration.

veneer   a thin layer of surfacing material adhered to a base material, e.g., face brick over CMU or wood veneer over a pine trim material.

vent stack   a system of pipes used for air circulation and prevent water from being suctioned from the traps in the waste disposal system.

vinyl   a resin-based thermoplastic material used for resilient flooring.

W

waler   a 2x piece of lumber installed horizontally to formwork to give added stability and strength to the forms.

water-borne preservative   a coating applied to wood to resist deterioration.

water-cement ratio   the ratio between the weight of water to cement.

waterproofing   preferably called moisture protection since there is no product that will permanently resist water penetration or deterioration; materials used to protect below- and on-grade construction from moisture penetration.

weatherproof   preferably called *weather tight* for the same reason as explained under "waterproofing."

welded wire fabric (WWF)   a reinforcement used for horizontal concrete strengthening.

wind lift (wind load)   the force exerted by the wind against a structure caused by the movement of the air.

wythe   a continuous masonry wall width.

XYZ

x brace   cross brace for joist construction.

yard   lineal measurement consisting of 36".

zinc   non-corrosive metal used for galvanizing other metals.

INDEX

D

E

F